EXPERIMENTAL ANIMATION

pp 40-41 Frankfurt not spelled correctly

Experimental Animation

An Illustrated Anthology

Robert Russett and Cecile Starr

VNR VAN NOSTRAND REINHOLD COMPANY
New York Cincinnati Toronto London Melbourne

Acknowledgment is made to the following periodicals for their permission to include their copyrighted material in this volume: *Film Library Quarterly*, *The American Film Institute Report*, *Filmmakers Newsletter*, *Magazine of Art*, *Film Culture*, *Sight and Sound*, *Image et Son* (Paris), *Bryn Mawr Alumnae Bulletin*, *Film* (London), *Films in Review*, *The Village Voice*, *Film Comment*, *Print*, *The Moving Image*, *The Silent Picture*, and *Source*.

Hans Richter's material on Viking Eggeling is from his book entitled *Dada: Art and Anti-Art*, published by McGraw-Hill Book Company and used with permission of the publisher. The excerpt on Harry Smith is from Jonas Mekas's Movie Journal, copyright by Jonas Mekas, published by the Macmillan Company, reprinted by permission of *The Village Voice*.

Copyright © 1976 by Litton Educational Publishing, Inc.
Library of Congress Catalog Card Number 75-21261
ISBN 0-442-27194-8 (cloth)
ISBN 0-442-27195-6 (paper)

Printed in the United States of America
Designed by Loudan Enterprises

The authors and Van Nostrand Reinhold Company have taken all possible care to make full acknowledgment for illustrations and quotations used in this book. If any errors have accidentally occurred, they will be corrected in subsequent editions, provided notification is sent to the publisher.

Published in 1976 by Van Nostrand Reinhold Company
A Division of Litton Educational Publishing, Inc.
450 West 33rd Street
New York, NY 10001, U.S.A.

Van Nostrand Reinhold Limited
1410 Birchmount Road
Scarborough, Ontario M1P 2E7, Canada

Van Nostrand Reinhold Australia Pty. Ltd.
17 Queen Street
Mitcham, Victoria 3132, Australia

Van Nostrand Reinhold Company Ltd.
Molly Millars Lane
Wokingham, Berkshire, England

16 15 14 13 12 11 10 9 8 7 6 5 4 3 2 1
Other books by Cecile Starr:
Discovering The Movies, 1972

Library of Congress Cataloging in Publication Data

Main entry under title:

Experimental animation.

  Filmography: p.
  Bibliography: p.
  Includes index.
  1. Animation (Cinematography) I. Russett, Robert.
II. Starr, Cecile.
TR897.E96   778.5'347   75-21261
ISBN 0-442-27194-8
ISBN 0-442-27195-6 pbk.

Contents

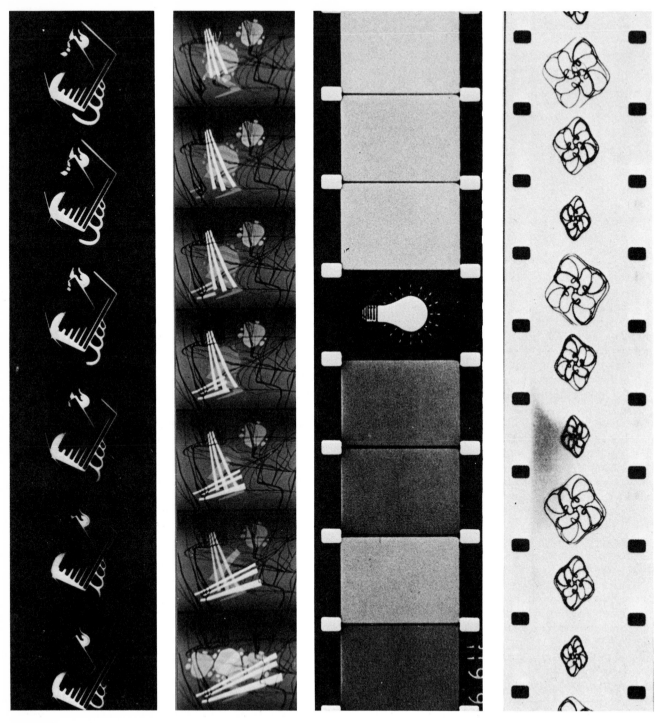

From left to right: Strips from the work of Viking Eggeling in the 1920s, Dwinell Grant in the 1940s, Paul Sharits in the 1960s, and Stan VanDerBeek in the 1970s.

Preface

This book originated with Robert Russett, who, as an independent animator and artist, wanted to examine in detail the significant artistic and technical achievements of his predecessors and contemporaries. Finding no volume of this kind, he began collecting material on those aspects of innovative animation which he felt would be most useful to himself and other animators and artists, as well as to critics, teachers, students of film, and the interested public.

The publishers suggested that Russett be joined in his undertaking by Cecile Starr, whose work as a film critic and teacher had brought her into close contact with a number of pioneer animators over several decades, and who had made film interviews with several important animators and had released a number of classic animation films in connection with her earlier book, *Discovering the Movies.* They divided the work into two main areas, Starr collecting material for the pre-1950 sections of the book, and Russett for the later periods—with some overlapping and sharing of responsibilities. Their common goal was to create a readable volume of lasting value, with the best and most informative articles, interviews, illustrations, and other source materials, to provide insights into the work of as many animators as possible, and at the same time to give a dynamic overview of this brilliant but little-known kinetic art form.

They settled on the title *Experimental Animation*, for want of a better term, as the only one broad and elastic enough to embrace the extraordinary range of cinematic works represented in the collection. Despite the obvious limitations of the word "experimental," the editors have used it mainly to suggest individual techniques, personal dedication, and artistic daring. A remarkable number of the films discussed in the book rise considerably above these specifications, and many clearly can be called recognized works of art. So much the better.

Traditionally, experimental animators have avoided the standard animation stand and the production-line procedures of the commercial studio. One common bond among all experimental animators is that, in varying degrees, they personalize their equipment and techniques, as does any fine artisan or craftsman. Although the film-artists included in this book are primarily concerned with animation as a form of artistic expression, they also fulfill another important need by providing others with innovative and exciting technical directions. Many of the techniques described in this book are minimal and direct; they can easily be adapted to the efforts of amateurs and young children in informal settings, and to budget-conscious students and independent filmmakers on more advanced levels. On the other hand, some animators have gone far beyond the conventional mechanisms by building complex devices or by using sophisticated computer languages, which have vast potential in the commercial field.

Although experimental animation is a unique art form with a bold and exciting tradition that dates back over fifty years, it has remained relatively isolated and undocumented within an area of filmmaking long dominated by the comic cartoon. To help balance the situation the editors decided to limit this volume to noncartoon animation. For space reasons, puppet animation was not included.

Because little has been printed on the work of the current generation of young animators, the book includes representative statements selected from their written interviews conducted especially for this volume. Translations from French and German about the work of some European pioneers have required many revisions; frequently the writings employed a figurative vocabulary whose meanings and implications were not entirely clear (and still may not be) when translated into another cultural environment after a lapse of half a century.

Dates, which are always a problem in film books, are even more so regarding experimental films, which rarely have an official release. The editors have avoided giving great importance to those who were "first" to achieve various effects or styles; they regard each film as a constellation of values, not as a winner or loser of a race in chronological time. Wherever possible, the editors have attempted to clear up often repeated inaccuracies, some of which have been perpetuated, knowingly or not, by filmmakers about themselves and their colleagues. The recently published studies on Oskar Fischinger and Viking Eggeling, though not yet the full and spirited renderings to be hoped for, point the way for other detailed studies that will surely follow.

The editors are grateful to the many filmmakers, or their families, who have loaned important documents and picture materials for inclusion in this book. While not entirely in disagreement with Len Lye, who rejects the idea of still pictures as suitable "illustrations" of his moving pictures, the editors have made a special effort to obtain the best possible picture material, and they consider it an integral part of the book. Unlike publicity stills for theatrical feature films, which are posed separately and may differ significantly from the filmed scenes they represent, the illustrations of animated films are usually exact reproductions of the material in the films, or even enlargements of actual frames and strips of film. The absence of color in this book, a serious loss, is at least partially compensated for by the inclusion of an abundance of illustrations in black-and-white, carefully placed as visual comments on many of the ideas and techniques explained in the text.

Ultimately, the only way to understand and appreciate the filmmakers is to view their films again and again, as one would hear a piece of music, read a poem, or look at a painting. In evaluating the works produced in the experimental field, it should be remembered that it is not only the film-artist who is called upon to confront new materials and to struggle with the continuing redefinition of art; the same responsibility, in another sense, falls upon the viewer. In order to fully experience these complex artistic works, therefore, the viewer must be prepared to constantly develop new standards of judgment and perhaps finally even new esthetic attitudes. Experimental animation, like other serious art forms, requires in varying degrees an active and empathetic response from its audience. In a world in which we are in danger of becoming passive receivers of processed and programmed entertainment, any creative activity which enables the viewer to function as a sensitive and discerning individual should be welcomed and encouraged.

Experimental animation, which is now enjoying a kind of renaissance, may have as much in common with music and painting as with commercial animation and film. Perhaps one day these films will be marketed through art galleries and "hung" in museums; perhaps they will be collected and played on home projectors and video machines, as long-play records are now heard on hi-fi sets; perhaps programs of these films will be presented in theaters and television, as recitals and concerts now are viewed with pleasure by mass audiences. The editors hope that this book will help its readers develop new and responsive attitudes and standards of appreciation toward the challenging and ever-changing concepts and techniques of experimental animation.

Cecile Starr and Robert Russett

1/A Rising Generation of Independent Animators

Robert Russett and Cecile Starr

INTRODUCTION

The young artists whose work is represented in this section form only a small sampling of the current generation of animators who began working within the last decade. Their selection was determined by two circumstantial factors: availability of published material about their work or their responses to written questions sent them by the editors.

The backgrounds of these young animators point out the importance of having first-rate facilities and equipment made available in a congenial atmosphere. Such surroundings have been found increasingly within college and university film departments in the United States, and in Canada, most notably at the National Film Board of Canada (see Chapter 5). Some of these young animators indicate that they made their first films in high school; they thus were ready for advanced work by the time they reached college or university level. Some animators have chosen to work in techniques that are as unsophisticated as the first animated films that were made, about 70 years ago; others are experimenting in highly technological areas that require considerable equipment and expertise. Most of these young film-artists also work to some extent in painting or graphics and some have made live-action moving pictures as well as animated ones.

Unlike the generation of independent animators before them, they have often found audiences and some financial support, although usually only within modest terms. A number of their films, depending on individual styles and subjects, have been placed in commercial 16mm distribution and already have gained wide circulation in schools, colleges, and public libraries. Several have been shown on educational television, or placed in theatrical distribution, with considerable recognition (including an Academy Award) but rather little financial gain. Since short films do not enhance box-office returns, they rarely make much money for their creators.

Museums and independent showcases in many large cities are showing the works of young animators more frequently these days. Through the Whitney Museum of American Art and the American Federation of Arts, both in New York City, animated films are being circulated to museums and other groups across the country in specifically organized and annotated programs. New animated films are frequently presented at film festivals here and abroad—ironically the prestigious New York Film Festival offers no compensation for the films, while a number of local groups (like the Sinking Creek Film Celebration in Tennessee and the Ann Arbor Film Festival in Michigan) offer token payments and small cash prizes as recognition and encouragement to the filmmakers.

Still, animation is not a ready source of prestige or financial gain for its creators. Their basic motivation is generally more personal—the fascination, often the compulsion, of seeing their entire creation take on life of its own, moving freely in time and space. Perhaps hundreds of young animators like those presented in this section of the book are now working on advanced levels; perhaps thousands are beginning to work as students or novices. With such growing interest in the field, future creations are impossible to imagine. And that, by definition, is the nature of experimental animation.

Adam Beckett

Adam Beckett, self-portrait in pen and ink (1975), drawn by the filmmaker for this book.

Adam Beckett was born in Los Angeles, California, in 1950. He attended Antioch College, and is currently doing graduate work at the California Institute of the Arts where he is studying animation with Jules Engel and Patrick O'Neill. As a student he has produced a number of artistically innovative animated films including *Evolution of The Red Star* and *Flesh Flows*, which have been shown extensively in this country as well as screened abroad. Beckett, who this past year formed his own production company, Infinite Animation, Ltd., is presently in the process of completing his latest film *Life In The Atom*.

INTERVIEW WITH ADAM BECKETT
Q: How did you start making animated films?

Beckett: Throughout high school I had been drawing and painting as well as doing a little cut-out animation. Just before going off to Antioch College I saw some fantastic films done by James Gore which somehow enabled me to make a connection between my graphic work and filmmaking. When I saw his films I thought I can do this too. So I did a film on my own at Antioch using full line animation. The drawing was done on typewriter paper and the images were held in registration with nails.

Q: As an art student at Cal Art you have made a number of outstanding films including your best known work, Evolution Of The Red Star. *Exactly how many films have you made altogether?*

Beckett: I have finished four films, namely *Heavy-Light*, *Evolution Of The Red Star*, *Sausage City*, and *Flesh Flows*. In addition there are two more films in the works. One is *Dear Janice* and the other is *Life In The Atom*.

Q: As a student, how has working in an educational environment affected your film production and what, specifically, do you feel schools can do to effectively develop the creative potential of student animators?

Beckett: Besides those impalpable qualities of talent and drive, otherwise known as inspiration and perspiration, there is one thing that every artist must have and that is a great deal of free and uninterrupted working time. Schools can help the student-artist in this regard by providing 24 hour access to facilities, flexible mandatory requirements, adequate living arrangements, and other similar kinds of conveniences. The teaching is probably best done by people who are professional artists themselves and who are so wrapped in their own work that they don't have time to interfere too much in the activities of students. They should be there primarily as examples of what it is to be a working artist in the field of animation. In a medium like animation, which is so dependent on technology, the best possible equipment and facilities are, of course, also extremely helpful. As far as I can see it is a matter of the most extraordinary circumstances and luck, when an individual manages to emerge from the educational system with the autonomy of spirit and knowledge needed for him to be an artist. Too much direction is probably more harmful than too little. Ideally, the school should be a place where one can develop the independence and self-confidence to make some headway against the incredible inertia that exists in the commercial arena. I think we are at the beginning of a wonderful golden age of animation, now that the last nails are in the coffin of the big studios. Schools, I believe, can in the future be very important as production centers for animated films.

Q: Would you discuss the idea behind your film, Evolution Of The Red Star, *and how it developed graphically?*

Beckett: Evolution Of The Red Star was my first technically successful attempt to apply my one and only original film discovery—animation of a cycle under the camera. There are several films involving painting under the camera such as Oskar Fischinger's *Motion Painting No. One*, [see Chapter 2], and some of Norman McLaren's work [see Chapters 5 and 7], but to my knowledge this type of film has always involved the manipulation of a single image. *Evolution Of The Red Star* was made by photographing the evolution of a six-drawing cycle, or repeating image, over a five- or six-week period. During this period pen-and-ink lines were continually added to the growing formation. Once the complete image was drawn and filmed I used optical printing procedures to produce many color variations. Carl Stone did the music when the filming was complete, and the final editing of the color variations took place after his music was finished. The idea of a cycle has, needless to say, many obvious philosophical, esthetic, and scientific implications. Cycles occur in nature on all levels from the astronomical to the psychological. The filmic idea of cyclical evolution mirrors the anti-entropic process of biological evolution.

It provides an escape from static repetition by a process of positive feedback or continual addition. Aside from all of this, it is great to be able to make nice, long, fully animated films from 6 or 12 or 48 drawings.

Q: Although Evolution Of The Red Star *is a totally visual film it does, in an unconventional way, tell a story. Are you basically interested in creating non-verbal forms of narrative animation?*

Beckett: I came to animation with a background in the graphic arts, and my main interest is still in the visual image itself. Although I do use a form of narration, I am basically interested in the problems of creating coherent and organic visual compositions in time.

Q: Which filmmakers, artists, or animators have most influenced your work?

Beckett: J. S. Bach, W. A. Mozart, Goya, Ingres, Rembrandt, Saul Steinberg, M. C. Escher, R. Crumb, B. Bartok, Walt Disney and company, Marcel Duchamp, Jordan Belson, Oskar Fischinger, Norman McLaren, James Gore, John Whitney Sr., Pablo Picasso, Dick Williams, Jules Engel, Robert A. Heinlein, Harry Smith, Goedle, Hokusai, and many, many others.

Q: What special attraction does animation, as a form of expression, have for you?

Beckett: It moves; it can be a one-man show or even a spectacle.

Q: What are you working on now and what are your plans regarding the future?

Beckett: I am trying to finish *Life In The Atom*, which I have been working on for nearly five years. It consists of some rather ornate animation of an attractive young couple and their activities. I am also interested in continuing my work with special effects. For example, this past year I did the main title for the 9th International Tournée of Animation. In the future, then, I plan to continue to make animated films, hopefully better ones than in the past.

(From a written interview conducted by
Robert Russett, November 1974.)

From *Evolution of the Red Star* (1973) by Adam Beckett. A unique form of cyclic animation is used.

Laurent Coderre

Laurent Coderre.

Laurent Coderre was born in 1931 in Ottawa, Canada. He attended several Canadian universities and art schools, including the University of Ottawa, Ontario College of Art, Ecole des Beaux-Arts in Montreal, and the University of Montreal. During the years following his formal education he worked as an artist, designer, musician and medi-

cal illustrator. In 1960, under the auspices of Norman McLaren, he joined the National Film Board of Canada (see Chapter 5). His artistic activities at the NFBC have involved making titles, film strips, and educational films, as well as producing purely artistic forms of experimental animation. Coderre has created experimental works which have won special awards for animation at Cannes, Venice, and numerous other film festivals. Presently, under the sponsorship of the NFBC, he is preparing three new animated films, *Arabesques*, *Acrobatics*, and *Chanson*.

INTERVIEW WITH LAURENT CODERRE

... I could say that animation, being an extension of my being, does not require any equipment during the creative process, but simply a way of jotting down an idea which finds itself on the spur of the moment, during a clash of strong contrasts. To animate a dot or line, to the rhythm of our accelerated contemporary life, is perhap's life's truest mirror. What better way to reflect an explosive decade than by explosive lines or three-dimensional textures moving across the screen in a tempo of frenzy.... Coming to animation after having lived painting, music, and other artistic disciplines is like a rebirth, a renaissance...

My being in animation is pure accident, following a series of happy circumstances. It was mentioned that Norman McLaren was to give a short, concise workshop to half a dozen people. My interest in this field having been there for a long time, I joined the group. I became fascinated by the unusual unsophisticated materials which could be used to convey so much. It is then that I asked McLaren for one hundred feet of 16mm film, to see if I could animate. During a week, at nights, I shot a three-minute test, on a half-dismantled animation stand. McLaren recommended that I become part of the animation unit. So this is how I came to animation, which I consider a field of infinite discovery. *Metamorphoses* was this first test...

I was given a sponsored series to do for retarded children, so I spent some time meeting with these kids trying to communicate and understand better their needs and their reactions. Then I made over half a dozen short films on problems to solve through their own initiative, within their limits. Some of these films were reduced to educational loops so the child could handle it himself. Problems worked on were: size relationship, color differentiation, categorization of shapes, identification of objects through metamorphosing shapes, counting, discovery of objects in their own world, and miscellaneous other problems. I was told by psychologists that these had broken a certain barrier in communication with the retarded, which helped them progress much faster because of their clarity in getting to the point in a way that talking, giving examples, or teaching could not do. Then there were complex mathematical problems for university students which were overcome in no time because of animated films. Further on, I enjoyed animating a technical film on electronic transducers for the fisheries department, to help fishermen with their catch on high seas. All of this was useful for discipline and training plus the satisfaction of knowing that they are serving some purpose.

...I have also experimented in several films (*Metamorphosis*, *Fleurs de Macadam*, *Zikkaron*) with control of shapes and forms to a simple rhythm; animating to words on a musical beat that seemed impossible; moving lines, dots, and masses to the pulse of life—all this

on relatively slim budgets so that I could see results quickly and learn from my mistakes, to go on to further, more precise projects. For example, in *Fleurs de Macadam*, I chose to make use of water color on cel instead of cel paint, to achieve very specific textures. While in *Zikkaron* I chose linoleum particles on black background, because to me it seemed for this film a better material to convey a certain dimension within the screen, that is, to draw and destroy the ephemeral state of things. That technique permitted me to concentrate more on content and movement.

I feel that my present films are to animation what sketches are to painting. But the unknown lies ahead....

(From a written interview conducted by Robert Russett, November 1974.)

From *Les Fleurs de Macadam* (1969) by Laurent Coderre, an animated version of a popular French Canadian folksong.

From *Metamorphosis* (1968). Laurent Coderre's first film was made with animated paper cutouts.

From *Zikkaron* (1971) by Laurent Coderre. Small particles of linoleum were animated to create a statement about man and his environment.

Caroline Leaf

Caroline Leaf.

Caroline Leaf was born in 1946 in Seattle, Washington, and studied art at Radcliffe College in Boston. After receiving her degree in 1964 she worked as a free-lance animator for several years making and directing animated films for television. In the spring of 1972 she began to work for the French section of the animation department at the National Film Board of Canada. Leaf, whose best known works are *Sand, or Peter And The Wolf* and *Le Mariage du Hibou*, creates her organic and stylized images by spontaneously animating textures and materials directly under the rostrum camera, without the use of prepared graphics or painted cells. Currently she is working for the English section of the NFBC, making an animated film based on a story by Mordecai Richler.

INTERVIEW WITH CAROLINE LEAF

I tell stories with my animation, and I have always worked directly under the camera, drawing, shooting it, changing the drawing, etc. To me it seems to be more alive than conventional cel animation, both to make it and to see it, for it is all made in one stage and the finished film shows my hesitations and miscalculations and flickers with fingerprints and quick strokes....

My images and techniques come from the materials I use. My first film, *Sand*, or *Peter and the Wolf* is made with a technique I developed animating with fine beach sand. The sand is set on a piece of milk glass and underlit and manipulated with my fingers. The sand becomes black on the white glass. I found I could adequately describe a form by its silhouette. The only elements I had were black and white, figure and ground. When the options are limited, my fantasy is most creative to exploit them. I have made four films with sand and still find new things to do with it. Likewise, techniques I use, such as suggesting objects and environments with a few shapes as I need them, and them wiping them out, come from the nature of the sand. Presently I am working with colors and inks, and I handle them in the same way as the sand, smudging, wiping, using my fingers....

I began to animate when I was a student at Radcliffe College. I like to control everything within my frame. I like the quiet of animation, though sometimes the length of time it takes to see a result from an idea frustrates me. I like to make things move. It is like making them alive.

I have wanted to tell stories with my films, and I used animal legends and myths, as you can tell by the titles: *Peter and the Wolf*, *Orfeo*, *How Beaver Stole Fire*, and *The Owl Who Married a Goose*, also known as *Le Mariage du Hibou*. Now I am working on more dramatic expression, dialogue, characters, and human problems. The film is tentatively called *The Street* and is an adaptation of a story by Mordecai Richler about the death of a grandmother in a poor Jewish family. Perhaps dramatic expression is not ultimately the best form for animation, but still, I do not try to do what live action can do better...

I believe every person's work is personal and therefore new. There are as many forms of expression as there are people. No one will do a thing in the same way as someone else. Therefore something new does not mean a world-shattering breakthrough of technique or idea. I find that when I am searching for new techniques, new materials to animate, I am usually barren of content ideas, whereas a content idea will take the shapes of the techniques I have at hand...

The strongest influence on me is from literature rather than film. Kafka, Genêt, Ionesco, Beckett, have affected me most with the depths of their visions and world views, and ways of breaking up time to tell a story...

(From a written interview conducted by Robert Russett, November 1974.)

From *Le Mariage du Hibou* (1975) by Caroline Leaf, an animated version of an animal table.

From *Le Mariage du Hibou* by Caroline Leaf.

From *Sand*, or *Peter and the Wolf* (1969) by Caroline Leaf. Beach sand was manipulated to produce images and graphic effects.

Frank Mouris

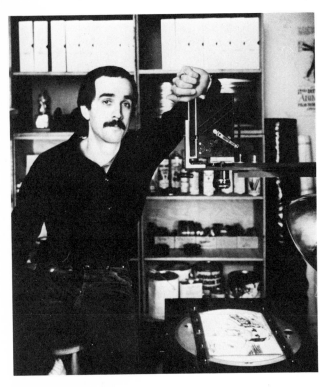

Frank Mouris, about 1974.

In Frank Mouris's first film, one of the two narration tracks tells the story of his life in his own words. Here are a few excerpts:

"I WAS BORN IN KEY WEST, FLORIDA [in 1944], WHEN MY FATHER WAS IN A NAVAL STATION THERE AND I WAS THE FIRST OF FIVE KIDS AND IT WAS, I GUESS, A GOOD TIME TO BE BORN.... I HAD A VERY STRICT RELIGIOUS UPBRINGING, WHICH I FEEL HELPED ME IN MY WORK LATER. IT GAVE ME A KIND OF ASCETICISM, A CALVINISM, ALMOST A PRO-TESTANT WORK-ETHIC, EVEN THOUGH IT WAS A SUPER-CATHOLIC ENVIRONMENT.... WE LIVED IN RATHER COMFORTABLE, MIDDLE-CLASS SUR-ROUNDINGS.... FROM AN EARLY AGE, I ALWAYS WANTED TO WORK IN MY FATHER'S GAS STATION.... THEN I HAD THE USUAL TEENAGE SEXUAL FANTA-SIES WHICH I WON'T GO INTO TOO SPECIFICALLY. I HAD A NUMBER OF CRUSHES ON GIRLS IN SCHOOL...AND, FOR THE FIRST TIME I STARTED RELATING TO PEOPLE OUTSIDE ME.... AND THEN IT WAS TIME TO GO TO COLLEGE. I SPENT MOST OF MY TIME STUDYING. I WASN'T EXACTLY SURE WHAT I WAS GOING TO DO. I THOUGHT MAYBE I WOULD WRITE LETTERS TO PEOPLE AS A PROFESSION— THAT WAS SOMETHING I ENJOYED DOING.... I HAD TO MAJOR IN SOMETHING, SO I STUDIED ARCHITEC-TURE...JUST BEFORE I GRADUATED [I] DECIDED THAT ART WAS THE ANSWER AND I WOULD BE A PAINTER OR A SCULPTOR, BECAUSE THEN YOU CAN DO THE THING ENTIRELY YOURSELF.... I DECIDED TO GO TO GRADUATE SCHOOL AND LEARN SOME-THING VAGUELY MECHANICAL, THAT IS, GRAPHIC DESIGN.... THROUGH THAT I GOT INTERESTED IN PHOTOGRAPHY, AND THEN SUDDENLY THROUGH PHOTOGRAPHY I GOT INTERESTED IN FILMMAKING, SPECIFICALLY ANIMATION, AND ALL OF A SUDDEN, THERE IT WAS...THAT WAS WHAT I REALLY WANTED TO DO, WAS TO WORK WITH ANIMATED IMAGES AND MAKE MY WORLD WITH THEM, AND SO FOR MY THREE YEARS IN GRADUATE SCHOOL I MUST HAVE PLAYED AROUND WITH DIFFERENT WAYS TO ANI-MATE DIFFERENT KINDS...OF THINGS AND HOPE-FULLY THEY WOULD BE THINGS THAT HADN'T EVEN BEEN ANIMATED BEFORE. SO THAT WAS ABOUT HALFWAY THROUGH MY GREAT SAVING-UP PERIOD OF ALL THESE IMAGES AND THAT LED TO MY FANTA-SIES OF WHAT WOULD HAPPEN WHEN...ALL OF THAT CAME TOGETHER AND I WAS SENDING MY FILMS TO INTERNATIONAL FILM FESTIVALS AND WINNING AWARDS AND BEING A FAT CAT...AND THAT'S ABOUT AS FAR INTO THE FUTURE AS I CAN FANTASIZE...."

Since completing his multi-award-winning *Frank Film*, which took nearly six years from start to finish, Frank Mouris and his wife Caroline have finished two films:

Coney, using single-frame, live-action techniques in a real location, and *Screentest*, using animation with actors. In the spring of 1975 Mouris received a John Simon Guggenheim Memorial Foundation fellowship to write and direct his first dramatic, fictional film; in the fall of 1975, he became a Directing Fellow at the Center for Advanced Film Studies of the American Film Institute in Beverly Hills, California.

INTERVIEW WITH FRANK MOURIS

I would say that major studio animation is based primarily on drawing and my work isn't. I come to animation more through the experimental animators of that same era that aren't really that well known. I only discovered the possibility of my doing animation when I saw VanDerBeek's work [see Chapter 8] about 10 years ago and then, suddenly, there was the possibility that I could do animation even though I didn't draw a lot, and I didn't draw well. My kind of animation deals with found objects, found images, which I rework into my own kind of universe which they make completely from scratch through drawings. . . .

Most of the animators that I know individually do not only do drawn animation or collage or object animation, but they're also involved in regular live-action filmmaking, production, shooting, special effects.

Q. Where do you think the future of animation lies?

Mouris. Everywhere and anywhere. I really have something against strict definitions. I've had a lot of flack because a lot of people don't think of animation as an art form. Animation is generally considered to be a very specific area of filmmaking and I've run up against people with that kind of attitude and I turn it around all the time and say I consider filmmaking a very special part of animation. Just technically, animation, I mean filmmaking, really is frame by frame.

There's so much unexplored territory that's very exciting like computers, xerography, video, and things that we can't even dream about yet. I think it's all over the map, it's not in any one area of film. Some people say the future is definitely in computer animation. I find that when someone makes up the definition, I take that as a welcome challenge to prove the definition wrong. When they say *that* is animation, or when the Bolex booklet comes out with the instructions which tell you *this* is how you film well, do not do *these* things, I find that I check out first with a dealer whether if I do these things, it will hurt the camera. Then, if it won't I go ahead and do them, and see what kind of effect it gives.

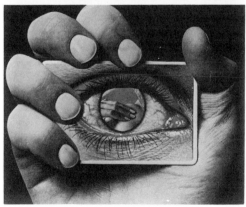

From *Frank Film* (1973) by Frank Mouris, collage animation recounting significant events in the filmmaker's life.

Q. How would you compare the differences between animation in America today and animation abroad?

Mouris. I think American animation is fantastic. I would combine it. I think that there is an English speaking animation—Canada, the United States, and England have the same kind of approach to animation, the same kind of vitality, and wit, and dash and style. There is a lot of foreign animation that I really like; I like the seriousness of it and I like the fact that they are more inclined to treat animation as an art. When I say animation here, people say "Oh, you draw cartoons," but I think in Europe especially, animation is much more highly regarded as an art form. And while I like the toughness and seriousness of a lot of those things, I think that just as a lot of American animation falls into caricature and witless violence and comedy, a lot of European films get very pretentious and heavy. It's almost like you aren't allowed to laugh.

Q. What do you think are the most important needs of animation right now?

Mouris. Distribution for one. For short films, theatrical distribution has been disastrous. We're all waiting for the cassette revolution to come along. Of course we may be waiting 10 years from now. The problem with both live-action and animation is that when you're starting or when you don't have much money or don't have any backing, you have to do short films, and there's no real way that short films can do that well. Cassettes can hopefully not only solve the technological problems but the financial ones. . . .

Esthetic needs are somewhat special for animation. When you make up everything yourself, there is more of a tendency to become precious about your work or what you have made up than in live-action filmmaking. What some people think is self-indulgence. But when you spend hours, days, weeks, and years doing art work, it's very hard to throw something away if it doesn't work. The most critical point is after it's finished but before it's publicly released, and you have to really sit down and decide what is it, what does it do, why is it seven and a half minutes long; maybe it should be three and a half minutes long.

Q. Did the work of any of the people working in the major studios in the thirties, forties, and fifties have any effect on you?

Mouris. Only recently have I been able to sort out the names and influences, but they've definitely been on an almost subliminal level. I was watching that stuff from the time I could turn on the television or go to a theater, and I miss a lot of that kind of excellence and discipline. I go to retrospectives of the older kinds of animation. I loved it,

From *Frank Film* by Frank Mouris.

and I still love it. I realize that it's not what I can do or could ever do, but maybe it's been an influence. I think, though, I've been much more influenced by VanDerBeek and McLaren [see Chapters 5 and 7], and Len Lye [see Chapter 2] and Borowczyk and other people like Belson and Kubelka and Brakhage. Many of the uncommercial filmmakers are very much in tune with animation though they aren't specifically doing animation. I think it's because they exercise the same high degree of control over their work that is so important in animation.

Q. Is there anything specific you are trying to accomplish in your work?

Mouris: Yes, and it's unspecific. I'd like to work with the unknown. I don't want to re-do or re-learn what someone else has already done or learned. That's why my two new film projects are different from *Frank Film*. It means I'm no longer plagued by boredom, but it also means I'm plagued by indecision. One day I think it's fantastic and the next I think, why am I wasting my time on this film. I would like to approach film the way Borowczyk does or Norman McLaren. Just go out and discover some area that suits you and push it as far as it can go, do the best you can, then finish that and go find something else. I would also like to be doing something new, but not to the point of being so eclectic that nothing is really related to anything.

(From *The American Film Institute Report*, Vol. 5, No. 2, Summer 1974.)

ANIMATION AND OTHER OBSESSIONS
by Frank Mouris

The typical reaction to my *Frank Film* is some comment upon its obsessive nature. For me, animation *is* an obsession. In fact, it is the very latest and most powerful of a long list of obsessions in my life. And it is certainly the most satisfying one, since it legitimizes all the other obsessions that possess me. Before I discovered the medium of animation, no one could understand the weird things I did. Now that I am a productive animator, people just figure that those are the kind of weird things animators have to do in order to animate. Let me explain . . .

All my life I have been obsessed with magazines. More than a compulsion to read everything that crossed my path, it was an entrancement with the magic worlds displayed in all those colorful photographs. And the advertisements were at least as powerful as the editorial pages, and usually more fanciful. I couldn't understand why anyone would ever want to throw a magazine away— it wasn't as if you could use up or digest all that fantasy and color in just a couple of viewings. So, I saved magazines. I asked my friends to save them. I got my mother

to have all her friends save them. I scoured the neighborhood sidewalks on trash collection days. I haunted the waiting rooms of doctors and dentists, waiting for the opportune moment to grab some of their accumulating treasure. Occasionally, I even *bought* magazines, but in my more rational moments I knew that my habit was much greater than my financial resources, so I would have to avoid paying for it as much as possible.

Eventually, I ran out of storage space for all those magazines, so I made a reasonable compromise: I would only save the best images from each magazine and discard the rest. Then I could continue to collect magazines as if there were no tomorrow. Tomorrow came rather quickly, as all those loose pages took up nearly as much space as the magazines, and created a terrible mess. So I hit upon a solution. Why not sort out the images by category, then cut them out and store them in cardboard boxes? Why not, indeed. Soon I had a room filled with cardboard boxes, and a seemingly lifelong occupation of saving, sorting, cutting, and filing. Even *I* began to be overwhelmed as this obsession increased. I was annoyed that all those images were just sitting there doing nothing useful while I was working myself into exhaustion. So I began to make collages with them: collage letters, collage books, collage artwork for *magazines* (recycling!). I learned a lot about combining images, but I wasn't satisfied with the results.

I'm a very active person, constantly moving, and I love to dance. I wanted my collages to have that liveliness. And their great moment came. My wife Caroline and I were stalled in the filming of my autobiographical film; the footage was disappointing. It was mostly live-action, so it was undeniably me—but it wasn't *really* me. So we decided that I should just use my cutout images, and by the time they were shot and Tony Schwartz added his genius to the soundtrack, it really *was* me, *Frank Film*. And so after years of collecting and cutting and collating, a product emerged and finally other people could relate to my weird behavior. So animation has legitimized my obsessions and has now become my very biggest obsession, ordering and channeling my other obsessions. Even as you read this, my current obsessions with Coney Island, felt-tip pens, and zany New York characters are working their way toward becoming animated films. I am also obsessed with collecting empty salted peanut jars, but wherever that is leading is still a mystery, even to me.

(From *Film Library Quarterly*, Vol. 7, No. 1, 1974.)

Eliot Noyes, Jr.

Eliot Noyes, Jr.

Eliot Noyes, Jr., was born in 1942 in Washington, D.C., and was educated at the Putney School and Harvard College. He first began experimenting with animation while attending Harvard, and, following his graduation, he continued his film work with Charles Eames and the National Film Board of Canada. Since then he has co-founded Cyclops Films production company with Claudia Weill and has produced animated films for WNET in New York, *Sesame Street*, and the Learning Corporation of America. Currently, with the aid of an American Film Institute Independent Filmmaker grant, he is working on a new animated film tentatively called *The Dot*.

INTERVIEW WITH ELIOT NOYES, JR.

I view myself as an artist who uses animation the way a painter would use paints and a canvas. The reason I am in animation is that it is a form of self-expression; what I want to get across is mostly a very personal view of the world. Animation for me right now isn't a collaborative kind of a process, and it isn't the kind of thing like the studio set-up in the thirties and forties where a lot of people got together and wrote a story, a lot of people animated it, and a lot of people contributed to the music. It's a way that I have found to make films where I can control everything, and I think that's part of why I like to do it, because I have control over everything.

The purpose of animation back then was to entertain, and I'm not sure that the purpose of my films is entirely entertainment. I don't design them as entertainment. I do them as much to satisfy myself as anything else. I have faith that if you do something that satisfies yourself it will be interesting to other people.

Q: How about getting your work distributed and shown— is that a great consideration when you are making your films?

Noyes: Well, it is getting to be now. It didn't used to be. I wasn't ever getting them shown. I was really thinking about getting them made, and I think I am going to another phase now where I want to make sure that where I spend a lot of energy on something, it isn't kind of just going to sit on the shelf.

Q: What kind of avenues are open to you?

Noyes: I think the standard avenues which have been open for the last 10 years are still valid and good. But I don't think that I like them that much anymore. You know the small 16mm distributor who has prints and then he sells them to libraries and then some enterprising school teacher somewhere out in Kansas sees your film in a catalog and maybe it will get shown in a classroom. I really would like to make theatrical shorts. If a market opened up there, I would love to make 10-minute animated theatrical shorts....I couldn't possibly make a 90-minute film if I did it myself without it taking forever, so

I would have to find some way to direct it and have some other people animate for me. And if I did that, I would have to find some way, some technique (I don't use cel animation) that would allow other people to carry out my directions and still have that kind of crazy, spontaneous quality that a lot of my work has. . . .

Q: How and why did you get into animation?

Noyes: . . . One of the things that is becoming clearer and clearer to me is that as a child I was very isolated from people and the only way I could deal with things was to kind of create my own world, to create alternate kinds of realities. The only way I could relate to people was by showing them these realities. It was fun, and I got good at being able to make up things. I also come from a very art-conscious background, and I've been aware of my abilities to make things for a long, long time. I used to make model airplanes, I used to draw, I used to play a lot of music, and I see animation as very much connected with those kinds of pleasures. Then I really got interested in film during the sixties. I saw a lot of films from the National Film Board of Canada and it seemed like the ultimate thing to do—to make statements about the world. Personal statements that then were blown up big on a huge screen so that lots of people could see. . . .

Q: Where do you think the future of animation lies?

Noyes: I'm not sure that there is a future, or if there is a future, I'm not sure that it is apparent yet. A lot of films are made and they aren't seen. I think if there was a return of the theatrical short market in this country, that would be an incredible outlet. I know that *Sesame Street* was a place where these individual animators who are dotted across the country could go to and get a way to make films that weren't entirely commercial—that had a lot of their own personal touch in them. People are getting interested in animation as an art. I don't know what is going to happen because the structure hasn't changed yet. The way people get to see films is still the same as it was 10 years ago. I keep thinking about cassettes, and that someday I will be able to make a five-minute animated film and it will sell like a 45 rpm special and I will make a lot of money. Five-minute films are just not commercial. A five-minute animated film about a personal subject doesn't make much money. Nobody really has a way to get hold of it and see it and that probably won't change for a while, so I think the future of animation is going to be if people who are animating can find some sort of way to bind together and make works that are difficult to ignore.

From *Clay* (1964) by Eliot Noyes, Jr. Whimsical clay sculptures are animated in the film, producing a metamorphosis of abstract and representational forms.

From *Sandman* (1973) by Eliot Noyes, Jr. Sand animation creates granular textures and silhouettes.

Q: What do you think the most important needs of your field are today? You mentioned cassettes might be one thing that would help out independent animators.

Noyes: I think that Europeans have always looked at animation as a high art form, and this country's mind has been polluted by the Disney people who have made animation cartoons. In fact, I think the Academy awards up until a few years ago used to give awards for the best cartoons. They didn't call them animated shorts. One need is for animation to be shown and understood so that people start to recognize it as an incredible force. The only place people regularly see films in controlled screening situations is in movie houses, so they have to see them in movie houses. The big problem in TV is that an animated film just gets swallowed up by all that kind of garbage. Animated film is so intense that unless you had a program of it that lasted half an hour—that might be a way of getting animation over the air.

Q: What are you trying to accomplish in your animation?

Noyes: Somebody asked Freud, "What are the most important things in a healthy person," and Freud said, "To be able to love and to be able to work," and I am working on both of those things. Animation is my work and if I can work through animation and find out who I am through animation, that would be the best thing that I could want. That is really what I am trying to do. I am really trying to get in touch with who I am and what I have to say, and I really want to have fun, and I am beginning to much more than I ever used to.

(From The American Film Institute Report, Vol. 5, No. 2, Summer 1974.)

A page of preliminary character studies for the one-minute film, *41 Barks* (1972) by Eliot Noyes, Jr., which is a clever audio-visual joke.

From *41 Barks* by Eliot Noyes, Jr. One of the 41 dogs, each of which barks a note of "My Country 'Tis of Thee." All drawings were made on paper.

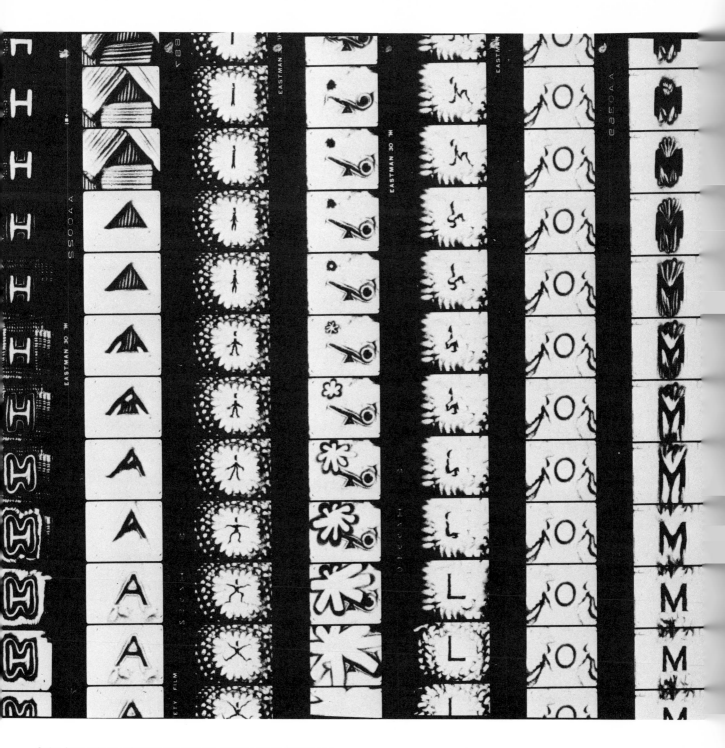

Strips from animated footage produced in 1973 by Noyes for Sesame
Street, with sand on illuminated glass.

Dennis Pies

Dennis Pies.

Dennis Pies, whose early education and background was in the field of drawing and printmaking, began making animated films in 1972 as a graduate student at the California Institute of the Arts. During the two years he worked toward an M.F.A. degree in animation there, Pies produced an outstanding series of four films, while experimenting with unusual graphic techniques and exploring atmospheric forms of abstract imagery. His films have had many showings including those at the International Animation Film Festival in New York, the Whitney Museum, and the World Festival of Animation in Zagreb, Yugoslvaia. Pies is presently living in Rio Nido, California, where he is working on his new animated film *Sonoma (Valley of the Moon)*.

INTERVIEW WITH DENNIS PIES

I was 25 years old when I made my first animated film. I had been involved in printmaking for a number of years and I wanted to see my imagery become dynamic—more performance oriented. I found that the California Institute of the Arts had an excellent animation program which was geared to the fine arts and which would accommodate a wide range of approaches . . .

During my two years at CAL Art, I completed a total of four films. With each I experimented with a different approach. In the first film, I generated a large number of drawings with no preconceived structure and shot these drawings in many different ways—some animation and some film graphics. From the 800 feet that I shot, I edited a 250-foot film, *Nebula*, just as one would edit a live-action film. My second film was *Merkaba*, and it was based on a dream that I had. Using the dream as a story board I conceived the structure in every detail before beginning the art work. The word MERKABA is my use of the Jewish work MERKABAH, meaning vehicle of light from Jewish literature. It is a word that sounds like the imagery and reads well on the screen. It has other suggested meanings such as the KABA, the religious stone in Mecca that once glowed. In the dream that I had, it was about 2 A.M. at night and I looked up and saw that the stars were swarming like bees. They began to mass in a circle, then a thin transparent shell, like an elongated jellyfish, congealed around the star cluster. The center crystallized and formed what looked like a city of translucent glass. *Merkaba* is a long animated film, ten minutes in length. The timing was structured to present a very intense, yet quiet and meditative effect.

My third film was *Aura Corona*. Here I was experimenting with choreographed movement by means of "straight-ahead animation." I used as my subjects for this dance two vertebra-like creatures. I used an improvisational approach for the movement and timing. This simple idea began to build on itself as I did the drawings. Eventually, the structure of the film began to make itself known to me. This, for me, is the most exciting way to approach animation. My two vertebra beings had developed auras—in scientific language, corona discharge. The film ended with an aura corona, so *Aura Corona*, with its almost musical ring, became the title. My improvisation, however, did not end with this film. The process and imagery of *Aura Corona* generated the idea for another film called *Luma Nocturna*. *Luma Nocturna*, which means night light, is the double or dark twin of *Aura Corona*. Both of these films, then, are conceptually part of the same project.

I am presently working on my fifth animated film. In this film I am traveling on a journey. Again, I use the improvisational "straight-ahead" approach and I employ actual incidents and dreams from my life. It is a fantasy/journal/documentary, and it is the most personal work I have attempted. I hope to complete it before the end of 1975....

Technically, the effects in all my films are made with the artwork. No optical effects printer was used. The luminous colors are iridescent lusters that I originally made for doing my prints. These lusters, when applied to my graphic work, light up nicely under the Oxberry camera and show well on film. I like to work on both black and white fields using various drawing techniques, including air brush and certain painterly techniques. I use some camera moves and dissolves ... but for the most part the technical aspect of my films is conventional. It is the content that I consider experimental....

I do not feel that my films are entirely abstract, but I conceive each to deal with a certain central idea or subject. Even in my first film, *Nebula*, the most abstract of all, I was working with an idea from *Star Maker*, a book by Olaf Stapledon. To quote from Stapledon's book: "Gradually I discovered that I had made contact not with microorganisms, nor yet with worlds or stars or galactic minds, but with the minds of the great nebulae before their substance had disintegrated into stars to form the galaxies."...

Q: Your films have been compared to the works of Jordan Belson and James Whitney. Have these west coast filmmakers had a direct influence on the development of your style?

Pies: Jordan Belson and James Whitney have most definitely been an influence on my film work. Their film imagery was very much like the imagery of my prints, and seeing their films made me aware of what this type of image could do in the dynamic medium of film....

I am more influenced by the fine arts area, on the whole, than by filmmaking. I am still very active in the graphic arts and continue to work extensively in the field of drawing and printmaking.... My future plans are to work within the tradition of personal cinema as an art form.

(From a written interview conducted by Robert Russett, July 1974.)

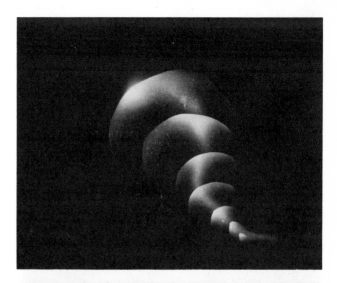

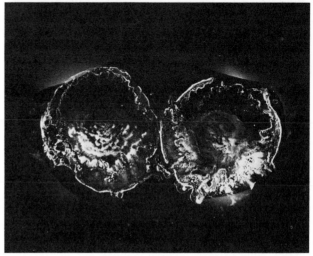

From *Luma Nocturna* (1974) by Dennis Pies, an atmospheric animated film with iridescent forms.

Robert Russett

Robert Russett.

Robert Russett was born in 1935 in North Adams, Massachusetts, and was educated in the visual arts, receiving a B.F.A. from the Rhode Island School of Design and an M.F.A. from Cranbrook Academy of Art. Following his graduate work at Cranbrook, Russett continued his studies for one year in Paris at Atelier 17 and, in the mid-sixties, with a background in painting and printmaking, turned to animation as a form of expression. His abstract animated films, which he views as a kinetic extension of his work in the graphic arts, have had numerous showings in this country and abroad. In 1968 he received an American Film Institute grant to produce an experimental animated film, and in 1971 he was the first filmmaker to be awarded a MacDowell Colony Fellowship. Russett, an associate professor of art at the University of Southwestern Louisiana, has recently been at work on an abstract film, *Thalamus*.

FROM "ABSTRACT ANIMATION"
by Robert Russett

Abstract animation, despite many significant advances, is still in its infancy. When compared, for example, with other visual arts such as painting and printmaking, it is a relatively new and unexplored form. Most artist-filmmakers today would agree that the plastic and kinetic potential of abstract animation is far from fully understood. In my own work with abstract animation I am particularly interested in exploring the optical effects of color. I have found that certain optical systems when mechanically diagrammed in time can produce unique color structures. These color structures have their own synthetic quality—a luminous appearance—which cannot be produced in other art forms. Basically, I use two techniques to achieve these effects: (1) color after-image, an illusion produced from animated black and white patterns, and (2) optical color mixture, a form of temporal pointillism.

The color after-image effect is produced by a very intriguing technique. Black and white images are systematically programmed, frame by frame, to achieve the vivid illusion of color. This effect, called Benham's Top, is one of the more interesting and complicated aspects of the after-image phenomenon. The principle of Benham's Top is usually demonstrated by a rotating disk which is designed with a black and white pattern.

From *Neuron* (1972) by Robert Russett, Strips of fim showing abstract patterns which explore the optical effects of filmic color and geometry.

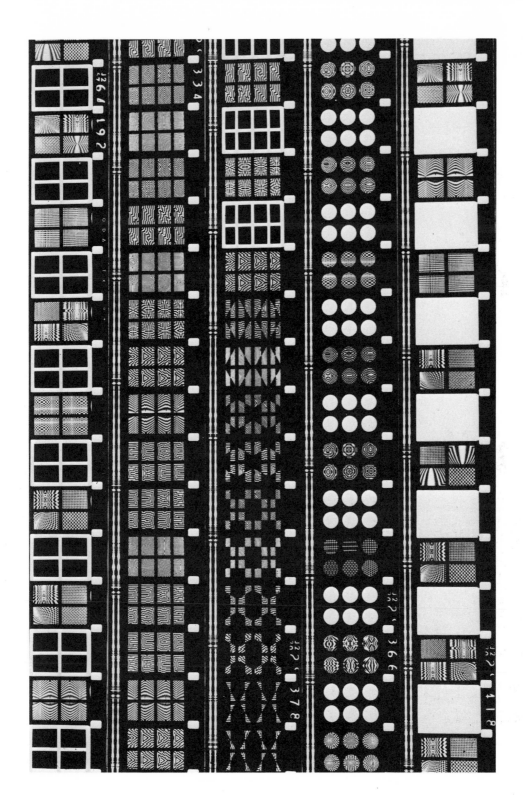

Changing the speeds of the disk will cause varying frequencies of flickering white light to generate a wide range of colors. The single frame process, like the rotating disk, can also cause retinal changes in sensitivity which will produce the illusion of color. My work with this color technique has just begun, but it is apparent that an un-catalogued range of creative possibilities can result from the after-image effect.

My approach to optical color mixture in animation is based on the same phenomenon as pointillist painting, but with one important difference. In a pointillist painting, colors are placed next to each other on a static two-dimensional canvas. Essentially, the pointillist technique consists of organizing small brush strokes of separate hues so that they visually merge into a single color. In animation, optical color mixtures can be achieved by organizing hues on separate frames in linear time. These individual color frames, when frenetically animated, appear to simultaneously co-exist in the same frame. The results of this temporal structure is a pulsating multi-colored image. Many artistic and perceptual variations on this technique are possible, depending on the flow of images and the linear interval of colors. . . .

(From *Filmmakers Newsletter*, Vol. 5, No. 9/10, Summer 1972.)

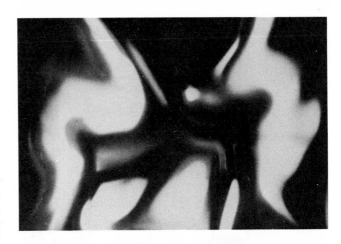

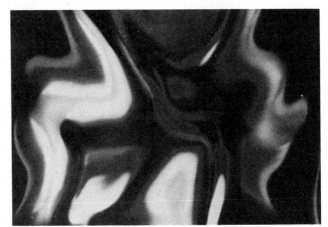

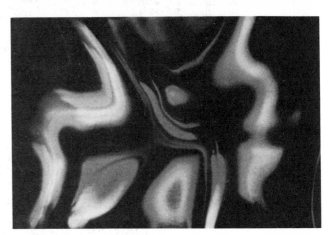

From *Neuron* by Robert Russett. Individual frames are composed of multiple images.

From *Thalamus* (1973—) by Robert Russett. Various forms of light manipulation create pulsing chromatic forms.

John Stehura

John Stehura.

John Stehura was born in 1942 in Chicago, Illinois, and attended UCLA where he received a B.A. degree in film and an M.A. degree in art. He began studying computer programming while enrolled at UCLA and later also studied engineering in the Ph.D. program at the University of Waterloo, Canada. In 1965, after four years of computer research, Stehura programmed the complex and fascinating images used in his film *Cibernetik 5.3*. Since then, he has spent most of his time developing a special computer language for unifying music and graphic animation systems. His work in recent years has basically consisted of experimenting with various models of animation software and filming test sequences. Below are excerpts from Stehura's *Program Notes For The Film* CIBERNETIK 5.3.In his original text, computer characters and phonetic spelling were used to describe his approach to animation.

PROGRAM NOTES FOR THE FILM "CIBERNETIK 5.3"
by John Stehura
DURING THE LAST FEW THOUSAND YEARS PEOPLE ON ALL CONTINENTS HAVE ASSISTED IN THE CREATION OF FOOD PLANTS AND ANIMALS, WHICH AS AN INDIRECT AND PARTLY SELF SUSTAINING ART HAS HAD GOOD YIELDS AND BENEFITS. AND IN A SIMILAR MANNER WITH REGARD TO COMMUNICATIONS, AND THE INSTRUMENTS INVOLVED, THE ELECTRONIC PROCESSOR OFFERS SOME PARALLELS WITH REGARD TO PERSONAL AND RESPONSIVE, OR INTERACTIVE APPLICATIONS.

DURING 1961 I HAD DESIGNED A NUMBER OF MECHANISMS WITH REGARD TO GRAPHICS, TO STUDY THE RANGE OF GRAPHIC POSSIBILITIES AVAILABLE WITH DIGITAL SYSTEMS, AS WELL AS INDEPENDENT SELF-REGULATING AND GENETIC-ORIENTED CONTROL MECHANISMS, AND VARIOUS INTERACTIVE SYSTEMS WITH HIGHLY RESPONSIVE CHARACTERISTICS. THE EARLY PROJECTS, TILL 1965, CONSISTED OF WORK ON A SERIES OF BASIC APPROACHES THAT CAN BE USED TO MAKE ANIMATED IMAGERY. EACH SYSTEM OR APPROACH IS BASED ON A UNIQUE AND BASIC THEORY OF DESIGN:
1) THE GENERATION OF IMAGES USING MOSAICS, LIKE COLOR TILES, OR SCANNED 1 THRU 3 DIMENSIONAL ARRAYS.
2) GENERATION THROUGH MOBILE BUT FIXED LINKAGES, LIKE THE HAND AND ARM.
3) DESIGN GENERATION THROUGH THE USE OF REFLECTIVE SURFACES, AND THE RECORDING OF 1 OR MANY OPTICAL TRAJECTORIES.
4) IMAGE PARTICLE ARRANGEMENT THROUGH POSITIONING VARIABLE POSITIVE AND NEGATIVE FIELDS IN 2 OR 3 SPACE.
5) SHAPE GENERATION THROUGH ADDITIVE, SUBTRACTIVE OR LOGICAL MASKING OF MOBILE FORMS.

IN THEORY EACH APPROACH COULD BE USED TO GENERATE A LARGE RANGE OF ANIMATED IMAGES, BUT EACH APPROACH ACTUALLY POSSESSES

SPECIFIC FAVORABLE CHARACTERISTICS, FOR SPECIFIC CIRCUMSTANCES. (WE CAN EASILY RECOGNIZE EACH OF THESE TECHNIQUES AS THEY ARE USED IN OTHER CRAFTS OR SIMPLY AS NATURAL PHENOMENA). THE FOLLOWING STEP INVOLVED THE INTEGRATION OF THE SEPARATE DESIGN SYSTEMS INTO ONE UNIFIED PROCESSING SYSTEM, NEXT, 'INSTRUCTING' THE SYSTEM HOW TO CONTROL ITS OWN PARAMETERS, AS AN ORGANISM WITHIN AN ENVIRONMENT, ALLOWING VARIOUS FORMS OF INTERACTION BETWEEN THE IMAGES THEMSELVES, AS WITH A PROTOZOAN OR PLANETARY SYSTEM.

THE FILM 'CIBERNETIK 5.3' WAS GENERATED BY A FULLY AUTOMATIC ANIMATION PROGRAM (SYSTEM FIVE VERSION THREE) WHICH TO SOME DEGREE INTEGRATED ALL OF THE BASIC IMAGE FORMATION APPROACHES AS WELL AS HAVING THE ABILITY TO BE INSTRUCTED IN GENERAL TERMS AS TO THE USE OF ITS CONTROLS IN THE CREATION AND MAINTENANCE OF THREE DIMENSIONAL GRAPHIC AND ACOUSTIC ENVIRONMENTS. IN SOME AREAS OF DESIGN, FULLY AUTOMATIC DESIGN MECHANISMS ARE THE BEST WAY TO ACHIEVE A RESULT, WHILE HAND WORK MIGHT BE BEST IN A SLIGHTLY DIFFERENT SITUATION. IN ANY CASE I BELIEVED THIS EXPERIMENT WAS SIGNIFICANT TO PERFORM, AND ITS POTENTIAL TO GENERATE INTERESTING IMAGES WAS BETTER THAN I WOULD HAVE GUESSED, AND THE FIRST TEST RESULTED IN THE FILM. THE FILM WAS GENERATED IN 1965 AND SHOWN THE FOLLOWING YEAR AT UCLA, AND ACCIDENTALLY GOT ITS FIRST LARGE SHOWING AS BACKGROUND MATERIAL FOR A JIMI HENDRIX CONCERT AND LATER AT VARIOUS FILM EXHIBITIONS, AND AGAIN THROUGH 'THE SINGLE WING TOURQUESE BIRD-LIGHT SHOW' IN THE MOVIE 'THE BABY MAKER.'—THE NEXT SEVERAL YEARS WERE SPENT BUILDING A META DESIGN SYSTEM THAT COULD RAPIDLY GENERATE A LARGE NUMBER OF SYSTEMS, SUCH AS USED IN MAKING THIS FILM, AS WELL AS ANY PREVIOUS SPECIAL SYSTEMS OR FUTURE COMBINATIONS. . . .

CIBERNETIK 5.3: IMIJ KONSTRUKTSHUN MODEL 5 VERSHUN 3 (1962-65) IZ A SPESHALIZED CIBERNETIK SISTEM UV MOSHUN PIKCHER PRODUKSHUN. IT IZ AN INISHEL EKSPLORASHUN IN PRINCIPELS UV PATTERN FORMASHUN AND VARIASHUN, OPTIKAL AND AUDIO TEKHNIQUES. BASED ON PRINCIPELS UV DESIEN THE SISTEM KAN PRODUUS AN UNLIMITED

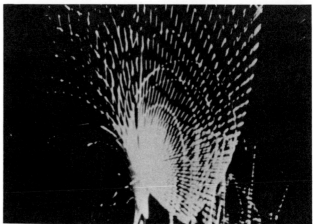

From *CIBERNETIK 5.3* (1962–1965) by John Stehura, a sequence of computer generated frames showing whirling clusters of geometric forms in three-dimensional space.

NUMBER UV MOSHUN GRAFIK AND AUDEO PRODUK-SHUNS EECH WITH ANI REQUESTED DURASHUN. <T2> <T4> PATTERN FORMASHUN: THE BASIK PATTERN UNIT IZ KALLED AN IMIJ. UP TU 25 IMIJES MAE BE UZED AT WUN TIEM. EECH IMIJ IZ SPESIFIED AZ A KONNEKTED SEREEZ UV LINZ. IMIJES AER JENERATED AT THE BEGINNING OV A NU FILM AND DUURING ITS PRODUKSHUN. THEER AER 2 METHODS OV IMIJ JENERATSHUN, SIMMETRIKAL AND RANDOM. THE FORMASHUN UV SIMMETRIKAL IMIJES IZ ESTABLISHED BI INTERFERENSS UV 2 OR 3, LO SUMMASHUN SEERES NUMBERS, PRODUUSING A SERIEZ UV LINZ. FOR EKSAMPEL, THE 2 NUMBERZ: 3 & 5 KAN DESIGNAET A KOMPLEET BILATERAL SIMMETRIKAL PATERN OVER 15 UNITS IN LENKTH WITH THE SEQUENSHAL PROPORSHUNS UV: 3,2,1,3,

1,2,3, BI THE SQUAER WAEV INTERFERENS OV THE 2 NUMBERS. THIS MODEL UZES THE RESULTANT PROPORSHUN LIST AZ A LIEN LIST & PROCEEDS TU ROTAET THE ANGULAR CHAANG BETWEEN EECH LIEN, IN PROPORSHUN TU THE LENKTH UV THE LIEN, SO THAT THE START POINT MEETS THE END POINT, FORMING A KLOZED LIEN LUUP. THE RANDOM IMIJ IZ KONSTRUKTED WITHIN REKTANGULAR SPAS BOUNDZ WITH A SPESIFIED NUMBER OV RANDOM LINZ, WITH RANDOM RANGGS UV POINT TRAJEK-TOREE MOSHUN.

(From technical notes, May 1975.)

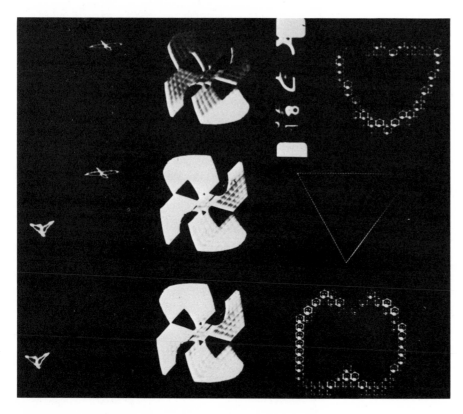

Test images from Stehura's experiments in computer graphics: animated line drawing of a bird in flight (left); the technique of mobile surface shading (center); mosaic elements defining a linear shape in motion (right).

Emile Reynaud's Optical Theatre, Paris. 1892–1900.

A Note on the Origins of Animation

In the beginning all animation was experimental. It derived from Emile Reynaud's Optical Theater (1892), which, though not photographed for mass reproduction, surpassed other motion-illusion devices (such as Joseph Plateau's Phenakistiscope and Reynaud's own Praxinoscope) in its ability to depict a full story before a large audience on a larger-than-life-sized screen.

The first generation of animators to use motion picture photography before 1910—Emile Cohl, Ségundo de Chomon, J. Stuart Blackton, Arthur Melbourne-Cooper and Winsor McCay—had little or no contact with each other; possibly they knew each others' work, since films at that time were an easily exported commodity. Arthur Melbourne-Cooper is said to have produced an animation commercial in England for Birds' Custard Powder as early as 1897, and an animated matchstick film in 1899 to aid British soldiers in the Boer War. Ségundo de Chomon in Spain made his first animation film in 1905—a stop-motion film of animated objects entitled *El Hotel Eléctrico*, which is thought to have inspired J. Stuart Blackton's *Haunted Hotel* in 1907 in the United States. These films have much in common with the fantasy films of George Méliès, in spirit rather than technique; Méliès used elaborate drawings as moving props, settings, vehicles, even characters, usually within a stage setting, not on a frame-by-frame basis.

Emile Cohl, perhaps the best-known animator of the early period, was 51 years old when he made *Fantas-*magoria (1908), the first of a long list of animation films he made in France; later he worked in the United States with cartoonist George MacManus on a series entitled *Professor Bonehead* (1912). Another well-known American cartoonist, Winsor McCay, made some 4,000 individual drawings to bring to life his popular comic strip, *Little Nemo*, in 1911. (McCay's well-known *Gertie the Dinosaur*, which is often incorrectly called the first American cartoon film, was made, copyrighted, and released considerably later, in 1914.

In 1913 the Canadian animator Raoul Barré created what is considered the world's first animation studio. John Bray set up a similar studio in the United States in 1914; his animation productions were already being released on a monthly basis through Pathé. Bray and Earl Hurd obtained the basic patents for cel animation in 1914 and 1915. From then on, the animation business proliferated. There followed generation after generation of immensely popular cartoon characters, from Koko the Clown and Felix the Cat to Mickey Mouse and Betty Boop, Bugs Bunny and Mr. Magoo. While these cartoons were innovative in style and technique, sooner or later individuality and creativity tended to subserve assembly-line techniques, deadlines, and marketability, as in any mass-production enterprise.

The artists whose films concern us in this book set forth from entirely different origins into completely new areas of animation.

2/Pioneers of Abstract Animation in Europe

Cecile Starr

INTRODUCTION TO THE EUROPEAN ANIMATORS
"It's the thing of the future," the French poet Guillaume Apollinaire wrote in 1914. "It has to come if our art is to have any relation to this rhythmic moving cinematographic age of ours." Apollinaire was writing about the plan of Léopold Sturzwage (later Survage) to set a series of abstract paintings in motion, using the newly established techniques of film animation.

Survage began his series of nearly 200 abstract water colors in 1912, only two years after Wassily Kandinsky had made his first entirely nonrepresentational painting. Finding no one willing to animate his Colored Rhythm designs, Survage went no further with the project and devoted the rest of his life to painting.

During the same period, the Swedish painter Viking Eggeling, who also lived in Paris, was struggling with the concept of a universal language of abstract images, as yet unaware that the motion picture was the medium to which these struggles would lead him. No concrete evidence has yet been presented that Eggeling knew of Survage's proposed film; but it seems likely enough that, in the interconnecting circles of modern artists in pre-war Paris, Eggeling had heard or read of the Colored Rhythm sketches. Eggeling's friend and neighbor, Amedeo Modigliani, whose studio was just across the hall, knew Survage well enough to paint his portrait; and the writer Tristan Tzara was a close friend of both Eggeling and Survage.

It was Tzara who introduced Eggeling to the Dada group in Zurich after the war, and to the German painter, Hans Richter, in particular. The subsequent collaboration between Eggeling and Richter took them on to Berlin where their pursuit of a meaningful system of abstract forms took ultimate shape in moving pictures: Eggeling's *Diagonal Symphony* and Richter's *Rhythm 21*, *Rhythm 23*, and *Rhythm 25*. But before these films were completed, another artist, Walter Ruttmann, had presented his finished hand-colored abstract film entitled *Lightplay Opus I* in several German cities.

Ruttmann's film was first reviewed on April 2, 1921, by a Swiss critic and dramatist named Bernhard Diebold, under the heading "A New Art, The Vision-Music of Films." We do not know what role Diebold may have played in influencing the early abstract animators (he had written about a proposed synthesis of painting, dance, music, and film as early as 1916). But we do know that at the first screening of Ruttmann's film, Diebold was accompanied by his young friend Oskar Fischinger, who had clipped and saved Diebold's earlier articles (which he kept for the rest of his life); Fischinger was just beginning his own first steps into experimental animation at that time, with Diebold as his mentor.

In addition to their backgrounds in painting and graphic art, and their close association with the avant-garde writers of the time, music was another bond these early abstract animators shared. Survage, son of a Russian

33

piano manufacturer, had given up music for painting, but worked as a piano tuner in his early years in Paris. Eggeling, whose father owned a music shop in Sweden, was also a pianist, as was Richter. In Zurich, when they were struggling with their first abstract designs, the Italian pianist-composer Ferruccio Busoni turned their attention to *time* as a factor to be reckoned with; Busoni suggested that Richter enlarge his understanding of visual counterpoint by playing Bach's little preludes and fugues. Eggeling called his system of visual systems "The Thorough Bass of Painting," borrowing a term that applied specifically to Bach's music. Walter Ruttmann was a cellist and violinist as well as a painter, engraver, and lithographer, and Oskar Fischinger was apprenticed to an organ builder before becoming an engineer.

Fischinger, the first of the group to combine technical as well as musical and artistic talents, was also the first to make his life's work in abstract animation. In addition, he had his films shown as popular entertainment in movie theaters, facilitated no doubt by his choice of light classics as musical accompaniment for many of his early sound films. (Richter and Eggeling thought of their films as visual music, and provided no sound accompaniment for them; Ruttmann had special scores composed for his *Opus* films.)

Within a few short years, both Richter and Ruttmann moved away from animation into other aspects of filmmaking, where they won more widespread recognition. Viking Eggeling's work came to an end with his early death in 1925. By 1935, when abstract painting was outlawed in Hitler's Germany, the abstract animation film found new life across the Channel in England, where it was given freshness and vigor by Len Lye and Norman McLaren (see Chapters 5 and 7), with sound and color as added elements for increased experimentation. The London Film Society, which had showed virtually all the important animated films produced in Europe in the 1920s and early 1930s, had also helped finance Len Lye's first film, in 1929. It is perhaps fitting that some of Lye's wartime abstract films carried slogans to help raise British morale against Germany's seeming invincibility—free film fighting against controlled film, so to speak.

Oskar Fischinger had left Germany for North America early in 1936; McLaren followed a few years later, and Len Lye after that. Abstract animation, which first had taken root in continental Europe, flourished in London for a while, then was transplanted across the ocean in the United States and Canada. It has since remained an essentially North American art.

In singling out these early pioneers in abstract animation, we overlook others whose films no longer exist or who worked only partly in animation. A place of honor is reserved, however, for Fernand Léger, whose film *Ballet Mécanique* (1924) combined live-action near-abstractions, frame-by-frame animation of paper cutouts, and three-dimensional objects with a mastery of style and tempo that still astonishes the viewer today. Its influence upon other filmmaker-artists cannot be overestimated. At the other end of the line, we learn of a mysterious Mr. Jens whose film, entitled *Color Abstract*, is described in the program notes of the London Film Society as "direct hand-painting on the film" with a small amount of photographic material interspersed. The film is dated Germany, 1932. No further record of this germinal film or its filmmaker seems to exist.

While the work of the pioneer abstract animators in Europe is of inestimable historical importance as a movement, it is the quality of their artistry that deserves our greatest attention. Many of the films described in the following pages are individually striking, even dazzling achievements. They remain unrivalled by the subsequent works of later innovators, growing rather than diminishing in value with the passing of time, like all works of art. Yet these films, and the men who made them, have barely begun to receive their full recognition. Some day the names of Ruttmann, Eggeling, Richter, Fischinger, and Len Lye will be prominently inscribed in all the histories of art and film, as the first to cross into the future that had to come, and is still coming.

Léopold Survage

Léopold Survage painting one of his Colored Rhythm series, drawing by Pablo Picasso, 1912.

Léopold Survage was the first known artist to theorize and design a work of abstract animation. His colored "plates," made in the years 1912-1914, were never filmed; 59 of them are now owned by The Museum of Modern Art in New York, 12 by the Cinémathèque Française, and others mainly by Survage's family and artist-friends. While his position as a forerunner of abstract animation should not be minimized, Survage was clearly not an animator. Although he conceived the bridge between painting and film, which later artists were to cross, he remained a painter and continued painting in France until his death in 1968. Large sweeping patterns, which dominate the backgrounds of many of Survage's works, give them a sense of motion that is both characteristic and distinctive, the only reminder of his exploratory efforts in film.

Survage, born Sturwage in Moscow in 1879, attended the School of Fine Arts there, and found himself greatly impressed with the modern French paintings (Manet, Gaugin and the Impressionists) he saw in private collections soon after the turn of the century—"real art . . . absolutely different in spirit from what they taught us at the school." Disillusioned with both sides after the 1905 Revolution, he arrived in Paris in 1908, intending to earn his living as a piano-tuner and to study evenings at the studio of Henri Matisse. He first exhibited his paintings in 1912, at the Salon des Indépendants, in the Cubist gallery. Survage was a familiar, if taciturn figure in a circle of artists that included Picasso, Braque, Modigliani, Léger, Brancusi, and many others.

Inspired by the trends in abstract and cubist painting, Survage began his rhythm-color "symphonies" in movement. At the suggestion of his sculptor friend Alexander Archipenko, Survage presented a description of his Colored Rhythm series, with illustrations, to the avant-garde poet and critic Guillaume Apollinaire, who published them in the final issue of his review, *Les Soirées de Paris* (July–August, 1914), calling them the "ninth muse". At about the same time Survage registered a shorter description of his proposed work at the Academy of Sciences in Paris. He also presented his plan to the Gaumont Company, which had developed a primitive color process around 1911, but nothing came of it.

Survage had his first one-man exhibition in 1917, under Apollinaire's patronage. In an accompanying bulletin, Apollinaire wrote that Survage had "invented a new art of painting in motion," which was about to manifest itself by means of cinema. The writer called Survage "the glistening bridge" (*le pont chatoyant*), between the painters of the past and "the magnificent urge that is to transport the new painters." In 1919, another French poet, Blaise Cendrars, who like Apollinaire was enamored of the poetic possibilities in cinema, made a unique attempt to bring Survage's Colored Rhythm series to life through words, using analogies to living organisms.

COLOR, MOVEMENT, RHYTHM
By Léopold Survage

Painting, having liberated itself from the conventional forms of objects in the exterior world, has conquered the terrain of abstract forms. It must get rid of its last and principal shackle—immobility—so as to become as supple and rich a means of expressing our emotions as music is. Everything that is accessible to us has its duration in time, which finds its strongest manifestation in rhythm, action and movement, real, arranged, and unarranged.

I will animate my painting, I will give it movement, I will introduce rhythm into the concrete action of my abstract painting, born of my interior life; my instrument will be the cinematographic film, this true symbol of accumulated movement. It will execute the "scores" of my visions, corresponding to my state of mind in its successive phases.

I am creating a new visual art in time, that of colored rhythm and of rhythmic color.

(signed) Leopold Sturzwage
Paris, 1914

(Text of a sealed document, no. 8182, deposited on June 29, 1914, at the Academy of Sciences of Paris.)

COLORED RHYTHM
by Léopold Survage

Colored rhythm is in no way an illustration or an interpretation of musical work. It is an autonomous art, although based on the same psychological premises as music.

ON ITS ANALOGY TO MUSIC. It is the mode of succession of their elements in time which establishes the analogy to music, sound rhythm, and colored rhythm, whose realization I am advocating by means of cinematography. Sound is the primordial element of music. Combinations of musical sounds, based on the law of simple relationships between the numbers of vibrations of simultaneous sounds, form musical harmonies. These combine into musical phrases. Other factors intervene: the intensity of the sounds, their timbre, etc. But music is always a mode of succession IN TIME of diverse sound vibrations. Musical work is a sort of subtle language by whose means the composer expresses his state of mind, or to use a felicitous expression, his interior dynamism. The performance of a musical work arouses in us something analogous to this dynamism of the composer; the more sensitive the listener—as an instrument of perception would be—the greater the intimacy between him and the musician.

The fundamental element of my dynamic art is COLORED VISUAL FORM which plays a role analogous to that of sound in music.

This element is determined by three factors: 1) visual form proper (abstract); 2) rhythm, that is to say, the movement and the transformations of this form; 3) color.

FORM, RHYTHM By visual abstract form I mean all generalization or geometrization of a form, of an object, of things around us. The form of these objects, quite

Colored Rhythm, studies of the film, Léopold Survage, 1913, watercolor, brush and ink. (Collection, The Museum of Modern Art, New York.) Standish Lawder, in *The Cubist Cinema*, described the Survage drawings he saw in the Museum of Modern Art collection as simple hues of yellow, orange, green, blue, red, and purple, growing out of a black void, and retreating to it. They varied in form "from hard-edged, though rarely rigidly geometrical, to softer, blurred areas of color, shapes that were frequently rounded, curving or pointed. . . . Nowhere was there to be a sense of gravity or density. The forms floated weightlessly, without regard to up or down, transforming themselves at will . . ."

simple and familiar like a tree, a piece of furniture, a man, is in fact so complicated. The further one studies the details of these objects, the more they rebel against simple representation. The means proposed for representing abstractly the irregular form of a real body is to reduce it to a geometric form, simple or complex; and these transformed representations would be with respect to the forms of objects of the outside world, what musical sound is with respect to noise. But this is not enough to represent a state of mind or arouse an emotion.

An immobile abstract form is still not expressive enough. Round or pointed, oblong or square, simple or complicated, it produces an extremely confused SENSATION; it is only a simple graphic notation. Only when it begins to move, when it transforms itself and meets other forms is it able to arouse a FEELING. Through its role and its destination it becomes abstract. In transforming itself in time, it sweeps through space, it encounters other forms in the process of transformation; they combine together, sometimes travelling side by side, sometimes battling among themselves or dancing to the rhythm imposed by a certain cadence, itself obeying the soul of the creator, successively gay, sad, dreamy, meditative... There they are arriving at an equilibrium. No! that equilibrium was unstable and the transformations begin again; in this way visual rhythm becomes analogous to sound rhythm in music.

In both these domains, rhythm plays the same role. Consequently, in the world of plastic arts, the visual form of each body is precious to us only as a source, as a means of expressing and evoking our interior dynamism, and not at all to represent the meaning or importance that this body may take, in reality, in our life. From the point of view of this dynamic art, visual form becomes the expression and the result of a manifestation of form-energy, in its ambience. So much for form and rhythm, which are inseparable.

COLOR Produced by coloring matter, whether by radiance or by projection, it is the cosmos; it is the energy-ambience, at the same time, for our receptive apparatus for perceiving light waves: the eye.

Psychologically, it is neither color nor sound, absolute, isolated, which touch and influence us, but the alternating series of colors and sounds. As a result, thanks to its principle of mobility, the art of colored rhythm increases this alternation which exists already in ordinary painting, but only as a group of colors simultaneously fixed on an immobile surface and without changing relationships. By means of movement, the character of these colors acquires a force superior to that of immobile harmonies.

From this fact, color in its turn allies itself to rhythm. Ceasing to be an accessory to objects, it becomes the content, the very soul of abstract form. The technical difficulties reside in the realization of cinematographic films for the projection of colored rhythm.

For a three-minute piece, one must consider the registration of one thousand to two thousand images. That is quite a lot! But I do not propose to execute them all myself. I will provide only the essential steps. From these, the draftsmen, with a little good sense, will know how to deduce the intermediary images, of which I will have indicated the quantity, hence the cadence. When the plates are finished, they will be passed in succession before the lens of a three-color cinematographic apparatus.

(From *Les Soirées de Paris*, July–August 1914.)

COLORED RHYTHM
by Guillaume Apollinaire

I had foreseen this art which would be to painting what music is to literature. The artist who has taken the pains to give it birth is named Léopold Sturzwage. He lives in a sixth-floor walk-up in Montrouge. He has communicated the characteristics of his idea to the Academy of Sciences and seeks a cinematographic company willing to pay the costs of the first attempts at colored orchestration.

One can compare Colored Rhythm to music, but the analogies are superficial, and it really is an independent art having infinitely varied resources of its own.

It draws its origin from fireworks, fountains, electric signs, and those fairy-tale palaces which at every amusement park accustom the eyes to enjoy kaleidoscopic changes in hue.

We thus will have beyond static painting, beyond cinematographic representation, an art to which one will quickly accustom oneself and which will render its followers infinitely sensitive to the movement of colors, to their interpenetration, to their fast or slow changes, to their convergence and to their flight, etc.

There is no doubt that the name of Léopold Sturzwage, to whom we owe a new Muse, will soon become famous.

(From *Paris-Journal*, July 15, 1914)

THE BIRTH OF THE COLORS
by Blaise Cendrars

Mr. Léopold Survage is the author of a theory on the rhythmics of colors. He has discovered the genesis of animated colors. His reflections and his studies on contrasted color waves led him to imagine a film to display this genesis in the cinema. Alas! The direct filming of colors is

still unrealizable in the cinema. I am going to try to render in words as photogenic as possible the forceful way in which Mr. Léopold Survage manages to recreate and break down the circular movement of color. He has more than 200 sketches. One would think oneself witnessing the very creation of the world.

Red little by little invades the black screen and soon fills the whole visual disk. It is a somber red, of a rough nature, wrinkled like seaweed. It is composed of a multitude of little flat scales placed alongside each other. Atop each of these little scales is a tiny blister which trembles softly and ends by bursting like cooling lava. Suddenly, the seaweed red divides in the middle. The scales regroup themselves to the left and to the right; the blisters increase their movement. A blue streak appears which widens and grows rapidly, from above and below. Frondlike, this blue extends its branches in all directions and grows little trembling leaves on the red, wedge-shaped like the leaflets of the maidenhair fern. The red scales and the blue leaflets now alternate two by two, quiver, turn gently, disappear. There remain on the screen only two large bean-shaped spots, one red, the other blue, facing each other. One could call them two embryos, masculine and feminine. They approach each other, join together, divide, reproduce by cells or by groups of cells. Each spore, each tiny spore is surrounded by a fine violet line which soon grows larger, swells and distends like a pistil. This pistil becomes plump, its head grows larger as you watch it. Little orange-colored lozenges grow bigger in turn, and multiply extremely rapidly. The orange and the violet devour and tear each other. Branches, boughs, trunks, all tremble, lie down and rise up again. Suddenly the orange spreads out like the flower of a gourd lightly striated with gold. At the bottom of its calyx, two violet pistils curve over a red and blue stamen. Everything turns dizzily from the center to the periphery. A ball is formed, a dazzling ball, of the most beautiful yellow. It might be a fruit. The yellow explodes. Confetti-like multi-colored fruit seeds scatter in every direction. Multiform seeds which fall again majestically, from above downward. This movement goes faster and everything falls thick and fast like hail, and uniformly green. Some threads take shape, chains and bonds. Thin branches, knotted stalks, rising tall or creeping. One might call it a pastureland which turns brownish, turns grayish little by little in order to dissolve slowly into a fog of vague forms. Vanishing to white. The white fixes itself and hardens, the disk, the black disk reappears and obstructs the visual field.

(From *La Rose Rouge*, July 17 1919.)

Walter Ruttmann

Walter Ruttmann, around 1921.

"A New Art, The Vision-Music of Films." Diebold and his young friend Oskar Fischinger were "greatly impressed with this work", which was according to William Moritz, Fischinger's biographer, "not only the first abstract film to be shown in public, but also a film hand-tinted in striking and subtle colors, with a live, synchronous musical score composed especially for it."

While no copies of the film are known to exist, the original score by Max Butting has been placed in the Swedish Film Institute, bearing Ruttmann's crayonned sketches to the music as guides to its synchronization.

Ruttmann continued his abstract experiments for the next few years, with his *Opus II*, *Opus III*, and *Opus IV*, which were widely shown and written about. The three films were screened at the London Film Society on October 25, 1925, with program notes describing them as "studies in pattern, with a drum accompaniment." The following day *The London Times* described them as "Absolute Films—a series of moving patterns which produce the liveliest response in the spectator." While *Opus IV* was found the least successful, *Opus II* had a "delightful grace" and *Opus III* "an astonishing suggestion of vastness and strength in the abstract." The review concluded: "Mr. Ruttmann's three works opened the afternoon and lasted not long, but we shall remember them after the rest has been forgotten." (As *Opus I* was not included in this program, we may wonder if there were no existing prints even at that early date. Max Butting, in his memoirs, wrote that "this *Opus I* was nevertheless soon antiquated." Conceivably Ruttmann did not wish it to be seen, after he had made improvements in the later films.)

The techniques Ruttmann employed in these four films have not been adequately recorded in film literature. Richter wrote in the mid-1940s that Ruttmann turned plasticine forms on horizontal sticks, changing their shapes between film takes. Lotte Reiniger has recalled that Ruttmann painted the films "on a very small glass plate," and Standish Lawder in *The Cubist Cinema* proposes that mirrors were used to distort and animate the painted designs. Possibly these and other techniques were used in combination.

Walter Ruttmann was born in Frankfort in 1887, studied

In the spring of 1921, Walter Ruttmann showed his short film *Lichtspiel Opus I* (*Lightplay Opus I*) in Frankfort, Germany. This is thought to be the first screening of an abstract animated film seen by a general audience anywhere in the world. The film was reviewed by Bernhard Diebold in the *Frankfurter Zeitung* under the heading

painting as a young man, and served as a lieutenant in the German Army from 1914 to 1918. He is quoted as saying, after the war, that it made no sense to paint any more, unless the painting could be set in motion. He had been a life-long film enthusiast when he began his animation experiments. During the years when the *Opus* films were created, Ruttmann also made short abstract films for advertising purposes in Munich and in Berlin. In 1923 he created the "Dreams of Hawks" sequence for Fritz Lang's *Siegfried*, which was thought quite daring in its time.

He joined Lotte Reiniger (See Chapter 3) for her feature length silhouette animation film, *The Adventures of Prince Achmed*, working out the special fantasy effects and backgrounds. For some of the fantasy effects, most notably in the opening of the film, Ruttmann used the wax-slicing machine he had commissioned from Oskar Fischinger the year after their first meeting in Frankfort.

Prince Achmed was completed in 1926, and after that Ruttmann gave up animation and turned to editing and making documentary films. His *Berlin, Symphony of a Great City* (1927), scripted by Carl Mayer, with photography by Karl Freund and others under Ruttmann's direction, won worldwide acclaim as an avant-garde documentary. It opens with a 30-second segment of abstract animation. *Weekend*, a 15-minute sound-montage evoking an escape to the country, commissioned by the Berlin Broadcasting System, was recorded and edited on film, the most flexible medium then available. Hans Richter has called it "one of the outstanding experiments in sound ever made."

After a short stay in Paris in the late 1920s, Ruttmann went to Italy and filmed *Accaiao* (*Steel*) in 1932, based on a theme by the playwright Luigi Pirandello. On his return to Germany, he made a German version of the film, as well as other films about urban life. These documentary films often reflected the early attention he had given to moving forms and light patterns. In 1936 Ruttmann collaborated on the editing of Leni Riefenstahl's impressive *Olympia*.

According to an obituary in *Film-Kurrier*, Ruttmann died in Berlin on July 15, 1941, after a serious operation, which contradicts the report that he was killed while filming on the Russian Front.

THE FILMED SYMPHONY
by Leonhard Adelt

The lights go out, the projector starts, writing appears and disappears on a white wall so quickly you can barely read: "Opus I, Symphony in Three Movements." The composer, if I understand it right, is named Brunning [Butting—*ed.*], the painter, Walter Ruttmann.

And it's the painter that matters. Wrapped in the darkness of the room, he is among us. I saw him briefly before the change in light merged our existence into the nothingness of the white screen. Tall, haggard, an American type, of uncertain age, with sleepless lids over his transcendent look, he answered curious questions with only a helpless smile on his thin-lipped mouth.

Now his work is talking for him, without words, without sound, in changeable form. The gentle hues of the planes—sky-blue, dusk-red, dawn-green—playing according to rhythmical laws, are changing into geometrical forms, uni-colored and two-dimensional: angles, squares, circles, wavy lines. Fiery tongues, stinging, the sun's disk glowing fiery-red, then disappearing; stylized clouds lowering and moving away, colored balls rolling like children's balloons, white waves rearing into a crescendo with foamy paws like polar bears, overlaid with a leitmotif of dolphin-like arabesques. In the final movement squares rush by like letters in a sorting machine at a post-office. The concepts of sound painting or tone color seemed literally to fulfill their meaning; content and character of the musical piece express themselves, silently moving in the forms and colors of the continuous motion picture.

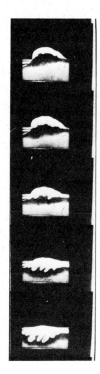

From *Lichtspiel Opus I* (1921) by Walter Ruttmann.

That an artist with the means of his art achieves effects in the field of another art is not without example; dance and opera also, silently or eloquently, are able to express musical values. Not so, the fine arts. If a painter wanted to represent the effects of music, he could do it only indirectly by showing a circle of listeners seemingly moved by a Beethoven sonata, with the master's death-mask in the background so there would be no misunderstanding as to the meaning of the picture. The obstacle to a direct presentation was that fine arts remain closely tied to frozen form. Music, however, as a rhythmical sequence of sound, is movement, so that these two media are mutually exclusive. This antithesis is now bridged through the moving picture of the music-painter Ruttmann.

He does it through the medium of the film, mind you, not through film *per se*. The film *per se*, which does nothing but photograph continuously, is totally without art; only by transcending its automatic naturalism will it become the servant of the arts, will it serve the poetic imagination, the dramatic *mis-en-scène*, the mimic presentation, and in animated film the graphic inspiration. Even then film is not art in itself, but just its technical medium of expression, thus not to be equated with poetry or painting but only with the scenic frame and the canvas which only creative imagination can fill with the figments of its pre-destined art form.

The painter Ruttmann, who sees music as a painterly movement of form, just as other people might perceive it as an emotional experience or a law of harmony, technically continues the tradition of the animated film in order to find an immediate expression for his vision. His technical production procedure is very painstaking: with seemingly microscopic exactness, the painter must produce a series of many thousands of drawings and then color them. This continuing pictorial sequence, like music—that is the bridging element between the two—is basically an element of eurhythmy, moving form whose rhythm fulfills itself according to the laws of harmony of the presented symphony. The baton of the conductor also describes invisible forms and lines in the air; if these lines were to become visible, they would coincide with the form-play of the symphonic film up to the point where the translator connects the individual freedom of his painterly imagination with the deeply experienced musical piece.

Ruttmann, as an artist who aims for direct expression of experience, is an expressionist, which means that in place of traditional schemes of communication he substitutes a completely subjective expression. He therefore maintains this free interpretation, which is the individuality and downfall of expressionism, in contrast to the strict commitment of the conductor. For expressionism, at best, realizes only one postulate of art, namely, to form the individual experience—but more or less deprives itself of the other, that is, letting others share in this experience. The moving picture offers an exit from this impasse—not intellectually like the score—but out of his just feeling for rhythm and harmony, Ruttmann's painterly paraphrase of the score, full of imagination and on the wings of his fantasy, conjures up musical associations, thus communicating his experience in a painterly as well as musical way, just like the dance, whose two-dimensional companion-piece the music-film is.

The projector has stopped, the daylight reveals a circle of professionals and artists, and then cedes again to darkness; because we are so delighted, we have the projectionist run the mute symphony for a second time.

(From *Berliner Tagblatt*, April 21, 1921.)

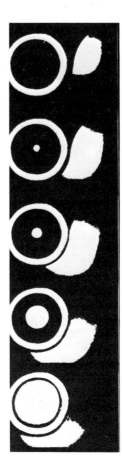

From *Opus II* (*ca.* 1922) by Walter Ruttmann.

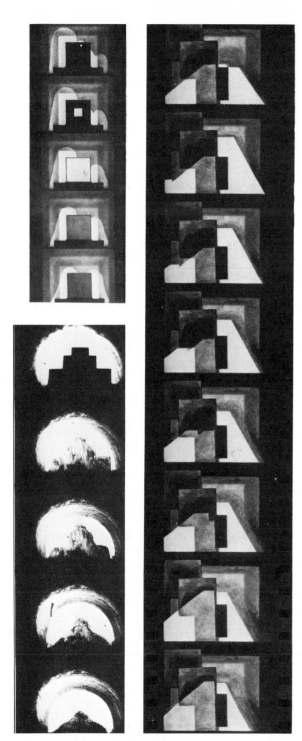

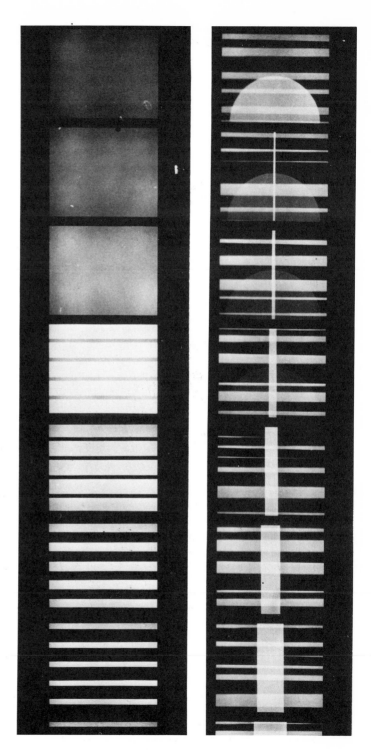

From *Opus III* (*ca.* 1923) by Walter Ruttmann.　　　　　　　　From *Opus IV* (*ca.* 1924) by Walter Ruttmann.

43

Viking Eggeling

Viking Eggeling, around 1924.

Viking Eggeling's importance and originality were well known to many of his contemporaries, although in the fifty years since his death, his name has been all but forgotten. Laszlo Moholy-Nagy, in his book *Painting, Photography and Film* (Munich, 1925) wrote of Eggeling: "Not only was he first to discover the all-prevailing, revolutionary importance of an esthetic of time in film, he set forth its principles with scientific precision and attempted to carry them over into his creative work. His experiments at first leaned upon musical frames of reference, such as the division of time, regulation of tempi, and over-all structure. Slowly, however, his perception of optical timing asserted itself, and so his first work, based upon form-drama, became a veritable ABC of the phenomena of movement, as expressed by light-dark and by variations in direction."

While correcting proofs of his book, Moholy-Nagy learned of Eggeling's death, and added: "Among present-day artists, he was one of the most lucid thinkers and creators. His significance will be heralded with fanfare by somnambulant art historians in years to come."

Viking Eggeling was born in Sweden in 1880, studied and worked in Germany, Switzerland, and Italy before settling in Paris in or around 1911. Among his artist friends were Amedeo Modigliani, who had a studio across from Eggeling's in Paris, and Tristan Tzara and Jean Arp, with whom Eggeling joined hands as a fellow Dadaist in Zurich (1917).

Through his later years, in Paris, Zurich, and Berlin, Eggeling strove to create a new universal language of abstract symbols, searching for "the rules of a plastic counterpoint" (in Arp's words), which he set down on large rolls of paper in "a sort of hieratic writing with the help of figures of rare proportion and beauty." These figures, Arp wrote, "grew, subdivided, multiplied, moved, intertwined from one group to another, vanished and partly reappeared, organized themselves into an impressive construction with plantlike forms." Hans Richter, recalling his first meeting with Eggeling and their subsequent collaboration, has written: "He was far ahead of me in the discovery of the principles of plastic expression when I met him in 1918."

Tristan Tzara described Eggeling as "one of those creatures who in their solitude exceeded the limits of their time, a precursor in all the fullness of this term." Arp admired "his unyielding character, his fanatic love for his work and the work itself," over which, he adds, Eggeling "tormented himself to death."

From 1919 until his death in 1925, Eggeling lived in or near Berlin, collaborating with Hans Richter on scrolls and films, and later with Erna Niemeyer finishing *Diagonal Symphony*, on which Eggeling worked for three or four years. The film was first shown in Berlin at a private screening on November 5, 1924, under auspices of the Curator of National Arts, with comments by the critic Adolph Behne. The first public showing was on May 3, 1925. Eggeling died on May 19th, after an illness of several months.

VIKING EGGELING
by Hans Richter

One day early in 1918, Tzara knocked on the thin partition between our rooms in the Hotel Limmatquai in Zurich, and asked me to come and meet the Swedish painter Viking Eggeling. He had mentioned this artist several times before, and had hinted that he was "experimenting with similar ends in view". I found a burly man of average height, with an aquiline nose and the brilliant blue eyes of a viking. Eggeling showed me a drawing. It was as if someone had laid the Sibylline books open before me. I "understood" at once what it was all about. Here, in its highest perfection, was a level of visual organization comparable with counterpoint in music: a kind of controlled freedom or emancipated discipline, a system within which chance could be given a comprehensible meaning. This was exactly what I was now ready for.

While I, using surfaces, could only produce a limited number of pairs of opposites, he had an inexhaustible supply of such pairs in the realm of the line. Whether this was Art or Anti-art, to me it was the occasion of new insights into the realm of mental and spiritual communication. These brought within my reach the famous "balance between heaven and hell".

In our excitement at the startling similarity of our aims and methods, we became and remained friends. The enthusiastic approval with which I greeted his work was something that had hitherto been denied him, and must have been as much of a surprise to him as was to me the discovery of the artistic possibilities I had been seeking.

In the enthusiasm of our first meeting he presented me with the drawing, which he later borrowed back from me and gave to Arp. (Later Tzara had it.) I was so delighted with this gift that I asked him to come at once to my studio, so that I could give him one of my own pictures. In his presence, I painted a medium-sized abstract canvas, impromptu, in exactly one hour. This he found impossible to understand. How could even one brush stroke be applied, without painstaking analysis and preparation, and without a clearly-defined theme? And in color, too! But the contrast between us, which was that between method and spontaneity, only served to strengthen our mutual attraction, I sought method and discipline to control my spontaneity; he discovered in me the directness of feeling that would allow his methodical art to take wing.

Like me, he had arrived at his theory by way of music, and always explained it in musical terms. He came from a very musical family (to this day there is an "Eggeling's Music Shop" in Lund, Sweden, where he was born). My own first encounter with the arts also took place through music. As a child, I often used to hide under the piano at my mother's weekly musical evenings and listen, overcome with emotion.

As his starting-point, Eggeling had taken the most elementary pictorial element, the line, and he was working on what he called its 'orchestration' (a concept first used by Gauguin in speaking of color). This was the interplay of relationships between lines which he had arranged (as I had done with positive and negative surfaces), in contrapuntal pairs of opposites, within an all-embracing system based on the mutual attraction and repulsion of paired forms. This he called "*Generalbass der Malerei*" [Thorough Bass of Painting]. The drawing that had impressed me so much at our first meeting was, he told me, the product of his systematic creative use of this "*Generalbass.*"

Over and above this, he had an "all-embracing philosophy" which had led him to formulate rules of everyday conduct which had, for him, absolute validity. The interplay of "opposites" and "affinities" was for him the true principle of creation so much so, indeed, that he recognized no exceptions. It was not in my nature to agree with this sort of exclusive thinking. But how could one create a new order of things without insisting on dotting all the 'i's? How else could a vision of the world be achieved in which the greatest was exactly mirrored in the smallest and the smallest in the greatest? It was overwhelming. His incisive mind, his intense personality, his whole heart and soul—all were dedicated to the furtherance of his ideas, even in his choice of food. For instance, he refused to have eggs and milk at the same meal on the grounds, expressed in the same terms as he used for his "linear orchestrations", that "eggs and milk are too 'analogous'."

We were no longer interested in "form" but in a principle governing relationships. Form could be placed in con-

Elementary Tablet, 1917–1918, Viking Eggeling, sketches.

text only by its opposite, and could be brought to life only by the establishment of an inner relationship between the two opposites. This was the only way to create a unity, that is to say, an artistic whole.

At the time we were convinced that we had set foot in completely unknown territory, with musical counterpoint as its only possible analogy.

In fact, however, this idea of the "unity of opposites" has been known, under the name of "contingence", for a very long time. But what we had found still constituted a "discovery". Our scientific and technological age had forgotten that this contingence constituted an essential principle of life and of experience, and that reason with all its consequences was inseparable from *un*reason with all its consequences. The myth that everything in the world can be rationally explained had been gaining ground since the time of Descartes. An inversion was necessary to restore the balance.

The realization that reason and anti-reason, sense and nonsense, design and chance, consciousness and unconsciousness, belong together as necessary parts of a whole—this was the central message of Dada.

(From *Dada: Art and Anti-Art*, 1965, McGraw Hill.)

ABSTRACT FILM ART
by B. G. Kawan

...Eggeling discovered a new territory for graphic art in film. His fundamental insights go beyond the boundaries of a special art genre. He investigated their basic conformities in a *Thorough Bass of Painting*, which would hold true for all art forms, and he found polarity as a primary principle of art. Polarity was a basic ground rule since within itself it reconciled Analogy with Antithesis. In every art work the similarities and dissimilarities of component parts must be presented in order to bring unity to the entire work. Where an ostensibly subordinate part stands unrelated to the whole, the completeness of a work, its identity is destroyed...

Contrasts and relationships of direction, light-intensity, position, speed, etc., unfold and change in a strict regulated sequence. Certain directions (vertical, horizontal, diagonal), or forms, are dominant. Dominants alternate. With the enlargement of one motif, in rhythmic counter-movement, another diminishes. There are corresponding proportional changes as well as regulated variations in tempo. As time is the primary dimension of music, in the making of the first art films, some elements of music were retained. As in music, associations to objects or models from nature were excluded here...

(From *Film-Kurier*, Berlin, November 22, 1924.)

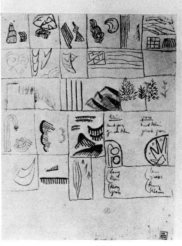

Studies for the *Thorough Bass of Painting*, Viking Eggeling. In his sketches of striations, radiations, and other linear forms, Eggeling set out "to develop a vocabulary of abstract forms and then to explore its grammar and syntax by combining these forms into 'contrapuntal pairs of opposites'..." (Lawder, *The Cubist Cinema*).

VIKING EGGELING
by Adolf Behne

On May 5, [1921] as Viking Eggeling's film was being shown publicly for the first time by the November Group, Eggeling lay ill with blood-poisoning and had been already given up by his doctors. His triumph thus coincided with his death—and one should speak here in terms of triumph. When Eggeling returned to Berlin from Switzerland one year after the war, to finish the abstract film on whose "score" he had labored since 1917, the opposition and obstacles were so enormous that anyone else would have lost heart and given up the fight. But not Eggeling, who went on with his work . . . in a field that was completely new.

Here and there, unknown to each other, a handful of men were dreaming of similar things, without benefit of experience, equipment, method or model. Each first had to create these things for himself. With no other means than his own great effort and intense faith in what he was doing, Eggeling step by step attained his goal. His *Diagonal Symphony* surely did not attack all the problems of the Absolute Film, but I believe that all in all Eggeling has rendered crucial service to inspire others and make their work easier. Undoubtedly he began with the most radical, the most elemental problems and went on to the most complex. I am convinced that a new film by Eggeling would have looked quite different. The graphic style that clings to *Diagonal Symphony* was not so much his style as a step along the way that Eggeling had looked on as essential to his further development.

Viking Eggeling was certainly the first to recognize the artistic, nonliterary possibilities and consequences of films with full clarity. He was one of the few really modern artists, that new breed of artist who is more at home at the drawing board than at the easel, who prefers a ruler to a palette. Although he had an extraordinarily fine sense of color, Eggeling rarely painted in his last years. In light and movement, whose structural aspects he tried to delineate, he found a fresh, pure and vigorous medium of expression.

Not much of Viking Eggeling is now found in museums, but the best of his precise craft will become part of modern culture.

(From *Die Weld am Abend*, Berlin, May 23, 1925.)

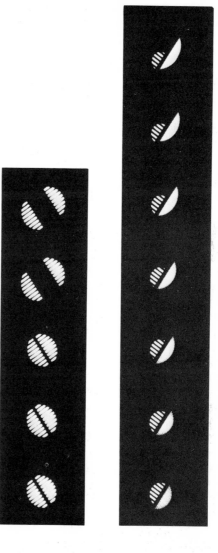

From *Diagonal Symphony* (1921–1924) by Viking Eggeling. "A pair of comb-like forms, first angular and then curved, perform a kind of mechanical dance, one growing, the other shrinking, each moving in perfect response to the gesture of the other." (Lawder, *The Cubist Cinema*).

From *Diagonal Symphony* (1921–1924) by Viking Eggeling. "...In more complex composition, curved and straight lines sprout and retract in regular rhythm, one answering the other." (Lawder, *The Cubist Cinema*).

Hans Richter

Hans Richter, in 1921.

ture films (the quote is from Richter himself): *Inflation* in 1927, for the film entitled *The Lady with the Mask*, and *Race Symphony* in 1928 for *Ariadne in Hoppegarten*.

Born in Berlin in 1888, Richter was active in pre-World War I modern art circles, and in 1916 after his discharge from the Army joined the short-lived but influential Dada group in Zurich. A chance meeting—and after all, chance was everything to the Dada view of art—brought Richter and the Swedish painter Viking Eggeling together in a collaboration that led them from abstract sketches to scroll paintings to films, each in different graphic styles.

In a letter to Alfred Barr (November 16, 1942), Richter explained the basic form and principle on which *Rhythm 21* was designed: "I used the square (or rectangle) as the simplest way of dividing the square *film-screen*, after I had discovered that our scrolls were paintings and followed the laws of painting not of filming. The simple square gave me the opportunity to forget about the complicated matter of our drawings and to concentrate on the orchestration of movement and time."

Once into film, Richter abandoned painting for long periods of time between 1927 and 1939, but he always returned to it with ideas learned from film (just as his first film ideas had come from his painting). In the 1930s Richter travelled, lectured, and made films in a number of European countries. In 1940 he came to New York where he later made three feature-length color films, *Dreams That Money Can Buy* (1944–47), *8 × 8* (1954–57), and *Dadascope* (1957–61), each composed of episodes suggested by well-known artist-friends—Duchamp, Arp, Léger, Ernst, and many others.

From 1942 to 1957, Richter directed the Film Institute of the City College of New York, where he originated the Robert Flaherty Award for the best documentary films each year. During these years he befriended and encouraged or taught Maya Deren, Frank Stauffacher, Jonas Mekas, Shirley Clarke, and others who helped create the post-war American avant-garde movement.

Richter's articles on film and art have been reproduced in many periodicals and anthologies, perhaps the most widely known being "The Film as an Original Art Form."

Hans Richter devoted only the first years of his film work to animation, creating the films *Rhythm 21*, *Rhythm 23*, and *Rhythm 25* in the years between 1921 and 1925. In his *Film Study* (1926) and *Ghosts Before Breakfast* (1927), abstract and object animation sequences are interspersed with nonrealistic live-action photography. During the late 1920s, Richter made a living in advertising films and in expressionist documentaries which were incorporated into the beginning of "not so good" fea-

49

His writing goes back to the 1920s when he published and edited the magazine *G* (for *Gestaltung*), edited with Mies van der Rohe and others, stressing form and order as the necessary polar opposites of eccentricity and chance. In 1929 Richter published a book on film demonstrating film techniques with stills and word explanations of significant avant-garde films of the time. The book was reprinted 50 years later in the original German; no English version has yet appeared. He has also written a number of art books, mainly about the Dada movement.

In his eighties, Richter remained an active and energetic painter, writer, and collage artist, living in Switzerland with his wife Friedl, and spending summers in their Connecticut home. After visiting him there in 1973, when Richter was 85, Jonas Mekas wrote: "Seeing Hans

Hans Richter, in 1974. (Photo by Robert Naughton.)

restored my faith in humanity....He refreshed my dream, my longing of seeing, of being occasionally with, men and women who are old and wise and beautiful and who are like bridges or examples or signposts for the others, and also crowns of humanity—they are the furthest extensions of man's body and spirit in time and space. If you want, you can look at them as humanity's works of art, crowns of Life as Art."

Richter died in Switzerland on February 2, 1976, at the age of eighty-eight. Two hours before he died he told his wife he had an idea for a new film he wanted to make.

EASEL—SCROLL—FILM
by Hans Richter
"The square is the sign of a new humanity. It is something like the cross of the early Christians." That is what Theo van Doesburg told the Swedish painter, Viking Eggeling, and me on his arrival at our country retreat in Klein Koelzig, Germany, in 1920. We were a little perturbed and skeptical about van Doesburg's statement, but we understood its spirit. We felt as he did. Through some magic, a new unity of purpose in the arts had developed in Europe during the isolation of the war years. Now that the war was over, there suddenly existed a kind of esthetic brotherhood, secretly developed. Whether or not the square was its symbol seemed to us of no importance in comparison to the fundamental issues upon which we could all agree.

We had seen, after 1910, that representation of the object had declined. We saw it finally vanish as a goal of painting. The self-respect of abstract art was increasing. A new set of problems arose. The overwhelming freedom which the "abstract," "pure," "absolute," "nonobjective," "concrete" and "universal" form offered (which, indeed, was thrust upon us) carried responsibilities. The "heap of fragments" left to us by the cubists did not offer us an over-all principle. Such a principle was needed to save us from the limitless horizons of possible form-combinations, so that we might attain a sovereignty over this new matter and justify this new freedom.

The upheaval of World War I, I am sure, had something to do with this urge for "order." I myself felt the need to establish an Archimedean standpoint, to penetrate the chaos which threatened from every direction. It appeared a physical necessity to articulate the multicolored darkness with a definite simplicity. But whether it was a desire for "security," as the psychologists would see it (to find order in chaos), or an overwhelming general trend towards collective standards, as the sociologists might call it, or the all-penetrating influence of science—the fact remains that a new generation approached this task with the energy of pioneers, the curiosity of explorers and the unperturbed objectivity of scientists.

Fugue, Hans Richter, 1920; fragment from the painted scroll.

It was with this aim, in this spirit, and at this time, that Malevitch in Russia decided to start from the very beginning again, from "nihil," with his *White on White;* that in Holland, fifteen hundred miles to the west, Mondrian, Doesburg and their friends discovered in the "equivalence of opposites" a working principle, a principle of style which they termed "neo-plasticism," based on the opposition of horizontal and vertical (excluding all others); and that six hundred miles to the south again, in Switzerland, the Swedish artist Viking Eggeling and I found another way to tackle the same task: by approaching it with the principle of counterpoint in mind, from the standpoint of polarity. The principle of counterpoint is not limited to music. For us, it was more than a technical device; it was a philosophic way of dealing with the experience of growth.

So strong was this historical impulse to establish "a 'New Order' that might restore the balance between heaven and hell" (as Arp put it), that it expressed itself practically simultaneously, though independently, in various places on the globe. It carried Eggeling and me (painters and nothing but painters) eventually, and half against our will, out of the world of easel painting to that of scrolls, and finally into film.

An account of the path we followed, our considerations and doubts, the experiences we went through thirty years ago, may be of some value to the ever-increasing number of artists who prefer the world of non-representational visions to the temptations of the representational object. It may also help to break down the stupid prejudice that plastic problems in the art of our time can be solved only on canvas or in bronze.

Influenced by cubism and its search for structure, but not satisfied with what it offered, I found myself between 1913–18 increasingly faced with the conflict of suppressing spontaneous expression in order to gain an objective understanding of a fundamental principle with which I could control the "heap of fragments" inherited from the cubists. Thus I gradually lost interest in the subject—in any subject—and focused instead on the positive negative (white-black) opposition, which at least gave me a working hypothesis whereby I could organize the relationship of one part of a painting to the other. In doing so, "form," as such, became a handicap and was replaced by straight or curved divisions of the canvas, which in itself became a surface on which opposites were to be organized. Repetition of the same element on different parts of the canvas, and repetitions with minor or major variations, permitted a certain control . . .

As much as we [Eggeling and Richter] both loved the

early work of Kandinsky, we still thought that such free improvisations as his would have to come "later," after a general principle had been established. (What made it right in Kandinsky's work was the still existing impressionistic basis, or at least a definite contact with a definite object.) This principle would be the challenge, a point of resistance, against any anarchistic abuse of freedom and, as such, a psychological stimulus—not a chain.

We saw in the completely liberated (abstract) form not only a new medium to be exploited, but the challenge towards a "universal language." This, as we wrote in a pamphlet called *Universelle Sprache* [*Universal Language*] which we published in 1920, was to be a means of emotional and intellectual experience for all, one which would restore to the arts its social function.

We sought to achieve a more than purely subjective solution; we felt very definitely prepared to sacrifice whatever had to be sacrificed of individual spontaneous expression, for the time being, in order to clarify and "purify" the material—form and color—until the very principle itself became expressive: "to carry on in the same way as Nature organizes matter, but to use only its principles, not its forms," in Eggeling's words.

Two years after our first meeting, these ideas were to bring us into association with van Doesburg and later with Mondrian, Malevitch, Gabo, Mies van der Rohe, Lissitzky and others.

The collaboration between Eggeling and myself had a number of consequences: 1. Our research led us to make a large number of drawings as transformations of one form element or another. These were our "themes," or, as we called them, "instruments," by analogy with music—the art form which inspired us considerably. We felt "the music of the orchestrated form." 2. This methodical contrast-analogy, "orchestration" of a given "instrument" through different stages, forced upon us the idea of a continuity. 3. When in 1919 we finally established a definite line of continuity on long scrolls, we became aware of a multiple and dynamic kind of relationship which invited the eye to "meditate." The contrast-analogy process had created an energy which grew as the relationships multiplied. The beginning set up, as planned, rapports with the end, the first part with the second, the second with the third, left with right, top with bottom, every part with every other. Without intending to, we had arrived at a kind of dynamic expression which produced a sensation rather different from that possible in easel painting. This sensation lies in the stimulus which the remembering eye receives by carrying its attention from one detail, phase or sequence, to another that can be continued indefinitely. This is because the esthetic theme is just that: the relationship between every part and the whole. In so following the creative process, the beholder experiences it as a *process*, not as a single *fact*. In this way, the eye is stimulated to an especially active participation, through the *necessity of memorizing*; and this activity carries with it the kind of satisfaction which one might feel if one were suddenly to discover new or unusual forms of one's imagination.

These seem to me the main characteristics of the scroll, which offers sensations that the easel painting, by its very nature as a static form, cannot offer. Van Doesburg, though, tried to make a different point. "It makes no difference whether one who looks at a Mondrian canvas moves his eyes (from one 'opposite' to the other) or whether a scroll 'moves' before the eyes of the beholder." Well, I think he had a point there but only a polemic one, as the *attitude* of the creator and the spectator is different in each case.

I consider the scroll as a new (dating from 4000 B.C.!) art form which, despite "sociological difficulties" that it might encounter (such as being despised by art dealers as too difficult to sell, or finding no room for its display over a potential purchaser's fireplace) ought to become a modern medium of expression. It must; in fact, as there are sensations to be derived from it which can be experienced in no other way, either in easel painting or in film.

I see in the elongated, horizontal paintings of artists like Tanguy, Klee, Miro and others, the same impulse to express similar sensations. There are "messages" to be told and "messages" felt which make the traditional limits of easel painting inadequate as communication.

One may assume that the Egyptians and the Chinese felt the appeal of this particular form of expression, and that they enjoyed arresting time in this way. Otherwise this form would not have evolved nor been preserved, as it still is in China today. The static unity which binds together the dynamic sequences is the form of the whole scroll. The unity of time is the same as in the easel painting, although its expression is fundamentally different. In the scroll painting, the orchestration of all stages of development of form is seen and felt simultaneously—backwards and forwards. This is one of the main distinctions of this new plastic expression and a source of its real beauty. "Becoming and duration are not in any way a diminution of unchanging eternity; they are its expression. Every form occupies not only space but time. Being and becoming are one. . . . What should be grasped and given form are things in flux" (Eggeling).

The logical step we had taken to the scroll had already thrown us, so to speak, out of the world of easel painting. It precipitated us a step further. After each of us in 1919 had finished his first scroll, we began to understand that we had gotten more than we asked for: the necessity to release this accumulated "energy" into actual movement! Never during our collaboration had we dreamt of that. But there it was. And movement implied film!

Few people have ever come to this medium so unexpectedly and with so much inner resistance. We knew no more about cameras and film than what we had seen in shop windows.

In 1921 Eggeling finished the first version of his *Diagonal Symphony* (after his second set of scrolls) and I completed my film, *Rhythm 21*. We were in a new medium altogether. It was not only the orchestration of form but also of time-relationship that we were facing in film. The single image disappeared in a flow of images, which made sense only if it helped to articulate a new element—*time*.

We realized that the "orchestration" of time was the esthetic basis of this new art form. Eggeling stuck to the graphic elegance of the forms developed in his scrolls. He endowed the different "instruments" with certain well-defined ways of motion. He really used them according to the musical term "instrument." But as they were products of the painter, they put innumerable obstacles in the way of the "filmer." It was then, and especially for him, a non-professional, a Herculean task. His film was remade three times under the most incredible conditions before he was satisfied.

I dissented from the start. It had taken an UFA technician more than a week to animate a single drawing of my scroll, "Prelude." The technician was not very encouraging to begin with, and I felt like a blind man being led by another blind man. I wanted to understand better what I was doing and decided, very much against Eggeling's arguments, to start from scratch again— using the principle of counterpoint to guide me. This time I did not concentrate upon orchestrating *form*— but *time*, and time alone.

The simple square of the movie screen could easily be divided and "orchestrated." These divisions or parts could then be orchestrated in *time* by accepting the rectangle of the "movie-canvas" as the form element. Thus it became possible to relate (in contrast-analogy) the various movements on this "movie-canvas" to each other—in a formal as well as a temporal sense. In other words, I did again with the screen what I had done years before with the canvas. In doing so I found a new sen-

From *Rhythm 21* (1921) by Hans Richter. "My first film was *Rhythm 21*. I did the shooting partly on an animation table, partly in the printing machine by stop motion and forward and backward printing. The printing machines at that time were not fully automatic and you could use them like a camera. In these years, 1920, 1921, and the following years, I learned, by myself and by trial and error, the fundamentals of film techniques. The original title of this, my first film, was *Film ist Rhythmus*, (but since I made others in 1923 and 1925 I just called them *Rhythm 21, 23, 25*.) ... I made three *Rhythms* in between odd film jobs between 1921 and 1926 ... *21* was only square forms; in *23* I used line; and in *25* I used both bands and lines but I also painted it in color ... (*Film Culture*, Winter 1963–1964.)

sation: *rhythm*—which is, I still think, the chief sensation of any expression of movement....

In the meantime, the scope of the experimental film has grown. The principles which we followed with our first abstract film are not limited to the articulation of lines or squares alone. The rhythm of a swing or a clock, the orchestration of hats or legs, the dance of kitchenware or a collar—could become expressions of a new sensation. The experimental film has at last come into its own. It has created its own realm, which we may term "film poetry," in contradistinction to the "novel" of the entertainment film or the "reportage" of the documentary.

Twenty years ago, the documentary was shown and considered exclusively as avant-garde; today it is accepted as a legitimate film species. Twenty years from now, film poetry may well be accepted as a legitimate part of filmmaking and recognized as part of the tradition of modern art, whence it came and to which it belongs.

The artists of the coming generation will seriously consider the camera as well as the brush their medium of expression.

(From *Magazine of Art*, published by The American Federation of Arts, February 1952.)

RICHTER'S "RHYTHM 21"
by Brian O'Doherty

...To recover the pristine amazement of *Rhythm 21* demands an act of restoration, for our vision has been prejudiced by the thousands of abstract films made since. What is remarkable is the complete control of syntax, the exact coincidence of intent, means and result. It is a very conscious and classic piece. The repertory of movements are simply Richter's linguistics of movement *actually* realized. In this sense it is dialectic in motion, that modernist dialectic of opposites—but deprived of any mythic qualifications or "psychology." It presents itself as a rigorous purism.

The majority of motions are clearly transferred from the two-dimensional plane of the canvas—up and down, side to side, in series of exits and entrances. The third kind of movement, in which rectangles and squares rapidly increase and decrease in size, can be construed as in and out, an idea of depth. But such is the two-dimensionality of the screen that this motion remains exactly what it is—an *idea* or notation of depth. Strictly, all we see is things getting larger and smaller. Reading in depth is *our* projection. What is new here is the application to the screen of the two-dimensionality of the

canvas. What we see are literally "moving pictures." Treating one medium with the assumptions brought from another can be dangerous. But Richter removes the fictive space we habitually project onto the screen. He flattens it, so that his images are *on* it, instead of *in* or behind it, and so refuse to break through to the universe of illusion. In announcing the formal integrity of the screen as a flat surface, Richter made his first and perhaps most important contribution to the esthetic of film.

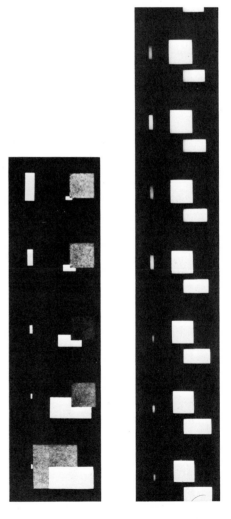

From *Rhythm 21* by Hans Richter. "...Its forms, like those of an abstract painting, seem to have no physical extension except on the screen... the film is a totally self-contained kinetic composition of pure plastic forms." (Lawder, *The Cubist Cinema*.)

54

All *Rhythm*'s forms are families of lines, squares, and rectangles in horizontal and vertical alignment. Compositions vary from very simple to complex—from the opening shots, where the screen itself is used as the major part of the composition, to compositions *within* the screen. The syntax is often serialized perfectly. Sometimes rectangles in different parts of the screen change size inversely in precise counterpoint. These serial occasions are used as blocks which are manipulated within larger, less serialized structures (i.e. timespans). Figure-ground switches are used as punctuations or modes of rephrasing a sequence that seemed to be locked into a programmatic development. (There is a particularly majestic example of this towards the end of the film when a large black square turns white). Such is the formal compression of the film that its few minutes seem very long.

This matter of speed is important. Unlike the scrolls, where we are free to compare and carry data back across blank intervals of canvas, the film forces its time on us. Thus memory becomes involuntary, since we cannot conceptualize and remember clearly (only after seeing the film repeatedly do we begin to see its structure). The rapid succession of images "collages" our memory, and instinctive processes are brought into play. The sharp, exact image before us is maintained in an ambiguous sea of remembering and forgetting. There are certain kinesthetic components to watching the film, kinesthesia of a very differnt kind from that of reading at the scrolls. In the scrolls we are constrained to locomote and remove our bag of viscera from one place to another, and this creates a kind of physiological static accompanying perception. In *Rhythm*, though we are at rest, there is a kind of conceptual kinesthesia, a paradigm of body reaction. The effect is tonic, sudden, and invigorating.

Taken out of context, some of the individual frames from *Rhythm* are formally very daring. There are dazzling degrees of marginal composition, minimal reductions, large vacancies, and single vertical strips, etc., that look like the advanced work of the fifties and sixties. However, Richter never aborted these discoveries out of the relational system in which they were discovered. In general, the composition of the frames has very marked connections to the purist art of the period. There are a few frames, amounting to less than a second, which are puzzling. Towards the latter half of the film, two oblique bars appear in the upper left-hand corner of the screen, breaking the vertical-horizontal rigor.

In *Rhythm 25*, now lost, Richter added color to the vocabulary he had used in *Rhythm 21*. This was done systematically in terms of primary and a few secondary colors with contrast as the vocabulary. This greatly increases the total vocabulary. Some idea of *Rhythm 25* may be gathered from the scroll "Orchestration of Color," 1923, and the sketches for the film 1923–24. Since the drawings are all available, one hopes Richter will remake this film. (Only one copy was made in 1925, and it was quickly lost.) Also of great interest is Richter's system of notation on graph paper, scoring *Rhythm 25*.

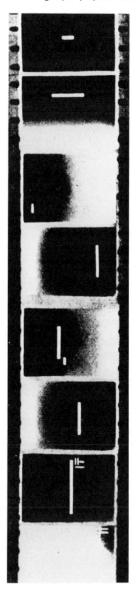

From *Rhythm 23* (1923) by Hans Richter.

55

This promised a method of composing films according to scores, where both musical and visual considerations could come into play. Richter did not follow up this idea. His other abstract work, *Rhythm 23*, is less classic than *21* or *25*, but it is another major film. After this, Richter made no more purely abstract films, though for years a sense of their structure underpinned everything he did, in effect contributing his idea of montage to film.

Film Study (1926), uses a larger repertory of abstract devices than any previous work. Circles, all-over patterns, soft-edge (out of focus) forms, dart-like shapes frequently produce formal occasions that break current compositional laws in painting. These forms are collated with objects, particularly artificial eyes and multiple repetitions of the same head. The attempt is to cut across the abstract-real dichotomy by using it as dialectic. The result, seance-like and spooky, is ambiguous. The expected exchange between poles (abstraction looking more psychologically motivated, the heads and eyes more abstract) takes place. But the use of the heads, lit from below, locate the film in expressionist country. From this on, Richter's films join the mainstream of film as it developed in Germany. . . .

(From *Hans Richter*, catalogue for retrospective exhibition, Finch College Museum, Contemporary Wing, 1968.)

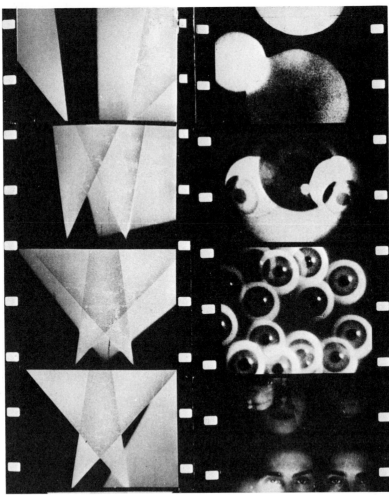

From *Film Study* (1926) by Hans Richter.

Oskar Fischinger

Oskar Fischinger, in 1937, working on *An Optical Poem* at MGM.

Oskar Fischinger's work in abstract animation spans more than 30 years, with over 100 minutes of film currently in distribution and numerous other reels lost or discarded as the nitrate stock disintegrated. His early background was as a draftsman and engineer; painting became an auxiliary to his film work in his middle years, and later a major activity. When he was only 16, Fischinger felt himself respond to the call for the new art of abstract moving pictures, in articles Bernhard Diebold published in 1916. Around 1920 the two became friends and Fischinger joined the literary club to which Diebold belonged and made graph-scrolls which visually analyzed two dramatic works.

With Diebold's encouragement Fischinger turned to film. Between 1922 and 1926 he made a number of abstract films with different techniques: several reels of moving graphs, experiments with his wax-slicing machine, and some of his early *Study* films. He also made cartoon and clay-figure animation films at that time. In 1927 Fischinger set off on foot from Munich to Berlin, filming a remarkable record of his two-month journey in one- and two-frame shots of people and places along the way.

Then began his most successful period. *Studies 5* through *12* were sold and shown in theaters throughout Europe, as well as the United States and Japan. The first eight *Study* films were drawn entirely by Fischinger, some 5000 separate charcoal drawings for each film. In his thorough study of Fischinger's work and life, published in *Film Culture* (No. 58–59–60, 1974), William Moritz writes that to achieve maximum smoothness of motion, Fischinger never photographed the same drawing twice. By 1931, Fischinger was joined in his work by his wife Elfriede, who filled in solid bodies and shadings, and by his brother Hans who later designed and made one abstract film on his own.

In 1932, with advertising films and assignments to create special effects for feature films, Fischinger added half a dozen employees to his studio. One German writer commented that Fischinger's "compositions of dancing lines are the only kind of abstract film which can be found in the regular programs of the German cinemas, and which are well received by the public." The films were also screened at film societies, written about in many newspapers, film magazines, and art journals, and included in film-lecture presentations by Ruttmann, Moholy-Nagy, and others.

Music was an important part of many of Fischinger's films, which in the early years were synchronized to phonograph records and then in the later years to re-recordings on film itself. In the early 1930s Fischinger also made his first synthetic sound experiments, and began working with Bela Gaspar to perfect Gaspar-color, the first European system of color film. His *Composition in Blue* won prizes at the 1935 film festivals in Venice and Brussels.

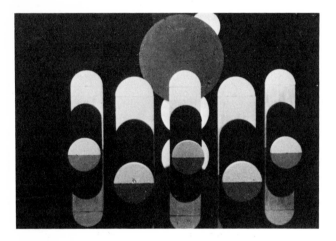

From *Composition in Blue* (1934) by Oskar Fischinger.

By this time, Goebbels had taken control of the German film industry. Elfriede Fischinger recalls that all production suddenly stopped. Everyone was a bit scared, although at first they did not realize the seriousness of the situation. Fischinger avoided difficulties by calling the films "ornamental," since abstract art was forbidden.

Early in 1936 Fischinger got a contract to work with Paramount Pictures and left for Hollywood. He spoke no English, was entirely unaccustomed to American production methods, and not surprisingly did not want to conform to Paramount's regimented system. The contract was soon terminated. In 1938 Fischinger travelled to New York to find backing for a number of projects, including a full-length abstract animation film based on Dvorak's New World Symphony, which he hoped to produce for the forthcoming New York World's Fair. No backers were found. Fischinger had

earlier contacted Leopold Stokowski about using one of his Bach orchestrations in a sequence for another film, an idea which Stokowski presented and sold to Walt Disney, resulting in a contract for Fischinger on the film that became *Fantasia*. A clash of taste, and most likely of personality too, brought about Fischinger's withdrawal from the one big commercial opportunity he had helped initiate and certainly merited.

The Solomon R. Guggenheim Foundation, through its curator Hilla Rebay, gave Fischinger several grants, one of which allowed him to buy from Paramount the unreleased film he had made for them. The film was re-titled *Allegretto*, since Rebay did not like its original title (*Radio Dynamics*). With Guggenheim funds, Fischinger produced *An American March*, in color, set to John Philip Sousa's Stars and Stripes Forever, as part of the foundation's effort to put refugee artists to work on patriotic themes.

Because of Fischinger's German nationality, work prospects grew dimmer than ever for him when war was declared. Orson Welles had approached Fischinger about making abstract images to accompany Louis Armstrong's music, and when that fell through, for Welles' Brazilian film, which also failed to materialize. During the time when Fischinger was not allowed to work in a film studio, Welles kept him on his own personal payroll, working on the two projects.

After the war, the Art in Cinema series at the San Francisco Museum of Art presented a large cycle of Fischinger's films, and he became a central and honored figure in the burgeoning West Coast experimental film movement.

For Solomon Guggenheim's 86th birthday, Hilla Rebay requested each of the foundation's grant-holders to create a special work; Fischinger made three Mutoscope reels, each composed of 600 abstractions showing colored circles moving in front of a black background. Mrs. Fischinger has subsequently released a 3-second part of Reel No. 1 in the form of a flip-book (1970).

Fischinger's last major work entitled *Motion Painting No. 1* was finished in 1947 with support from the Guggenheim Foundation. A second motion painting was begun, but was put aside unfinished. Fischinger did make several television commercials, and a brief experiment in stereo film based on his stereo paintings, but in the last twenty years of his life there was little beside his painting on which he could practice his talents. Oskar Fischinger died in Hollywood in January 1967. Although he had not fit smoothly into the American film scene, he never returned to Germany, indeed never left the United States once having settled here.

BILDMUSIK—ART OF OSKAR FISCHINGER
by Richard Whitehall

...Oskar Fischinger was born in Geinhausen, Germany, in 1900. After completing the then obligatory eight years of schooling he began, in 1914, to study organ-building but, after a year of this he entered the office of the city architect of Gelnhausen. From there he moved to Frankfort and was apprenticed to Pokorny and Wiedekind, one of the largest turbine manufacturers in Germany, studying, at the same time, engineering in evening classes at the Volkshochschule. His early training was exclusively technical, his cultural interests chiefly in literature and classical music. Yet in many ways, residues of this early interest and training in engineering reflect through all his work in art, the dominance of line, curve, circle, square, and the way they are used in space across the graphics of a painting or the frame of a film. And when in 1919 he joined a literary club, he took what was to be an unlikely but decisive step towards film.

Each member of the club was required, in turn, to lecture on some topic of literary interest. Fischinger, when his turn came, chose to analyze the structure of two works, Fritz von Unruh's *Ein Geschlecht* and Shakespeare's *As You Like It.* "In preparing for this speech I began to analyze the works in a graphic way," he wrote later. "On large sheets of drawing paper, along a horizontal line, I put down all the feelings and happenings, scene after scene, in graphic lines and curves. The lines and curves showed the dramatic development of the whole work, and the emotional moods, very clearly." This exposition of the dynamics of poetry seemed to baffle some members of the audience, however, and Fischinger began to understand that he needed movement and a time element to express his ideas with a greater clarity. Buying a camera, the young Fischinger taught himself the techniques of filmmaking, and was soon experimenting with hand-drawn animations (some of which, lovely, flowing silhouettes...still survive) and with machine-animation.

He invented a machine which pushed a block of wax towards a revolving, fanlike knife blade. The blade rorated, slicing thinly through the wax, as the camera photographed through an aperture in the blade to which the camera shutter was synchronized. Thus the camera recorded changing cross-sections of wax as art object in abstract movement. To get money to continue his film experiments Fischinger sold a license for the use of this machine to Walter Ruttman, painter turned filmmaker, the best-known German film experimentalist of the time....

It was at this time, too, that Fischinger began to create those short black and white films he called *Studies*, synchronizing music to image through a method he developed whereby a recording could be divided into sections and begun and stopped in precise alignment with the images. The first four *Studies*, made between 1921 and 1924, were shown at the Munich State Theater and at the Gesolai International Exhibition at Dusseldorf in 1925 in conjunction with Alexander Laszlo's newly invented Color Organ. Fischinger's film provided the motion for the colors of the organ, which were then projected on a single screen.

In 1927 Fischinger moved to Berlin where, amongst other things, he created special effects for Fritz Lang's science-fiction of space exploration, *Frau im Mond (Woman in the Moon)*, and continued with the *Studies. Study 5* was animated to a Spoliansky jazz recording, *Study 6* to Guerrero's equally jazzy Vaya Veronica, and *Study 7* to a Brahms Hungarian Dance.... The purity and simplicity of the black and white forms in the *Studies*, the sharpness and clarity of the play of light—the earliest animations, drawn in charcoal, had been projected in negative to achieve an even greater contrast in tone—have that quality of contemplative minimality and beauty so omnipresent in, say, the black paintings of Ad Reinhardt.

The dynamics of motion were inherent in and inseparable in Fischinger's films right from the beginning, just as the dynamics of sound were an inherent part of his film esthetic some years before a technical process became available to him that would allow a more subtle exploration of musical imagery. Music has been reduced

From Fischinger's untitled experiments with his wax-slicing machine, 1921–1926.

symbolically into a visual form—the notations of the score—for centuries, but Fischinger was after something much more Modernist and much more complex. In a sense he has done in film what Balanchine, that most musical of choreographers, has done in his plotless ballets, opening out as it were a graphic score in which a visual rhythm is closely related to an auditory one. Reduced to the simplest terms, Fischinger's work attempted to create a complete audio-visual harmony, as if the soundtrack is being projected optically along with our hearing of it. It is not that visual symbol, a line, a curve, a triangle, is equated with a note of music, indissolubly, so that, like a marriage made in heaven, the two may not be put asunder, but that Fischinger is exploring the

emotional content of a musical work in the way he had, at the beginning, analyzed the emotional content of a poetic one. For, to him, the music is the concentrated form of the thought and emotion of a composer. The unfinished *Study 8* was, he came to feel, the work which most fully explored his ideas on a sound/motion synthesis....

In the early '30s Fischinger moved into color and, in 1936, on to Hollywood. Paramount brought him out to California to create a color-abstract sequence for one of those indigestible musical extravaganzas of the time, in which an assortment of talent was gathered together to no good purpose, here *The Big Broadcast of 1937*. It was a first experience of the factory conditions of Holly-

Oskar Fischinger, around 1926, at his animation stand in Munich.

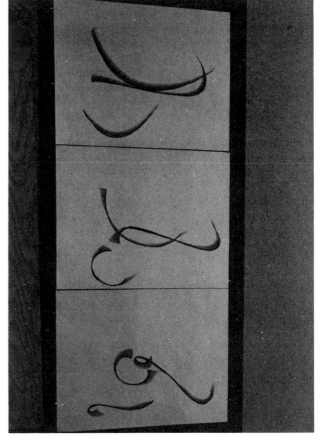

From *Study No. 7* (1930–1931) by Oskar Fischinger.

wood for Fischinger, and the beginning of an unhappy and not very fruitful period in his work. Paramount, who had planned the film in color, decided to release it in black and white. Fischinger departed the studio, buying back his completed section (which we now know as *Allegretto*). He moved over to MGM, staying just long enough to make *Optical Poem*. Eventually he was invited by Disney to work on *Fantasia*.

The hand of Fischinger is clearly discernible in the sequence on which he worked, the Bach Toccata and Fugue in D Minor, but never at anything like his best. One has only to compare this particular sequence from *Fantasia* with any of his other works to realize the extent of the vulgarization of his art and his ideas. There is, however, a subterranean stratum of Fischinger ideas embedded in the whole conception of Disney's feature (Fischinger's early work was screened weekly for Disney animators through those months when *Fantasia* was in production), vulgarized but recognizable. Especially this is true of the shaping of concepts of the sequence in which the sound track is brought on-screen to demonstrate, through action, its musical and visual potential....

For a time in the early '40s, Fischinger fell amongst film people who respected his talent. Orson Welles engaged him to work on a planned life of Louis Armstrong. But this, too, was not to be. Welles had a falling out with his studio, RKO, and the Armstrong film was abandoned. For the remainder of his life Fischinger was in Hollywood but not of it. In Germany he had made advertising films, including the famous Muratti commercial which used an animation of dancing cigarettes (much copied since), and the chief reason for putting *Study 8* aside was the necessity to fulfill commercial contracts. He refused, though, to subordinate his art to commercial requirements. *Fantasia* was not, on its original release, a commercial success and, in many engagements, the Bach Toccata and Fugue sequence was cut. This made it impossible for Fischinger to raise any interest in the Concrete feature he had dreamed of making. Returning to personal filmmaking, he completed *An American March* and what may well stand as his greatest individual achievement, *Motion Painting Number One*.

Although later there were to be some television commercials, and there were ideas for a three-dimensional film for which he created the 3-D paintings, *Motion Painting* is the last of his major works in cinema. It breaks with his earlier work, in that it is a free development of a painting in motion and isn't based on the strict laws of musical form he observed in his other work. Abstract images are painted across clear plastic sheets, with each few brush-strokes separately recorded on frames of film. When one sheet was filled another was placed before it, through six plastic sheets in all, with images on each side. There was also one first sheet on cardboard, painted on one side only....

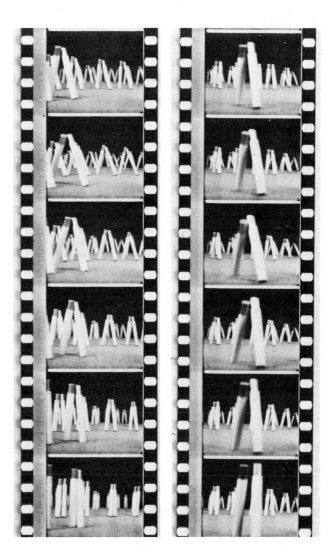

From *Muratti Greift Ein* (Murati Marches On) (1934) by Oskar Fischinger, strips from the cigarette commercial.

COMMENTS ON FISCHINGER'S FILMS
by William Moritz

STUDY No. 8 (1931)   One of the original German prints of *Study No. 8* ended with a title reading, "Left unfinished, February and March, 1930" (surely a mistake for 1931). At that time Fischinger did not have enough money to buy the rights for the second half of Dukas' *The Sorcerer's Apprentice*. Despite the lack of the finished ending of the music, this study remains the most complex, most stunning, and for the artist the favorite and most important of the black-and-white films.

Fischinger makes no attempt to tell Goethe's story of the magician's helper (Disney was to do that ten years later) but instead he uses the textures and movements of the sounds themselves as the jumping off point for creating an especially rich world in which a multiplicity of forms and movements perform in a deep environment.

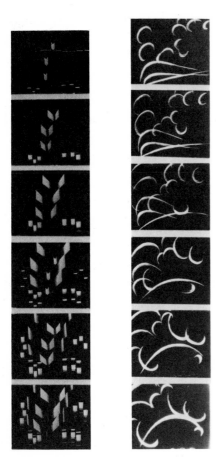

From *Study No. 8* (1931) by Oskar Fischinger.

Rectangles slink across the screen by rippling their contents through their volumes, then slide off into the distance, hovering in space as pure lines, then suddenly swing into action again, pivoting from one corner like fans. Again and again rectangles split in chain reactions, first as if they were merely being stretched and warped by a distorting mirror, then more positively into twos, then threes, then fours. Amorphous forms describe a series of fluid metamorphoses, one time curling into *art nouveau* swirls, one time flying apart as straight lines in various directions. Clusters of sharp crescents sweep into the frame from all sides, then suddenly melt into incredibly soft, sensuous swirls.

All of these disparate elements are cleverly balanced on the plane of time so that the action of the film becomes the tension between basic artistic polarities—shape vs. content, random grouping vs. ordered patterns, simple vs. complex structures, etc.—which are seen as mirrors of basic yin-yang polarities in the universe itself. Would the ending of the film have been able to provide a resolution to these tensions? We can never know, but as the film now stands, it is, like Goethe's *Faust*, a mirror of life itself: no resolution, continuous striving.

Fischinger was very proud of the atom-splitting sequence, and used to mention it in lectures along with the possible allegorical interpretation of Goethe's fable from the point of view of nuclear fission, a remarkable premonition for 1931....

AN OPTICAL POEM (1937)   An Optical Poem was executed almost entirely with paper cutouts which were suspended on sticks and thin wires, and moved around in front of *ca.*-four-foot-square backgrounds on a miniature stage with about an eight-foot-deep action area—a technique first employed two years earlier for the final sequence of *Composition in Blue.* This technique is by no means time- or labor-saving, but it produces some remarkable, almost eerie effects with modulating colortones and moving shadows.

Next to *Radio Dynamics* and *Motion Painting*, it is Fischinger's most important and mature statement. He has used the variety of moods or stances suggested by Liszt's Hungarian Rhapsody No. 2 (a music Fischinger had already had transferred to an optical track as early as December, 1935, but for *Optical Poem* the track was completely re-recorded by the MGM studio orchestra) to create a microcosm in which the circles, squares, and triangles act out a complete range of activities centering around the topic of relationships. They move in irregular clusters like traffic in a market place, they march, they dance, they fly, they orbit each other in twos and threes and fours, they melt into each other, they recoil suddenly away from each other, they expand and contract rhythmically and flicker, alone, together, and across stunning multi-plane perspectives. The "meaning" is for each viewer to contemplate: *An Optical Poem* is an instrument for meditation—microscopic, universal, personal.

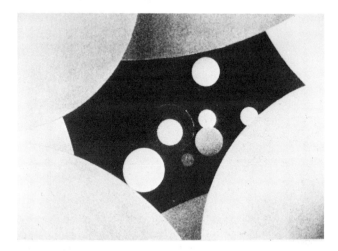

From *Optical Poem* (1937) by Oskar Fischinger.

MOTION PAINTING NO. 1 (1947) ... By all odds so delicate and difficult a process for a ten-minute film [oil-on-Plexiglas technique] might well have resulted in a failure or a weak film. At one point Fischinger painted every day for over five months without being able to see how it was coming out on film, since he wanted to keep all the conditions, including film stock, absolutely consistent in order to avoid unexpected variations in quality of image. Thus it is a tribute to Fischinger's skill and artistic vision that *Motion Painting No. 1* turned out in fact excellent.

Volumes could be written about this film which stands in length and complexity as Fischinger's major work. It is perhaps the only one of his films which is truly and completely (or purely) abstract (or absolute). Its images are actors in a complex being which modulates and transforms itself before our eyes, an object and an experience at the same time, something we must feel and contemplate, and meditate through....

First of all, it is a painting, and can be appreciated as an exercise in the painter's art. It shows a variety of styles from the soft, muted opening to the bold conclusion through a series of spontaneous changes prepared without any previous planning. All of the figures are drawn free-hand without aid of compasses or rulers or undersketching, even the incredibly precise triangles of the middle section. It is a remarkable, astonishing document of one creative process.

As the title suggests, it is also a painting about "motion," and the element of motion is exploited in many forms and variations, from the literal motion of the comet-like bodies in the opening sequence to the motion by addition or concretion at the close. Color and shape become elements in our sensation of motion, as the variegated spirals unwind themselves with seemingly variable dynamisms or speeds—the motion of music and painting. Even the placement and appearance of static objects becomes an instrument for manipulating the motion of our eyes, which renders all other activity relative—the motion of sculpture, happening, or pageant. And the final dramatic sweeps of the great wedges which form the mandala are rendered more exciting by the relatively static scenes that precede them—theatrical motion of dynamic duration in time.

It is tempting to see symbolic forms in the film, e.g., a human brain is the field of action in the opening sequence, with paths almost like a road map leading out of it into a world of architectural designs which grows in magnificence until they become structures of depth and power that collide in the end to form a beautiful, simple, pure mandala.

While this rendition of the film in representational terms is inadequate, unsatisfactory or untenable basi-

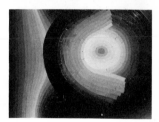

From *Motion Painting No. 1* (1947) by Oskar Fischinger.

cally, it lays bare an underlying structure which is appropriate. The opening scene of soft shapes and sensual action is amorphous like the thoughts of a child or an untrained thinker. Out of this develop connections first in the form of slow, logical enlargements of basic kernels, then by the direct connection of the kernels themselves. Then are added large blocks of material to form a new field of action—the process of education—on which logical construction takes place—cogitation and contemplation—which grows very gradually into more and more powerful and beautiful gestures—creativity and transcendent meditation. The film's structure is even richer and more flexible than this suggests, but there are elements of an archetypal pattern—childhood through initiation to maturity—which has a validity on many levels (e.g., the raising of the spiritual energy through the chakras in kundalini yoga) depending on the predisposition of the particular viewer at each time of his meditation/experience with the film.

(From *Film Culture*, No. 58-59-60, 1974.)

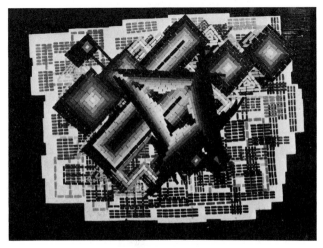

From *Motion Painting No. 1* (1947) by Oskar Fischinger.

Len Lye

Len Lye, around 1957.

Len Lye, another major innovator in abstract animation, was born in New Zealand in 1901, and made most of his animation films in England in the decade beginning in 1928.

In a review of his first film, *Tusalava*, by Oswell Blakeston in *Close Up* (January 1930), Lye is described as "a great artist with great ideas," and his film as symbolically "concerned with external influences corrupting the true spirit of the artist... One is reminded, from time to time, of the work of Kandinsky..."

Alberto Cavalcanti, a leading figure in avant-garde film and John Grierson's right-hand-man at the General Post Office (G.P.O.) Film Unit in Britain, has recalled the time when Len Lye came to tell Grierson that he wanted to make a film without a camera. It took "a lot of his personal charm to make us listen to him," according to Cavalcanti, but Grierson, "that King of Showmen," would not have missed such an opportunity.

Lye's first cameraless film was called *Colour Box* (1935), and is considered to be the first animation film painted directly on film and shown to general audiences. Lye made other "direct-animation" films—*Kaleidoscope* (1935) and later *Musical Poster* (1940)—but he also branched out into many different techniques. *The Birth of the Robot* (1936), a conventional puppet film notable for its abstract storm sequence, was made in collaboration with Humphrey Jennings for the Shell Oil Company.

Len Lye's *Rainbow Dance* (1936) used solarized and multiple images of the human figure within an abstract framework. Like *Colour Box* and other of his films of this period, the film had a tacked-on message: "The Post Office Savings Bank puts a pot of gold at the end of the Rainbow." Such brightly encased messages, according to Cavalcanti, kept audiences awake "by their wit, their quick tempo and their originality," and brought the sponsor a great amount of prestige.

For his next film, *Trade Tattoo* (1937), Lye stencilled abstract patterns on discarded documentary footage, which he transposed into color by an intricate plotting and printing system which involved so much time and equipment that Lye doubted that such complicated procedures could often be attempted.

During the war, Lye began directing documentaries. In 1944 he came to the United States, where he directed films until 1951 for the monthly news films, The March of Time, on such subjects as child development clinics and atomic power, and a long film on Basic English.

Since then Len Lye has made only sporadic animation films, financed and produced by his wife, Ann Zeiss. His one-minute advertising film called *Rhythm* won an award, from among 850 entries, as best commercial of the year (1957), but was subsequently disqualified because it had not been shown on TV. *Free Radicals*, which won the $5,000 second-place award at the Brussels World's Fair in 1958, brought little recognition in this country, and more disappointingly, no commissions for further film work. After having it turned down by several art theaters in New York City, Lye decided to give up film entirely, despite his 30 years of dedicated work. He turned energetically to kinetic sculpture, with which he won considerable recognition in museums and galleries, as well as in the press.

Recently Lye has renewed his interest in film as an independent art and in mixed-media works. A permanent exhibition of his work being installed in New Zealand's National Museum.

From *Rainbow Dance* (1936) by Len Lye.

TALKING ABOUT FILM
by Len Lye

...I'm personally not a literary type. I can't create anything out of a literary form that I think is as significant as anything I can create out of a figure of motion. I look at film in a different way from most people....

...I'm interested in composition with motion. I started making things wave about by turning hand-wound pulley belts...I'd just read of how Constable had done a lot of oil sketches of clouds in an attempt to convey their motion. I thought that was kind of a waste of time. If you're that intent on motion, why not get some kind of objects and push them around the way you think clouds might go? Then I thought, why bother with clouds? Why not just arrange motion?

I had the excitement of trying to discover things. No matter what area you're working in, if you think you're making a discovery, you get more enthused with the result of your efforts. Every painter, every artist, is making a discovery in just trying to isolate images that convey

what he thinks is significant. I had my own pet little subject, which was motion. So I was incessantly inventing my own exercises for this kind of development. I would jump on the back of a slow-moving horse and cart and sketch the movements in the garments of people walking past, or paint the reflection of a mast in the water, from left to right, which would create a repetitive pattern. This went on for three or four years.

At seventeen, I was making constructions. I would take the back off a box and then have a rectangular frame into which I'd put pulley-wheels and an old phonograph handle, and attach the strings of the pulley-wheels to another pulley-wheel, which would revolve something, and stick something that would wiggle-waggle on the other end of the shaft of one of the pulley-wheels.

I'm absolutely no engineer. I wouldn't dream of driving a car; I'd be up a tree in no time. So it took me a great study again to find out that if you put on a bigger wheel that thing would turn faster, and so on. I would wind it, look in the mirror, and see things moving about. Nobody knows what the hell you're up to, especially out in a place like New Zealand.

At the same time, when my teacher let me off the hook of traditional art, I found the only art I was interested in that was around in these places, Australia and New Zealand, was Ocean Island art. I became utterly convinced that they were the only vital things going in art and that they were much more exotic and creatively imaginative than, say, realistic Greek work. So I added to my theory the idea of trying to get significant looking things, as "significant looking" as the primitive Polynesian, Melanesian things that were in the museum there. I started with boomerang shapes and shield design shapes, but still no movement happened. They just turned around.

Well, I thought, this is very well. It's getting nowhere fast. How about film? About that time I'd seen one knock-out film, called *Pearls and Savages* by an Australian named Captain Frank Hurley. It was colored, I learned later, by Pathé in Paris. It was about some traders trying to get pearls in British New Guinea. There were fantastic native dances and headdresses and all that stuff. Of course, I was very impressionable and thought this was just the end. So it was decided film was the thing for me (by me). If you could learn about film, you could control motion with more than just turning a shaft by your hand. You could make the figure move in front of the camera, plan the next shot, and so forth.

I realized there was no film activity in New Zealand so I would have to go where there was...Sydney, Australia was where I learned animation. This was in 1921. I earned my living doing outdoor work, because that was where I preferred to be, rather than inside. I experimented with painting on film but I let it go, because there were a lot of other things I wanted to do. Mainly, I just learned cartoon animation. I wanted to go to Russia and work in the experimental theater. There was the Meyerhold Moscow Art Theater crowd who were doing extraordinary modern work of the kind I thought I could do in film. I hadn't got things sorted out in my own mind yet, so I thought I'd go to one of the best places in the world to sort things out: the South Sea Islands.

I settled on one for a couple of years, but I had to give it up because it was just too much. I couldn't do any work there—it was too wonderful for a young person. It was extraordinarily vital and interesting stuff all the time but nothing that gave you any stimulation for intellectual or creative endeavor. I had to get it at some world art hub.

So I went to London. There I struck lucky because I got a barge to live on rent free. So I didn't have to work much for expenses. I got a job in the theater pulling up the curtain, and the first film society in the world, the London Film Society, promised to pay the cost of photographing a cartoon film I wanted to make. It took two years drawing the different stages of movement in this film. I started in late '26 and ended in '28. [Usually the date is given as 1929—ed.] It was just a straight drawing animation, but the slowest thing on earth! These aboriginal-looking shapes just seemed to get nowhere at all. The images were good but the animation was too slow....

So I had this print of the ten-minute-long animation film. I showed it once in the London Film Society, and that was it. I accepted this as the way things are, for God's sake—slave like hell and be satisfied. It was called *Tusalava*, which is a Samoan word for "things go in full cycle." That was the start of my fine art film.

After this cartoon film, I would go out to the Ealing Studios, where I had friends, and cadge some plain clear film of n.g. [not usable] sound track film off them. I would paint right over the film and obliterate the sound track. I took this up to John Grierson and Albert Cavalcanti at the G.P.O. Film Unit....

I said, "Now with all this going on, all you have to do is put in a slogan there and you've got a film for your Post Office propaganda." He [Grierson] said, "Okay, how much?" I was surprised he was so ready for it and said, "Well, let's see, the cost of the paint..." So I gave him the cost of the paint. Anyway it was a success and I could get film work there anytime as long as I didn't rush it, say, once every six months or at least once a year. So this was the way I lived. I was painting batiks on the side to try to keep my hand in at primitive imagery.

I worked with an Australian composer in London, Jack Ellit. We made *Colour Box* in 1935.... I also made *Trade Tattoo*, which combined several techniques of animation. There would be three ways of following the rhythm, besides jump-cutting, which is an ordinary way. There would be the vibration pattern of a very formal pattern like stippling, or cross-hatching, which I had very geometrically designed, and which would be superimposed over the live action. You'd have the internal movement within the scene, such as a man's hand waving, which would have a rhythm and you could jump-cut that, make his hand wag faster or slower, and you could jump-cut the ends of the scene. You could make these visual accents synchronize with your sound accents. And this way you got a very tight tie-in of visual imagery with sounds and rhythms.

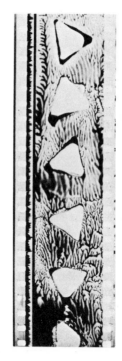

From *A Colour Box* (1935) by Len Lye.

Q: *How did you synchronize the sound?*

That's just a technical thing like knitting. First of all, the film is visual for me; then I search around until I get a sound with the same kind of tempo or rhythm that I want. The resonance, you know. Then I spot it up to get the length of the notes and the particular accents that I want it to follow, that appeal to me. Then I synchronize that sound accent with the visual accent. In *Trade Tattoo* I'm working at least three rhythms at once: I'm using maracas and I'm using something else; and the little dots are all in one rhythm . . . just to give texture to things, to stipple things. At other times in the course of that film, there might have been a passage that I liked so well in the music I found that I'll start designs very specifically (as in the double bass in *Swinging The Lambeth Walk*, boomp ta da boomp boomp) that looked to me like sound sounded; for instance guitar, where a guitar goes twang twang twang, I would accompany it with a twangy stringy image. I would get an image which matched the sound. . . . I've been asked a question which I found the answer to just the other day. Someone asked how my films look without sound. "Terrible," I said. They don't look at all good because they are done for sound, with sound.

Every film I got from the G.P.O., I tried to increase my interest by doing something new. Every film I did was something not previously done in film technique. The lab methods of optical printing and the transferring of black-and-white into color—they were done then for the first time. Leslie Oliver of Technicolor, London, was very helpful in this.

The films that I had color prints made of were all from lacquer paint, like acetate paint. I find that when you get an opaque orange it turns into a very deep Van Dyke brown. I find that if I'm using any of that lacquer color which is supposed to work on film, the best way to test it is paint the film on both sides on one strip, on one side on another strip, and then on the opposite side, so that you've got three strips, then put it on the radiator. If it shrinks at the same rate as the film stock, then it will stay on. If it doesn't, then throw it away and find some other paint that does. I also use an air brush. When I'm stencilling, the shapes are cut out of thin cardboard with a razor blade and in the measurements of the frame rack. Then you just spray this thin lacquer paint through the stencil designs. You can paint the back of the film and generally mess with colors.

I made *Free Radicals* from 16mm black film leader, which you can get from DuPont. I took a graver, various kinds of needles. (My range included Indian arrowheads for romanticism.) You stick down the sides with scotch tape and you get to work with scratching the stuff out. You spit on or dampen the celluloid with a sponge. Now the question is register. You've got sprocket holes to guide you. When you hold the needle you dig it in through the black emulsion into the film and then start doing kinds of pictographic signatures. You hold your hand at the right height and act as if you were making your signature. It goes on forever. You can carry a pictographic design in

your head and make a little design. You can't see what you're doing because your hand is in the way. That's why those things have that kind of spastic look. . . .

First of all, I worked for about three or four months with thousands of feet of film, scratching away before I went to see what I had. I wouldn't know what was there. When you see what you've got, you begin to get the control of what you want. You edit the best out of that. Once you've got the stuff and you're really working and you're not sure how it's going, then you look at it. If you're sure how you're going after two or three months, you're pretty sure of your

From *Trade Tattoo* (1937), by Len Lye.

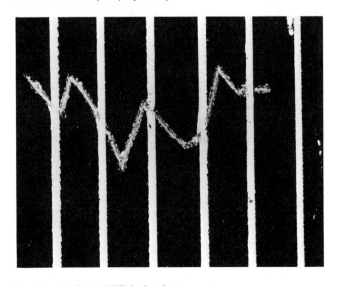

From *Free Radicals* (1957) by Len Lye.

results, so you just work away. Usually when you look at it you're disappointed. You draw a bit, then go to sleep, then draw a little bit more. It took about eight months. I stuck to it because I had to have it for the Brussels Exposition. . . .

I did about ten minutes worth of this stuff, collected the best bits, said "Oh, here're the best bits now," and looked at them. I realized that they were boring. I couldn't kid myself, after ten seconds they were absolutely boring to me. I had had it, although I knew that they were the best I could do. Then came the time I was looking for sound to go with them. I found an absolutely marvelous African field tape of the Bagirmi tribe. It had the same kind of feeling to it, the same resonance, the same attack as the visual attack in the tone of the drum and the way that the guy hand-drummed. I was absolutely fascinated. It was curious how I lost my involvement with the stuff after about ten seconds, but when I played both together I could stay with it for three or four minutes. I am totally involved with the sensory business about motion without any intellectual story, or anything else other than just motion. It occurred to me that the primitive boys were also very involved with dance patterns of rhythm. . . .

Q: You don't believe that experimental films, such as you have made, are made for any special audience?

Lye: Oh, goodness, no. They were just made for me. And if anybody likes 'em, fine. I made them and that's it. I only get the kick out of making them. If you start out with an inquiring mind, like I did. Nobody has numbed it. My excitement in life was to discover something that's significant to *me*. Now how the hell can I work it out if it has to be significant to an audience? It's the last thing on earth I'd be interested in. The main obsession is to find something that's significant and not to think: "Well, I wonder if so-and-so's going to like this."

You see, there are no incentives in experimental film, other than your own particular interest, because the value of basic film research, in techniques of screen presentation, isn't understood at all. The value of contemporary art isn't understood, let alone film, which has hardly any standards of reference in terms of fine art, or popular art, or pornographic art, or any other kind of art that you can say has established standards in popular films. There's a whole lot mixed up with nostalgia and humanism, but nothing much to do with fine art. For instance, all my previous films are commercial spots, glorified spots—that's not fine art. You can't go and put a pack of Chesterfields on the brow of Michelangelo's *Moses* and call it fine art. Folk art creeps into the domain of fine art. It's togetherness, not aloneness. It's a confusion of two different psychological levels. . . . To me, discovery is something

that is a workout on imagery I haven't seen done before, and that I haven't done before and one that I can make click for me. There are two areas of this for me. One is direct film and the other, live action. I've been reduced to painting *on* film, or scratching film, not that I want to, but because I want to deal with the *control* of three-dimensional motion. In direct film, if I can make something wiggle in a way that is fascinating to me, I'll take three months messing around with it, with a drive to find something that says: "Come on, you may get a kick out of it." And if you do, these are big kicks, and their shape lasts, you've got something to show for it. With your dope or your infatuation, you get great sensory kicks. O.K., but they go away, they fade. Not with art.

Q: I understand you're presently working with a form of moving sculpture?

Lye: Oh, yes. I'll tell you how that came. After making the rounds of the foundations and industry and knocking my head against their stone walls, I saw that I could just go on and waste my time, so I went back to animating solid three-dimensional objects, like motion sculpture, something I did as a kid, but now I realized that my particular sense of motion was tied in a lot with vibration. And instead of using an old handle to wind pulley-wheels, I used motors to transmit power to the object that they held: rods or blades or a whole lot of springy metals, and the motorized mechanisms would flip them about. If you shone a light on a reflecting surface, the light would be returned and flash away. The three-dimensional nature of the object would give you plenty of empathy with response. You'd get involved with a basic thing of existence—motion—the visually kinetic act of energy.

I'm working on a film now, one with abstract shapes, along the lines of *Free Radicals*, about rays in space. That's *what* they look like, anyway. That's what they *feel* like. As for live action, I won't be able to make a photographic film until I can get the means. Why? Because it'll take coin to demonstrate how to bust out of the live-action continuity confines of the film techniques of "pan," "dolly," "close-up," "angle change". . .

Q: Do you think the audience can be educated to appreciate experimental films more?

Lye: No. I think any public will accept the best if there's nothing else to take. It won't know the difference between the best and the worst. So, if the best is there and they won't know the difference, because there's no worse, then they take the best. They took it in Shakespeare's time. . . .

(From *Film Culture*, Summer 1963 and Spring 1967; interview questions by Gretchen Berg.)

THE *Tusalava* MODEL
by Len Lye

. . . The cartoon film *Tusalava* opens with dots rising in a black panel, left, . . . while a cog-chain affair rises straight up in a much thinner panel, (r.). In the white space, center, two grubs rise and assume a fertility pose (whatever that is), whereupon the dots in the panel become trapped in a cocoon which extrudes a huge grub. It sounds rather tame but I'm told "there's something about it." The grub divides. One half absorbs the other and then becomes metamorphosed into a cross between a huge spider and an octopus with blood circulating through its arms. Finally, this anxiety thing attacks an embryo totem figure that has developed in the cocoon and the scene ends with dots and welling circles. Life's gone full circle. The End.

Not really, because years later I saw that the grub and the attacking images were both a startlingly factual representation of anti-bodies and virus. The primitive side of my brain must have communed with my innate self enough to have reached down into my body and come up with gene-carried information which I expressed visually. I had always wanted to compose motion and the film came out of my instinctive learning of a body-English language which my primitive brain picked up without my consciously knowing I was learning that sort of alphabet.

This learning comprised various ways by which I'd devised what I called *models* for the practice of the art of motion, something like the way scientists make models to isolate facts. *Tusalava* was one big model for exercising my primitive penchant for primitive art. For the nearly two years of assiduous work making the thousands of drawings for *Tusalava* I was always imagining how it would look if an Australian Aboriginal was doing it . . .

Yes, I imagined the grubs I was interminably drawing on my sheets of cartoon paper were straight out of an Australian Aboriginal Witchetty Grub dance. I had never seen such a grub, much less an Aboriginal dance; but I remembered having seen some reproductions of Aboriginals daubing their black bodies with some sort of cottonseed flock in preparation for a Witchetty Grub dance. They were also shown standing in line—I suppose in readiness to mime the motions of the grub. I may have unconsciously chosen the grub for my film not only because I like Abo art but, also, because it would be something that would wiggle quietly and move slowly and give me plenty of time to think out its life span as I went along.

I plodded on making endless drawings for the film, hoping that the Aboriginal within me was looking after the growth of my grubs. This primitive stance in my creative attitude was one prime aspect of making the film. Other practices helped my primitive brain to dig up information out of my body, notably doodling. . .

Not only did it land me with my own original imagery (if I recognized anything I knew in a doodle, I'd stop) but, also, it taught me how to commune with my unconscious. This came about, I think, because I had already steeped my brain in primitive art. It helped to bring up the imagery of the doodles from the level of my own primitive side of the brain. Here's a model for practice I made up for getting the *feel* of primitive art: Lunchtimes and weekends I'd concentrate on some great primitive work in some

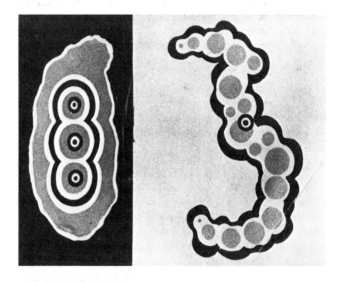

From *Tusalava* (1929), Len Lye's first film.

musuem. I would draw it very accurately and realistically and add color if need be. I would never read the label. This conscious block against knowing-versus-feeling went with the copying of some work from some tome in the library when I'd cover up the text beneath its reproduction with a piece of blotting paper. In that way I saw only the art, not the text. Before going to sleep that night I would look at my primitive art sketchbook and end up with the sketch done that day; then, when I had recalled its original feeling I'd put the book under my pillow. Goodnight . . .

One of the ways I had learned the body-English of art at the start was to be off on a sunny Saturday afternoon to go to a clean and uncluttered more or less deserted place like the handsome small-boat harbor of Wellington, N.Z., with its small wooden walk-outs. If it was a case of "you be me" it'd be this: You select a boat mast that's dancing on the water and really watch it. You take out your sketchbook and draw the left side of the pattern of mast wiggles. You do the same for the right, but you leave an open space between these two sides. Now you look at the middle line of the mast's dance on the water and shift your eyes back to the blank space on the page of your sketchbook and mentally transpose those middle wiggles to the paper.

Why? Because you've left it blank so that before sleeping that night you can look at the right and left contours of your sketch and again mentally fill in the backbone of the motion with which you had empathized down at the boat harbor. If what you're after without knowing it is to feel completely at one with your body which harbors your gene-pattern, you could put your book under your pillow like you've done with your primitive art book and simply go to sleep to dream of dancing waters . . .

Came the time years later when my wife Ann and I were asked to go to the Montreal Expo Film Festival where *Tusalava* was to be unravelled. Guy Metraux, who arranged it, saw us down in New York. He started talking about some film or other—some slow and rather dull-looking film he'd come across. It looked to him as if it would go on forever, he said, but by the time it was done he'd been caught up in one of the most holdingly inexorable of films. "The name of the film is," he said "*Tusalava*". "Oh", I said.

After the film was shown at Expo a film man named Sen asked me at coffee, . . . whether I knew anything about microphage.

"No, I don't," I said.

"Well," he said, "you've got a spitting image of a microphage in your film." He went on, "It's a kind of a virus; I'm doing a film on it for a scientist. It attaches itself to the wall of a cell, sticks a hollow needle through it, and injects its genes into the cell. Ping, you've got a fever, the sniffles, or whatever."

About three years afterwards I came across a scientific model illustrating the anti-body. It's the thing that takes on the job of blocking virus and protecting cells from intruders. The anti-body looked very familiar, so I got some stills from *Tusalava*. The grubs in them were the spitting image of the anti-body shown in the magazine. Therefore, two of the protagonists in *Tusalava* were dead ringers for both a microphage and an anti-body. So what?

So, maybe this: all art is a spin-off of the principle of genetic replication—self-replication. Every cell in our body is a prime example of it. . . .

Maybe it's related to the enhancement which occurs evocatively when any of us make discoveries about emotionally felt truths, such as the "evolutionary" feel felt by the fisherman standing in his boat in the rising sun, the gardener down into the earth and roots, the baker with his fire and his bread, the conscientiousness of the cabinetmaker, not to mention the truths we feel when the Arts hit something that remains evocative of man's sense of essential selfness. We take all the other stuff to the grave. Art lives.

(From an unfinished autobiographical
manuscript, dated 1973.)

From *The Birth of the Robot* (1936) by Len Lye.

3/Pioneers of Pictorial Animation in Europe

Cecile Starr

INTRODUCTION

The three European artist-animators included in this section—Lotte Reiniger, Berthold Bartosch, and Alexander Alexeieff—were among the first to develop new and distinctive styles of pictorial animation outside the bounds of the commercial animated cartoon. Each created a characteristic imagery: Reiniger in her sharply contrasting black-and-white fairy tales and adventure stories; Bartosch in his hazy, glistening caricature of modern society; and Alexeieff in his pointillistic half-tones that evoked real and fantasy life in turn-of-the-century Russia.

Lotte Reiniger was not the first to translate Oriental shadow-play drama into film animation. As early as 1912, Frederick A. Talbot (in *Moving Pictures, How They Are Made and Worked*) cited an Englishman named Mr. C. Armstrong who in the preceding two years had perfected a silhouette animation technique that consisted of moving and filming jointed flat models on a "one turn, one picture" basis, i.e., the jointed models were moved slightly for each picture between each individual turn of the camera. Armstrong's first film, *The Clown and the Donkey*, involved "a vast amount of patience and extremely delicate manipulation," according to Talbot, and was shown in London's Palace Theater where it provoked "unrestrained mirth." Armstrong also made a silhouette film advertising cigarettes, which Talbot wrote was well received and much copied. Talbot also reported seeing other subjects produced by European and American films which represented "possibly the high-water mark of this form of magic cinematog-raphy." Thus silhouette animation was clearly established well before 1912.

Other non-cartoon animation styles were developed almost as far back as the motion picture itself—using cutouts, clay, moving dolls, and object animation. These generally were made within the framework of commercial filmmaking, for profit and in some sort of systematized production scheme. Occasionally one finds information about pre-1918 films outside this framework. The animated clay figures of a New York sculptor named Helene Smith Dayton were described in *Scientific American* (December 16, 1916), for example. The publication stated that after she had learned to keep her grotesque men and women from moving too fast, and after she had learned to simplify her stories by limiting the main action to one figure at a time, Helene Dayton was able to turn out as much as 200 feet of film in a day. (Such speed being so far beyond the normal pace of single-frame animation, it can perhaps be dismissed as a journalistic miscalculation.) There is no evidence that the films were ever shown publicly.

A year later the same publication told of a five-reel film by a Chicago director named Howard S. Moss who animated dolls with the occasional addition of live animals and people in the same scenes. Mr. Moss admitted that many pins and invisible threads and wires were used in his film and that a corps of carpenters was employed for sets and props. His scheme for making the dolls smile, frown, pout, and wink was a secret he refused to divulge.

The first person to make a lifelong career of puppet

animation was the Polish-Russian Ladislas Starevitch. Originally a natural scientist, he made an intricate jointed wooden beetle and filmed it at two frames per movement to explain the anatomy of the insect. His first production, which parodied a popular Danish circus motion picture, was entitled *The Flying Frogs* (1911). His version of *Grasshopper and the Ants*, in 1913, won for Starevitch a medal from Czar Nicholas II. During the war he directed mostly live-action films. In the 1920s Starevitch again took up puppet films in France. His 50-minute *Roman de Renart* (sometimes called in English *Story of the Fox*), based on a collection of medieval tales, was completed in 1938. This ambitious work set as many as 75 animal puppets in motion at one time. The Starevitch puppets were finger-sized, the tallest being about six inches. Facial masks, as many as 300 for a single character, were used for different expressions.

Other significant developments in puppet animation were made in Europe in the 1930s by the Hungarian-born George Pal working in Germany and Holland (later in Hollywood), and by the Russian Alexander Ptushko, whose *New Gulliver* (1935) employed some 3,000 dolls made of rubber, metal, wood, and cloth in a politically oriented version of Swift's satire.

Puppet animation reached its fullest artistic recognition on an international basis with the work of the Czech artist Jiri Trnka in the two decades that followed World War II. As a youngster of fourteen, Trnka was apprenticed to a puppeteer. After a career as an illustrator of books and a stage set designer, he turned to animated cartoons, then to puppet animation. Among Trnka's long list of puppet films, those best-known in this country are the feature-length fairy tale, *The Emperor's Nightingale* (1948); the short parody of American Western movies called *The Song of the Prairie* (1949); and a social protest against enforced conformity entitled *The Hand* (1965), which won an Academy Award and was Trnka's last film. The expansive new directions of animation in at least several Eastern European countries owe a significant debt to Trnka as an artist, animator, and human being.

Lotte Reiniger's career in silhouette animation spans the years from 1918 to the present writing (1976), and is one of the longest and most productive in animation history. Most of her fifty short films are fairy tales (*Cinderella, Sleeping Beauty, Thumbelina*) with a sprinkling of fable (*The Grasshopper and the Ant*), legend (*Galatea*), opera (*Papageno*, based on Mozart's The Magic Flute), and Arabian Nights adventures (*Aladdin*). Her good taste and fine feeling for detail bring dignity and beauty to familiar stories that often have been de-

based for popular consumption in other films. Reiniger's magic transformations—birds change to slender dancing girls in *Papageno*, and eggs hatch human babies— add poetic moments to the prose of the stories themselves.

Jiri Trnka with puppets from his film, *A Midsummer Night's Dream* (1959).

From *The Hand* (1965) by Jiri Trnka.

Reiniger's work is interesting also in terms of her remarkable collaborations with Berthold Bartosch for nearly ten years, and with Walter Ruttmann (see Chapter 2) for the three years that *The Adventure of Prince Achmed* was in production. Concerning the use of their multi-plane animation stand, Lotte Reiniger has recalled that Ruttmann made his earlier *Opus* films on a very small plate of glass. On *Prince Achmed* they first divided their work, foregrounds and backgrounds, onto two separate stands, later joining the two negatives into a combined print. Then Ruttmann began working on a lower plate of glass, sometimes with sand, soap, or other materials. "To my knowledge," she has stated, "it is the first and perhaps the only time when two artists of completely different temperaments were working together on the same shot."

Berthold Bartosch also created moving backgrounds for *Prince Achmed* and for other Reiniger films of the 1920s. When Ruttmann abandoned animation, and Reiniger continued her silhouette films with less intricate background movements, Bartosch in Paris made his only completed independent film, *The Idea*. In it he paid at least as much attention to the buildings and lights and skies as to the characters and their evolving story. His single-handed mastery of four levels of images, with many superimpositions which he made always in the camera, is matched with what Claire Parker has called "his prodigious interior vision."

Alexander Alexeieff, an engraver and lithographer, was drawn to the motion picture medium after seeing Bartosch's style of animating the entire surface of the screen. With Claire Parker, Alexeieff invented a device called *l'écran d'épingles*, translated sometimes as the pinboard, sometimes as the pin screen. On this device, hundreds of thousands of movable headless pins are manipulated by hand to make single pictures which illustrate books (Pasternak's *Doctor Zhivago* and Dostoyevsky's *The Gambler* and *Notes from the Underground*), or moving pictures which illustrate music (Moussorgsky's Night on Bald Mountain and Pictures at an Exhibition, the French-Canadian folksong En Passant) or to retell a story in graphic pantomine (Gogol's *The Nose*).

A small pinboard has been acquired by the National Film Board of Canada, where recently Lotte Reiniger has also been a guest animator. It remains to be seen how these and other pioneer achievements in pictorial animation will be assimilated into current and future works by new animators.

Lotte Reiniger

Lotte Reiniger, in the 1920s.

Lotte Reiniger was born in Berlin in 1899, studied briefly at the studio of Max Reinhardt, and provided hand-cut silhouette titles for Paul Wegener's film, *The Pied Piper of Hamelin* in 1918, helping also to animate wooden rats in stop-motion, when real rats and guinea pigs refused to follow directions. The following year she made her first brief silhouette film called *The Ornament of the Loving Heart* and then other fairy tales and spectacles in quick succession.

In 1923, Lotte Reiniger, only 24 years old, undertook a full-length production of *The Adventures of Prince Achmed*, among the first all-animation feature films ever made. It took nearly three years to complete and was backed by a German banker named Louis Hagen who installed Miss Reiniger and her team of animators in a studio over his garage in Potsdam, outside Berlin. The film was produced by Carl Koch (Miss Reiniger's husband), with the collaboration of Walter Ruttmann, Berthold Bartosch, and Alexander Kardan. The story, from the *Thousand and One Nights*, is a tale of sorcery and splendor, a kidnapped princess, a magic horse, and friendly and monstrous creatures. It had a six-month run in Paris at Louis Jouvet's Champs-Elysées Theater.

Reiniger later made a Chinese shadow-play as part of Jean Renoir's *La Marseillaise* (in 1937), on which her husband, Carl Koch, collaborated with Renoir as scenarist. Koch is also credited as Technical Advisor on Renoir's *Grand Illusion* (1938) and as co-writer and assistant director on *Rules of the Game* (1939); late that same year he took over the direction of *La Tosca*, which Renoir had barely started shooting in Italy when the outbreak of war forced him to return to France. In his recently published memoirs, Renoir refers frequently to Koch as one of his closest and most valued friends.

In reviewing *The Adventures of Prince Achmed* in *Theatre Arts Monthly* (June 1931), Randolph T. Weaver wrote that he first heard of the film through Jean Renoir and his wife. He describes the film's "spirit and grace" and finds it as a whole "almost faultless." Freddy Chevalley writing in *Close Up* (June 1929) found only one fault—that the film was too long to hold the attention of the spectator. "Films of purely visual interest," Chevalley concluded "in which life manifests itself only under appearances far removed from reality, provoke a nervous tension which becomes the more pronounced the longer the projection." Chevalley recommended administering to audiences "by little doses surrealist poems and little works" ("opuscules," the name by which he refers elsewhere to Ruttmann's first abstract films).

Since *Prince Achmed*, Reiniger has made only short

animation films. Three *Dr. Doolittle* films, based on Hugh Lofting's books, were completed in the late 1920s, again with Bartosch working on backgrounds; they have circulated as individual reels. In 1929, with Rochus Gliese in Berlin, Lotte Reiniger co-scripted, directed and photographed a live-action feature film entitled *Running after Luck*, with Jean Renoir and his wife Catherine Hessling, Amy Tedesco, and Berthold Bartosch in the cast. The film was not successful, but a two-reel silhouette sequence was pulled from the feature and released separately.

With sound-on film in the 1930s, Reiniger created a number of films especially related to their musical backgrounds: *Papageno* (to Mozart's Magic Flute), *Carmen*, (based on Bizet's opera), *Harlequin* (based on 18th century music) and *Tochter*, (based on music by Benjamin Britten). Eric Walter White, who compiled the music for *Harlequin*, has described her animation technique in a charming booklet entitled *Walking Shadows*, published by Leonard and Virginia Wolff in 1931. The scenery, White tells us, is cut to the size of the animation table, or longer when travelling shots are needed, for it is the scenery and not the camera that moves. Similarly a close-up is made by substituting a larger figure and modifying the background proportionately. In *Prince Achmed*, for example, the main characters were filmed in at least three sizes, the largest nearly two feet tall. "The rhythm of the lines, expression of the features and details of dress all possess that unmistakable quality that comes from the subtle and incisive cutting of a pair of scissors," White indicates, "and not from the random wanderings of a pencil or a pen."

In the mid-1930s Lotte Reiniger worked briefly for the G.P.O. and Crown Film Units in England. After the war she made her home in England, working briefly for the Ministry of Health, and on a long series of myths and fairy tales for British and American television: *Aladdin*, *The Grasshopper and the Ant*, *The Calif Stork*, *Thumbelina*, and at least a dozen others. Later films have colored backgrounds made from transparent colored papers. Colored backgrounds have been added to some of the early films by special filter processes. Music has been added to those silent films still in release.

In 1936, Reiniger wrote, in *Film Art*: "Film is motion... just pure and simple motion on the screen." With the advent of sound, she found that the purity and simplicity of the motion was complicated by the need to transform *musical* value into *screen-space-value*. Each different score brought fresh problems of interpretation. "And this is perhaps good," she concluded, "for without it I certainly could not help feeling a certain amount of

bitterness towards an industry that fails to appreciate the hard work put into the creation of a silhouette film—after all an artistic achievement—yet is always ready to squander money on things of little importance."

Asked for his recollections and comments about Reiniger's work, Jean Renoir recently wrote: "She is an artist and her work would be as good if instead of working with film, she had been a painter or a musician.... Artistically I have to see her as a visual expression of

From *Papageno* (1935) by Lotte Reiniger.

From *The Grasshopper and the Ant* (1954) by Lotte Reiniger.

Mozart's music. I wish a film could be shot showing her hands during the making of one of her pictures. Her fingers clasping her only tool, scissors, make me think of a graceful classical dancer. I have no stories to tell about her. She is of herself a fascinating story."

In 1975, at the age of 76, Lotte Reiniger completed a new color film entitled *Aucassin and Nicolette*, as guest animator at the National Film Board of Canada.

Lotte Reiniger, in 1975, at the National Film Board of Canada.

From *Aucassin et Nicolette* (1975) by Lotte Reiniger.

"THE ADVENTURES OF PRINCE ACHMED"
by Lotte Reiniger

In the year 1919, I, Lotte Reiniger, was introduced by Paul Wegener, the leading figure of artistic filmmaking in Berlin by this time (*Student Of Prague, The Golem*, etc.), to a group of young people, who opened up a studio of scientific and artistic films. This group was called Institut für Kulturforschung [Institute for Cultural Research] under the leadership of Dr. Hans Cürlis, a friend of Paul Wegener. In this Institute I made my first silhouette film, followed by various others, and they did quite well in the cinemas and in advertising. It was the time of the inflation, and the dollars they brought in made us go along quite well.

We had not so much the idea to make money with these films, but more to be able to carry on. For at that time animation was in its infancy, there was just Felix the Cat, Fleischer's cartoons and so forth; Mickey Mouse was far away in the future. For the filmmakers of this period, those were the days: with each film we could make new discoveries, find new problems, new possibilities, technical and artistic, we were most eager to execute. The whole field was virgin soil and we had all the joys of explorers in an unknown country. It was wonderful.

Yet, when in 1923, a Berlin banker, Louis Hagen, visited the Institute and saw us at work, and asked us whether we could consider making a full-length picture in silhouettes, we had to think twice. This was a never heard of thing. Animated films were supposed to make people roar with laughter, and nobody had dared to entertain an audience with them for more than ten minutes. Everybody to whom we talked in the industry about that proposition was horrified.

But we did not belong to the industry. We always had been outsiders and we always had done what we wanted to do. Our friends were artists of the same calibre who approached films in their own ways, such as Ruttmann, Bartosch, Richter and Eggeling and others [see Chapter 2]. So we were not afraid of the challenge.

As the making of those silhouette films did not require very expensive equipment nor a great personnel, and money in this time of inflation became less valuable from day to day, our conscience was not overburdened in that direction. So we decided to accept that most tempting proposal.

The banker did not want this film to be made in the framework of the Institute and offered to install a studio for us above his garages in the vegetable gardens of his house in Potsdam. So we went there. We being me and my husband Carl Koch, who had married me meantime, and later on Berthold Bartosch, who had also worked with us in the Institute.

The studio was very low, being an attic under the roof, so the shooting field with its glass plate had to be very near the floor in order to get the camera up high enough in a suitable distance, with just enough space to place the lamps underneath. I had to kneel on the seat of an old dismantled motorcar to execute my manipulation. I liked this very much; it was a much more comfortable position for me than sitting on a swivel chair as I had to do later on.

The whole contraption looked like a four-poster bed, the camera being supported by sturdy wooden beams, on which we could fix and take off to our heart's content every construction we might need for our special effects. In the Institute I had obtained my stop motion with the aid of a bicycle pump, which worked very well.

But this time we intended to be as modern as possible, and so at the advice of cameraman Guenther Rittau, who worked for no lesser person than Fritz Lang, we had a motor of a special design installed. I did not take kindly to that motor at all, for it had to be set to work by a lever, a movement which distracted me from my attention to the figures on the glass plate, who demanded a rapt concentration throughout the shooting, whilst the reclining movement of pulling the string of the good bicycle pump allowed my eyes to be fixed on my scene perpetually. Furthermore, I could do it with my left hand and keep my right steady and free from blood pressure for the touch of the figures, which had always required utmost delicacy. Many years later, when I had a technically much more advanced rostrum installed, I ruefully went back to my old-fashioned bicycle pump.

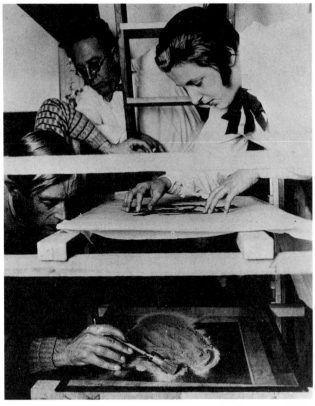

Lotte Reiniger at work with other animators, including Carl Koch (with glasses), Walter Ruttmann (with brush), and Berthold Bartosch (with cutouts).

As the theme for this long lasting enterprise we had chosen the Arabian Nights. The action had to show events which could not be performed by any other means. So from all the 1001 stories we sorted out all the events which fell into that category; the flying horse, magic islands, fantastic birds, djinns, sorcerers and witches, transformations and all there is to be found in abundance in these tales, and out of these items we formed the script.

I felt very bashful towards my serious collaborators, to engage them in such a fairy tale world, but for me it was real. "What has this to do with the year 1923?" said Walter Ruttmann. "Nothing," I could only say, "But that I am alive now, and I want to do it as I have the chance." But he did the most wonderful things for this film, and the bits I did together with him are the ones I am most proud of.

I am very proud also of the magnificent sea journey Berthold Bartosch composed and executed for Aladdin's flight. Nowadays, of course, waves are often seen in animation, but this was absolutely brand new. We could not stop Bartosch experimenting with waves afterwards. Only too natural, for one can do anything still better, but we had to finish the film one day. Here

it was to the great merit of Carl Koch, the producer, who stopped us from going to seed with endless experiments. He was a real gardener.

So we started in 1923 and finished in 1926. Starting with black-and-white only and gradually developing more scenery as movable backgrounds, using soap and sand and paint on different layers, sometimes two negatives, each done on different animation benches and composed by the different artists entirely after their own conception. The anxiety of this process was sometimes almost unbearable. Whilst working you only see your figures on your composition in one position. What will it look like when it moves, or what the two compositions, which might look all right in themselves, will look like when they are printed together, were riddles whose solution could only be awaited with hope. Many of the things we did are nowadays a household word, but we really did them for the first time. Often we had to experiment for weeks until we got them ready for shooting.

Although this was the time of the silent film, we were anxious to provide our picture with every support to ensure its coming over well to its audience. So we had the musician Wolfgang Zeller collaborating with us throughout this time, composing the score. When for instance a procession was wanted he composed a march; we measured with stop watches and tried to move the figures according to its beat. Or a Glockenspiel was executed to measure. In this period the better theaters employed an orchestra and for the more ambitious films special music was composed. In our own score, for this purpose, small pictures of the film were cut out and pasted in, so that the conductor knew where he had to place his intended effects. . . .

When the film was finished, we did not find any theater which wished to play it. So we arranged on our own a first performance at the Volksbuehne, a theater in the North of Berlin, where Wolfgang Zeller was in charge of the orchestra. His musicians had consented to play for us on a Sunday morning for his sake. We invited the press and all the people we could think of on postcards. As we had led a very remote life during the production, we had not had much contact with the press; our friend Bert Brecht helped us a great deal to invite the right people. It had to be on a Sunday morning, and as it was Spring and good weather had broken out, we did not think that many people would sacrifice a beautiful morning to see a mysterious, never-heard-of silhouette film in an out-of-the-way theater. But they all came and the theater was overcrowded . . .

(From *The Silent Picture*, Autumn 1970.)

Figures used in *The Adventures of Prince Achmed.*

From *The Adventures of Prince Achmed* (1923–1926) by Lotte Reiniger.

FROM "SCISSORS MAKE FILMS"
by Lotte Reiniger

...I will attempt to answer the two questions which I am nearly always asked by people who watch me making the silhouettes. Firstly: How on earth did you get the idea? And secondly: How do they move, and why are your hands not seen on the screen? The answer to the first is to be found in the short and simple history of my own life. I never had the feeling that my silhouette cutting was an idea. It so happened that I could always do it quite easily, as you will see from what follows.

I could cut silhouettes almost as soon as I could manage to hold a pair of scissors. I could paint, too, and read, and recite; but these things did not surprise anyone very much. But everybody was astonished about the scissor cuts, which seemed a more unusual accomplishment. The silhouettes were very much praised, and I cut out silhouettes for all the birthdays in the family. Did anyone warn me as to where this path would lead? Not in the least; I was encouraged to continue.

Now I was very fond of the theater and acting. But performing plays in a small flat made rather a confu-

sion, so it was a great relief to all when I began to use my silhouettes for my play-acting, constructing a little shadow theater in which to stage Shakespeare. There was peace for a short time; then came the film. I had refused to learn a profession, and I now had one desire—to make films at all costs. This was a problem, but the fairies must have pitied me and helped me. At this time, Paul Wegener, a great actor and artist, was in Berlin. He produced a number of beautiful and unusual films, and his ambition was to utilise to the full the possibilities of the camera for the development of the film.... Wegener saw me cutting silhouettes behind the stage in Reinhardt's theater, and he became interested. He liked my silhouettes; he thought they showed a rare sense of movement. He therefore introduced me to a group of young artists who had started a new trick [animation] film studio. Here I first began to photograph my silhouette figures, just as drawings are photographed for the cartoon film, and I was successful in making a film with my shadow figures.

This was in 1919, and the work was so interesting that from that time I have rarely done anything else. In the meantime I married one of the artists, and we started working together, as we have continued to do till the present time. That is my story.

And now the second question: How do the figures move? The technique of this type of film is very simple. As with cartoon drawings, the silhouette films are photographed movement by movement. But instead of using drawings, silhouette marionettes are used. These marionettes are cut out of black cardboard and thin lead, every limb being cut separately and joined with wire hinges. A study of natural movement is very important, so that the little figures appear to move just as men and women and animals do. But this is not a technical problem. The backgrounds for the characters are cut out with scissors as well, and designed to give a unified style to the whole picture. They are cut from layers of transparent paper.

When the story is ready, the music chosen, and the sound track recorded, then the work for the picture itself begins. Figures and backgrounds are laid out on a glass table. A strong light from underneath makes the wire hinges, etc., disappear and throws up the black figures in relief, while the background appears as a more or less fantastic landscape in keeping with the story. The camera hangs above this table, looking down at the picture arranged below. By means of a wire contrivance the film in the camera can be moved one frame at a time. After the first photograph, the figures are moved into their next position, and the whole photographed again. And so on.... The important thing at this stage is to know how much to move the figures so that a lifelike effect may be obtained when the film is run through.

The synchronization between sight and sound is secured by carefully measuring the sound track, and preparing a very exactly worked out scenario, in which the number of shots are calculated according to the musical value. These calculations are the basis for the picture which is then painstakingly photographed.

There remains a good deal to say about the artistic problems of this type of film, about its future, and about its value. But I am content to leave these matters to those people whose profession it is to bother about such problems. I feel that I do better to concentrate on making the films—and on making as many as my good luck allows. Each new film raises new problems and questions, and I can only hope to live long enough to do justice to them all.

(From *Sight and Sound*, Spring 1936)

Berthold Bartosch

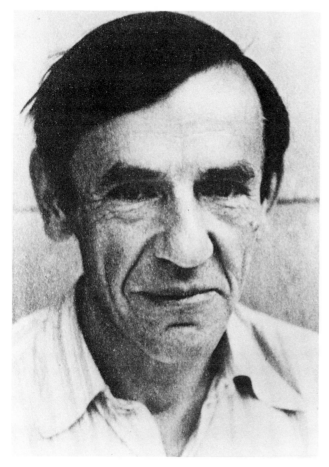

Berthold Bartosch, around 1947.

ophy. His interest in film seems to have derived from his association with Professor E. Hanslik, Director of the Cultural Research Institute in Vienna, who thought it foolish to write books which people would not read, and found cinema the most efficient means of reaching and educating the masses. At Hanslik's suggestion Bartosch set up an animation workshop for educational films, first in Vienna (1918–19), where he made a series of films illustrating the social ideas of Thomas Masaryk, and later in Berlin (1920), where Hanslik had opened a branch of his Institute.

In Berlin, Bartosch met Lotte Reiniger and cooperated with her in making the silhouette animation film, *The Ornament of the Loving Heart*. He also made several advertising films for Pinschewer Films, and others in Zurich. In 1922 he shot *The Battle of Skagerrak*, a commissioned animation film completed in eight days. None of these early films is known to have been shown in the United States.

In 1923–26, Bartosch collaborated on Reiniger's full-length animated film, *The Adventures of Prince Achmed*, together with Alexander Kardan and Walter Ruttmann. Bartosch's contributions are vividly described in Eric White's *Walking Shadows* (1931): "For an effect of stars he will take a piece of cardboard, pin prick it and photograph it moving slowly before the camera with a strong light behind. He will then take the same piece of cardboard upside down, move it in a different direction and at a different speed, and superimpose the second shot upon the first. The result is a sky of stars moving slowly and (apparently) in different directions and at different speeds; nothing could be simpler or more effective." Similar effects were made for the snowstorm in Reiniger's *Dr. Dolittle* films, and for the impressive opening of Bartosch's own film, *The Idea*.

Seascapes in motion were another of Bartosch's specialties, about which White wrote: "For years Bartosch has experimented with waves, making them out of superimposed pieces of semitransparent tissue paper. These he moves with such consummate skill as to convey the impression of the sea's natural sway and surge. Moonlit water he depicts by means of silver paper, in this case

Berthold Bartosch was born in Bohemia (now Czechoslovakia) in 1893. Between 1911 and 1913 he was an apprentice and then designer for the architect M. Hoffman in Vienna. From 1913 to 1917 Bartosch studied architecture and fine arts in Vienna; in this same period he became interested in Chinese painting and philos-

the waves overlap broadly, and the scene has to be lit from the front (above)." White added that at its first performance, the scene showing Dolittle and his animals crossing a moonlit tropical sea evoked an outburst of spontaneous applause.

It is perhaps an exaggeration, but Randolph T. Weaver in *Theatre Arts Monthly* (1931) credits to Bartosch "all the various mechanical devices for rendering the complicated scenic effects" of *Prince Achmed*. Lotte Reiniger has written that even after six months of working on one or another scene, Bartosch would have to be literally forbidden to go any further with his studies and experiments.

Bartosch was married in 1930 and settled in Paris. His wife, Maria, writes that in Berlin in the 1920s Bartosch is certain to have met the dramatist Berthold Brecht and the filmmakers Viking Eggeling, Hans Richter, and Oskar Fischinger [see Chapter 2], among others.

In Paris Bartosch created the 30-minute film entitled *The Idea*, which he completed in 1932. Alexeieff has described it as the first serious, poetic, tragic work in animation. The film was based on a book of the same name, consisting of 83 woodcuts by the Belgian artist Franz Masereel and published in Germany in 1927 with a preface by Hermann Hesse. Masereel had at first planned to collaborate on the film, but he was overwhelmed by the tedium and the technical details and soon abandoned the project to Bartosch alone.

On the mere technical level the film represents a prodigious achievement—some 45,000 frames, many of which were animated on four different levels simultaneously, often with as many as 18 superimpositions made in the camera—and all conceived and executed by the mind and hands of one man alone. While the theme and characters are taken from Masereel's original concepts, the sense of movement, space, and light derive almost entirely from Bartosch.

The characters in *The Idea* were of jointed cardboard; landscapes were made of different sorts of paper, from cardboard to semi-transparent tracing paper. "The exposure was an extremely important factor of Bartosch's art," Alexeieff has written, "because his method of creating animated shapes often required metamorphoses. For example, if he had to animate a cloud, he would blend up to four elements of the cloud, painted with transparent and luminous soap over each other in succession, and of such blendings he accumulated up to 18 on each frame of a sequence. In such an art he excelled, working—if I may say—like Renaissance painters layer by layer, thus obtaining incredible fineness of tone. These allowed him lyrical effects of luminous

fogs in his night city scenes, unequalled in real photography." Maria Bartosch has added that he used ordinary dampened soap on the glass plates, as his only means of light refraction. These and other effects helped create light, dark, and hazy tones with a striking vitality that presents Bartosch's multi-dimensional world partly as

Bartosch's starry background in *The Adventures of Prince Achmed* (1923–1926) by Lotte Reiniger.

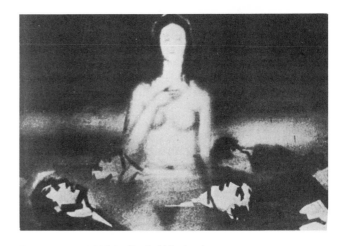

From *The Idea* (1932) by Berthold Bartosch.
"Men live and die for an idea,
But the idea is immortal.
You can persecute it, judge it, forbid it, condemn it to death.
But the idea continues to live in the minds of men...
He whom it penetrates no longer feels isolated,
For above all the idea remains..."
(From the opening titles of the film, 1932).

an idealized dream and partly as an unrelenting reality.

Arthur Honegger's score for *The Idea*, which was added to the already finished film, is thought to be the first to use an electronic instrument in a motion picture. Thorold Dickinson described the new instrument—called Les Ondes Martenot after its inventor—as played by the hands moving around an electrically charged rod. A recurring theme announced and accompanied the slender nude figure which personifies the idea men live and die for.

After finishing *The Idea*, Bartosch made an advertising film for André Shoes (1934), for which Alexeieff acted as business agent between Bartosch and the advertising company Publicis. Bartosch couldn't, or wouldn't talk to any businessman, Alexeieff reports—especially about money. The concept of this two- or three-minute film was to show different kinds of shoes being worn at different times for different occasions: a walk along the Seine, a business meeting, a tennis party, a dance. No legs or bodies were shown, only shoes. Alexeieff has written that despite being lame from birth, Bartosch excelled in the tennis and ballroom scenes, animating a number of pairs of shoes at once in the latter. Bartosch had learned the shoemaker's trade from his father, and in this film he used three-dimensional models a few inches long, with lead soles sewn inside for precise bending as the music required.

Between 1935 and 1939 Bartosch worked on an antiwar film tentatively titled *St. Francis* (or *Nightmares and Dreams*), partially financed by the British filmmaker Thorold Dickinson. About 2,000 feet of film had been shot when Bartosch and his wife were forced to flee Paris at the time of the Nazi occupation. All negative and positive material of the uncut film was deposited in a vault of the Cinémathèque Française; none of it was found again. Only a few test strips were saved, from which the illustrations included in these pages were made.

After the war, Bartosch made two advertising films, *Vitrex*, and *La Vie Heureuse*, for Etienne Raik. Between 1950 and 1959 he did light studies and research for a film on the Cosmos which was to portray the immensity of the universe, the fantastic spectacle of the sun and moon and stars moving endlessly in space. But for reasons of health, Bartosch was unable to realize the film. Between 1960 and 1967 he devoted himself to painting. An exhibit of 50 paintings—nudes, flowers, landscapes and abstract compositions—was held in Annecy in connection with the 1975 Animation Festival there.

Berthold Bartosch died in 1968 after a long illness.

Claire Parker has described her last conversation with him: "On his deathbed, Bartosch spoke still of a film he had dreamed of making for many years. He saw completely what he wanted to do. He said: 'It should be very, very simple. It is very difficult to be very simple, but it is necessary that it be very simple. During my years of work I have learned many things.' Then he smiled softly saying, 'Soap, it is quite extraordinary, with soap one can do everything.'"

ABOUT BERTHOLD BARTOSCH
by Alexander Alexeieff and Claire Parker

Alexeieff: It was in November or the beginning of December 1932 that *The Idea* was shown at the Studio Raspail. At that time, Claire Parker and I were thinking seriously of how to construct a pin screen to make films that would merit the name of engraved animation, for I was an engraver. I was thus doubly struck by the title announced in *La Semaine à Paris:* "Animated Engravings by Berthold Bartosch." Yet it was not at the Studio Raspail that I saw this marvelous film that so intrigued me, but somewhat later at the Théâtre Pigalle.

In the foyer of this theater (it had just been built and was not yet a year old), I met an astonishing couple: the man resembled a carved wooden nutcracker, right out of the *Tales of Hoffman*, and limped like Vulcan; he was accompanied by a slender young woman, among the most beautiful I have ever seen. They were Maria and Berthold Bartosch. They had come from Berlin, I learned later when we became friends.

Bartosch, born in a village in Bohemia, was Czech according to his passport, but he spoke German as his native tongue . . . Son of a shoemaker and born in 1893, he was thus formed by the liberal idealism of Central Europe before the first war and could not have been anything other than liberal and socialist.

Parker: Bartosch had worked with [Professor E.] Hanslik in Vienna, and with Reiniger in Berlin, in the twenties. He never returned to Germany after his arrival in France . . .

Alexeieff: How to explain the name of "Animated Engravings" which the Paris critics attributed to the film, *The Idea*. It was a misunderstanding. The film had been commissioned to Bartosch by the publishing house of Kurt Wolff . . . I think it important to add that Kurt Wolff was the one who discovered another Czech in the 1920s, Franz Kafka, and that he was the first to publish a work of Kafka.

The publishers had had the idea of making an animation film bringing to life Franz Masereel's woodcut illustrations for a book of socialist propaganda, which was called *The Idea*.

Parker: It was a book without words, of engravings alone.

Alexeieff: The publishers thought that since the book resembled a film, it would be quite simple to make a film of it. Bartosch discovered subsequently that it was not at all easy to animate the rather massive woodcuts. To do so, he had to adopt the same manner needed in translating poetry into another language, he had to re-create the whole thing. The chiselled engravings of Masereel would have become rather rigid animation in themselves, while Bartosch lame from birth, walking with difficulty, valued lightness in movements. It was thus necessary for Bartosch to make many inventions. He always wanted to do everything himself, with his own hands.

In 1931, he found shelter under the roof of the Vieux Colombier, thanks to its director, Jean Tedesco. He built in a virtual closet the smallest animation studio the world has ever seen. We are among the few who have seen his multi-plane workbench . . . On this workbench, Bartosch arranged the cut-out cardboard silhouettes which represented Masereel's characters, but these silhouettes moved about in an atmosphere of suppleness and extraordinary poetry . . .

The Idea was animated on sheets of glass with wash-tinted blacks and with soap. Some 100-watt bulbs obliquely lighted Bartosch's workbench from below, and the light became iridescent in the soap, giving some marvellous effects. The weakness of his lighting obliged him to make very long exposures which he created thanks to a relay with a bicycle pump. How proudly he pulled the string which made one think of an old-fashioned toilet flushing. Then one heard the release of the moving weights which descended slowly, weighing on the piston of the pump, and which made the camera's shutter turn for very long exposures. Animators will be interested to learn that Bartosch made many superimpositions, for he proceeded as painters do, working by successive layers. He was never assisted by anyone, not even by his wife. . .

Parker: One can hardly imagine how small his studio was—about 10 × 12 feet. Half the space was filled by the planes of glass which were layered into a sort of workbench. Bartosch stood before this workbench to pull the string of the bicycle pump. We later learned that this was not an ordinary bicycle pump. When we wanted to make the same thing ourselves, much later, for a film of compound pendulums, "our" pump proved very irregular. We asked Bartosch's advice. He told us that he had had a special pump made, that it was very well calibrated and that it gave him perfect regularity of very long exposures.

Alexeieff: The Idea, which runs about a half-hour, took Bartosch more than two years of work. Like many disabled people, Bartosch was spurred on by his very handicap to undertake herculean tasks. It must be said that the courage of his endeavors succeeded in surpassing human measure.

Berthold Bartosch, around 1956, shown at his animation stand in Paris.

From *The Idea* (1932) by Berthold Bartosch. The film was based on a book of woodcuts by the Belgian artist Franz Masereel.

From *The Idea* (1932).

Thorold Dickinson, a generous young Englishman, assistant director of feature films and far from rolling in wealth, admired Bartosch and proposed to sponsor a new film which he would finance by sending him part of his monthly salary. Thus Bartosch began a film which would have to be still larger and still more important than *The Idea*.... [It was an anti-war film in Gasparcolor, *St. Francis or Nightmares and Dreams*, which Bartosch worked on between 1935 and 1939, and which has entirely disappeared except for a number of strips from which the accompanying illustrations were made .].. .

When I had to leave Paris in 1941, I gave Bartosch up for lost. The occupation of the Sudentenland had made him a German. The Nazis were aware that Bartosch had refused their passport, that during his Viennese period he had worked on films on Thomas Masaryk's theses, and that he had begun an anti-Nazi film as propaganda against Hitler (1938). Lame as he was, not knowing how to speak French, he was far too distinctive and vulnerable to escape being quickly spotted.

When I saw him again in 1947 on the Boulevard St. Germain, and when I greeted him in German, with my Russian accent, he answered me in French: "Now I don't spik Cherman any more, I spik Franch." I asked about his film. "When they came to look for me," he told me, "they didn't find me, but they found my film and they destroyed it."

He planned to make a third film, a film still more grandiose, on the Cosmos. During the 20 last years of his life, he set about putting together all the details of this new film, whose secret he carried to his grave, November 13, 1968.

Parker: I don't think he had begun shooting it.

Alexeieff: It is difficult to know. He had showed me some pastel sketches. It should be mentioned that in Berlin Bartosch had been close to the artist circles grouped around the Bauhaus and that he had conceived the idea of animation films whose interest would be in moving form and not in story or caricature. . .

Also, among his Parisian friends should be counted Jean Tedesco, Jean Renoir, and the celebrated art critic Wilhelm Uhde who interested themselves in Bartosch's films and pictures; but not being an art critic myself, I did not know what to say about the numerous pastel sketches that Bartosch showed us. These sketches were destined to specify each step of his conception. The destruction of the second film had been too hard a blow, even for Bartosch's will of iron. He never complained about it, but I think that for the rest of his life he merely played with the idea of resuming his creative film work, while doubting

From Bartosch's unfinished anti-war film (sometimes called the Saint Francis film), on which he worked from 1935 to 1939. Both the negative and positive of the material Bartosch had filmed were lost during the German occupation of Paris in World War II. These illustrations are taken from the few ends of film that remain, in strips of six or eight images each. André Martin has described them as "extraordinary foggy urban landscapes which make one think of Seurat, fantastic bird-devourers of the moon, along with three meters of film showing a strange battle of airplanes."

his power to bring back to life what the war had crushed.

Bartosch would have been able to live comfortably making advertising films, but animation for him was a religion which would not permit compromise . . . Bartosch paid quite dearly for his beliefs . . . He lived with his beautiful Maria in extreme poverty, a poverty to which he accommodated himself quite willingly . . .

According to the theory of compensation which makes it natural for El Greco to be astigmatic and Beethoven inclined to deafness, Bartosch who moved with such difficulty had chosen animation, and no one had ever equalled the lightness of gait of certain of his characters. His intransigence, his incorruptibility, his artistic dignity will probably never be equalled, for the poverty of Bartosch, instead of being a handicap, was a stimulant to his fervor. Fortunately for animation today, animators know (artist-animators who make their films themselves— I do not speak for animators who work in teams) that animation today does not pay. This is sad, on the one hand, but on the other we animators should recognize with a certain pride that our way is hard as it was for the painters of the School of Paris, of the heroic epoch when one did not yet know how to sell paintings. The day when one knows how to sell animation, men will be drawn towards animation more often for gain than for the cultivation of the Art. . .

Bartosch's work influenced me very much. When I saw the words "Animated Engravings" in *La Semaine à Paris*, I said to myself: "How is it that you, whom poverty obliged to invent so many engraving techniques, have not been able to find a way of animating them?" Stimulated by the feeling of rivalry, I vowed my intention of trying to illustrate music after having illustrated books. I should also say that between Bartosch's detail (in the atmosphere, in the luminous fogs) and mine, there is certainly a familial kinship, less a kinship of Slavic temperament than a kinship of hazy wintry countryside, of snow or fog, characteristic of the North. We both loved light in the same way. Also, Bartosch showed that animation could be POETIC, and it is there, I believe, that his influence was unique. . . It was Bartosch who first dared to give animation the dimensions of a great art, trusting it to voice his pain, to lay bare his heart, to tell of his hope for a better future—which he never saw.

If I were a critic, I would draw attention to the importance of the cityscapes in the film *The Idea*, and I would compare Bartosch to that other painter of prisons: Piranesi. But I believe that the moral example of Bartosch prevails over everything else.

Parker: I knew Bartosch as wives know their husbands'

friends, observing a bit from the side, but not entering directly in the conversation. From this man emanated an extraordinary human warmth, a sustained passion. There was in him something essentially the peasant, or in any case the villager. In my opinion, he was not at home in the city. When we were at his place, under the roof of the Vieux Colombier, I always had the impression of being somewhere in the tower of the windmill, or in the steeple of a country church. It was his universe which he carried wherever he went.

During the war, they lived on a farm. . . . Bartosch could not work. They depended on strangers—well, not exactly—they had met the generosity which the Frenchman is capable of, when he senses another's need. And they became true friends of the peasants who took care of them; they worked in the fields, they learned French.

Without Maria, Bartosch would not have been able to exercise his art, to make *The Idea*, would not have been able to live. This beautiful woman, with a will of iron like her husband, worked all her life for him, not only to care for him and feed him, to keep house, but she also worked outside the house to earn their spending money.

Alexeieff: This life was dull only in appearance, for in the depth of their dreams, they lived, I am certain of it, one of the most fantastic lives that anyone has ever lived on this earth. I say in their dreams, for the role of dreams in a human life is important.

(From *Image et Son*, interview by Hubert Arnault, January 1969.)

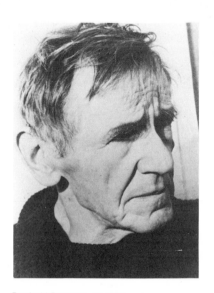

Berthold Bartosch, in 1965.

Alexander Alexeieff and Claire Parker

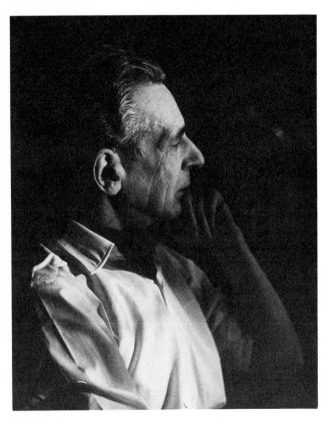

Alexander Alexeieff, around 1955.

Alexander Alexeieff was born in Kazan, Russia, in 1901, spent his first years in Constantinople, and as a young man travelled through the Far East and subsequently to Paris. In the early 1920s he designed and painted sets for the production companies of Pitöeff, Jouvet, Kommissarjevsky, the Ballet Suédois, and in 1936 the Ballet Russe.

Discouraged by the poor pay for stage designs, Alexeieff took up engravings, woodcuts, etchings, and lithographs for book illustrations, teaching himself because he could not afford lessons. His early works include

books by Baudelaire, Poe, Giraudoux, Morand, Gogol, Pushkin, and in 1929 his master-work, a three-volume edition of Dostoyevsky's *Brothers Karamazov* with 100 illustrations. in 1970 a volume containing two Malraux novels was published with 25 Alexeieff illustrations in color. Among his post-war book illustrations are the 12th century Russian epic *Song of Prince Igor*, *Tales of Hoffman*, and *Russian Fairy Tales*, the latter recently republished in the United States.

In the Autumn 1934 issue of *Cinema Quarterly*, Alexeieff and Claire Parker described their invention of pinboard animation as a means of creating films that are analogous to engravings, with "all the finesses of tone and shading" permitting all shades of gray, and even surpassing in brilliancy and delicacy of tint everything that is known in engraving."

John Grierson, in the same issue, reviewed their first film, *Night on Bald Mountain:* "...There is a soft shadowy quality in the form, and none of the hard precision of line associated with cartoons. The forms emerge from space, they have the appearance of dissolving to other forms. Three-dimensional qualities seem to be easily achieved, and models in animation can be introduced without disturbing the general style. The film, apart from its technical interest, is an imaginative performance, though difficult to describe. Imagine, however, a *Walpurgisnacht*, in which animated footsteps indicate spirit presences, goblins and hobgoblins appear and disappear and tumble fantastically, scarecrows do a fandango with their shadows on empty hillsides, white horses and black tear across high heaven, and skeletons walk. The animation is to the music of Moussorgsky. All film societies should see this film. It is as astonishing and as brilliant a short as they are likely to find."

The film was critically acclaimed, but as there was no way to earn a living from film society showings, Alexeieff turned to advertising films, which were shown in most movie theaters throughout Europe. Over a period of two decades, he made several dozen commercials, from one to three minutes long, animating objects, models, and puppets, among other things. A method for filming illusory solids, which he has called Totalization, is described in the following articles. Teams of two or three collaborators and assistants were often needed on these films, including most frequently Alexandra Grinevsky, Etienne Raik, and Georges Violet, in addition to Claire Parker. Music was a special element in Alexeieff's advertising films, sometimes taken from classical works of Chopin and Tchaikovsky, sometimes composed by contemporaries like Poulenc, Auric, and Milhaud.

During the war, while they were living in the United States, Alexeieff and Claire Parker made the two-minute pinboard animation film, *En Passant*, set to a French-Canadian folk song, for the National Film Board of Canada. Twenty years later, again on the pinboard, they made *The Nose*, based on Gogol's short story, which Alexeieff had illustrated in book form many years before. *Pictures at an Exhibition* (1972), set to Moussorgsky's music once again, used two pinboards, one of which revolved before a larger stationary one.

While working on *The Nose*, which like the other long films took nearly two years to complete, Alexeieff was asked by Orson Welles to make a number of pinboard stills for the prologue and epilogue of *The Trial*. He supplied the filmed still pictures; technical handling of the optical dissolves was left to Welles's staff.

Meanwhile Alexeieff has continued illustrating books, most often by Russian authors, including Dostoyevsky's *The Gambler* and *Notes from the Underground* and Pasternak's *Doctor Zhivago*, all published in the United States with serial illustrations made on the pinboard. Here, as in his films, one sees images from Alexeieff's recollections of Russia—street lamps guarding empty streets; houses with checkerboard window panes; snowflakes poised in mid-air; moons in all phases casting their beams below; mysterious men in black, and nameless creatures watching. In his films, many of these same images come to life in realistic and fantastic motion. "The future belongs to animation," Alexeieff has said. "The golden age of animation is soon to come."

Claire Parker has collaborated with Alexeieff on all his films and technical experiments and inventions. They have been married since 1941. She was born in Boston, attended the Winsor School and Bryn Mawr College, and studied drawing at the Massachusetts Institute of Technology and in Europe. In Paris she was drawn to Alexeieff's illustrations of *The Brothers Karamazov*, in which she found "a quality I had never seen before," she has said, "like paintings in black-and-white." She asked him to give her lessons in engraving, and with him began seeking ways to make engravings move. Together they built the first pinboard, of which several subsequent

From *The Nose* (1963) by Alexeieff and Parker, a film based on a story by Nicholas Gogol.

From *The Trial* (1963) by Orson Welles, pinboard illustration by Alexeieff and Parker used in the film's Prologue.

Claire Parker, shown moving pins with a roller on the negative side of the pinboard.

versions have been made. The pinboard is at times referred to as the pin screen, pinscreen, and/or pin board—its official name in French being "l'écran d'épingles."

In their work at the pinboard, Claire Parker operates the negative side of the image, and attends to all the camera work, both still and motion picture. She also works closely on the sound track analysis and synchronization. She directed one color animation advertising film during Alexeieff's absence from the studio. In 1936 she shot a color animation film on the Rubens exhibition in Paris that year. Except for a few years in New York during World War II, they have lived continuously in Paris, Alexeieff as a naturalized French citizen, and Claire Parker as an American. Both have been active in France on behalf of the animation film, and the general short film as well, particularly at the festivals of Tours and Annecy.

A sample of their work is seen in a one-reel film which shows how the illustrations were made for *Doctor Zhivago*, a unique collaboration in which the mind and eyes and hands of Claire Parker seem to respond in an instant to the mind and eyes and hands of Alexeieff. Without such empathy, it is unlikely that films as complex as theirs could ever have been made. The images are his, one is certain, but the films are of a necessity a joint effort. Alexeieff acknowledges this by giving equal credit to her on all three of their "long" films, each of which has taken close to two years of eight-hour days, sometimes seven days a week, to complete.

He acknowledged it further, on completing *Pictures at an Exhibition* at the age of 72 (Claire Parker is some years younger) when he said, jokingly: "I would be happy to go on and make films for the rest of Moussorgsky's music" (only one-third of the pieces are used in the film), "I would be happy to do it, but I don't think Claire has the strength."

REFLECTIONS ON MOTION PICTURE ANIMATION
by Alexander Alexeieff

I began to draw in 1905 at the age of four, in a villa where my parents lived on the shore of the Bosphorus near Istamboul. I began by drawing boats, because at each instant there were boats *passing* across the panorama which, like a Chinese scroll, unrolled itself before my eyes from the Black Sea to the Sea of Marmara against the background of the Anatolian shore. After the boats, I drew panoramas of the Bosphorus with crenelated fortresses (Rumeli-Hissar), with warriors *running* to the assault. What interested me was to render the *movement* of these summary figures drawn with a few lines. Later, toward the age of 7, I succeeded in drawing galloping horses in profile. It was at this time that I encountered the little tin

soldiers manufactured in Nürenberg. The elegance of their design and their *movement* which the German draftsmen succeeded so well in rendering constituted for me a marvelous drawing school. Later, when about 10 years old, I saw my oldest brother make a praxinoscope, the function of which was to give the illusion of movement; I imitated this by drawing in a little note-book a moving object phase by phase: there was a windmill with arms which turned, an aeroplane which took off, turned around, and landed. They were my first films.

At the age of 20 I helped destiny to bring me to Paris where I became the pupil of Serge Sudekin, set-designer and inspirer of the Bat (Chauve-Souris) Theatre. The actors of this theater mimed the movements of mechanical toys, developing the theme of the "Nutcracker" of Dumas who was himself influenced by Andersen, the true inventor of the animation of toys and objects. I painted and afterwards designed stage sets and costumes for 5 years. I then taught myself engraving and became an illustrator of de luxe books, an art which I practiced successfully for a decade. But this was the epoch of art films: Chaplin's earlier films, *Caligari*, *The Blue Angel*, Man Ray's three films, and finally Bartosch's film, *The Idea*, based on a book by Masereel, decided me to try my luck and to enter into contact with a larger audience (there being no more than 15,000 customers of de luxe books in France).

I was afraid of the Eldorado atmosphere which held the motion picture studios prisoner; the theater had already taught me the role played by chance in collective creations, distorting the intentions of the individuals who participate in them. I considered the animated cartoon good for comics, not for the poetic atmosphere which was the life-substance of my engravings. I would have to invent a motion picture technique such that I might, entirely alone, make pictures with half-tones, grays, and indistinct forms. I made this invention and built the first pin screen in association with an American, Miss Claire Parker of Boston, who later became my wife. We illustrated together *Night on Bald Mountain* of Moussorgsky, a theme used again after us by Walt Disney in the United States and Rigal in France. We had a success in the press unequaled for an 8-minute film; the newspapers and revues predicted the most brilliant future for us, but not a single motion picture distribution circuit beyond the motion picture theater Pantheon in Paris and the Academy Theatre in London asked for our film (released in 1934).

We decided to make no more animation films without having distribution assured in advance: this meant limiting ourselves to advertising films, which had in

France a real market but which paid badly. We were the first to make Gasparcolor films in France and obtained immediately a reputation for quality on the market. We established, I may say, a class of films in this domain without precedent and which were paid better and better by a certain number of progressive and powerful advertisers. The second World War interrupted this development; we resumed our small production in Paris in 1951. The only film made by us between 1939 and 1951 was *En Passant* which the Canadian National Film Board asked us to make for them during our stay in the United States, and for which we constructed a second pin screen, the first having remained in Paris. The first was composed of 500,000 pins, the second of 1,000,000 which made it possible to produce effects analogous to the charcoal drawings of Seurat.

From *En Passant* (1943) by Alexeieff and Parker. Illustrating a French Canadian folksong, this film was made for the National Film Board of Canada.

The pin screen, although conceived as a black-and-white technique, can serve theoretically for making color films as well. But for this, the pins must be thrice as fine and thrice as closely spaced as in the prototype we used to make *Night on Bald Mountain.* Such a pin screen being not yet available, all our color advertising films have been made by animating three dimensional objects. [Added in 1975 by Alexeieff and Parker.]

Since 1951 we have been developing the technique of a new kind of animation [Totalization]: instead of recording frame by frame a stationary object, we often record frame by frame moving objects which are connected with compound pendulums. We have built in Paris a robot, driven by a compound pendulum, which draws on one frame of the film while the camera makes one long exposure. After having thus made one frame, we rewind the robot which executes the following frame in a like way, etc. The results thus obtained are new, and very useful in certain particular cases, notably in the case of abstract pictures.

Our yearly production is limited at present to 3 or 4 minutes, and I find it sufficient: to augment the number of workers would tend to diminish the quality of the films: I believe it essential to avoid confusing the methods of mass production with those required to establish prototypes. Our films have an incomparably wider distribution than feature films: they are often seen several times by the same persons; their quality must therefore be more concentrated than that of feature films.

I am not qualified to speak of the direct motion picture. My main interest is for the animated motion picture, which can attain an artistic quality comparable to the masterpieces known in the older arts, like painting, the dance, music, sculpture, and above all poetry. The shortness of animation films appears to me relative. Most of Chopin's Preludes last about a minute; the Seventh lasts 32½ seconds but one remembers it all one's life; the Mona Lisa is a small picture in comparison with the immense canvases produced by the manufactory of Rubens: Rubens is a great painter only in his small canvases, painted personally by himself. And when I am told at the end of a screening which only lasts a minute: "What a shame that it is too short!" I am happy to hear it.

In Russia where I was born, the motion picture was called "Illusion"; we used to say: "tonight we are going to the illusion". I am interested in animation because the movement which we think we are perceiving is illusory: it never happened. I am less interested in the direct motion picture because it reconstitutes movements which once really happened. If words are the raw material of literature, and sounds of music, the raw material of motion picture animation is movement. Plastic form is necessary only because we cannot perceive movement without forms (two or three-dimensional). The "how" of movement is the real aim of animation. The rest, such as beauty of form and colour, is accessory, and even cumbersome.

I believe that all forms: words, sounds, colours, volumes, movements, have a meaning. They do not possess it of themselves; it is men who give them a meaning. Different meanings, in fact, in so far as the interests of human beings differ. Meanings, often erroneous or illusory. Such meanings are the more valued by the mind inasmuch as they are its own creations. For example, take a series of circles, each bigger than the last. They give on the screen the impression of an advancing circle. This impression does not correspond to what really happened, but it is far more impressive than the real advance of a circle because of an unreal rhythm in its growth. There must be a resemblance with, and a difference from, reality in a work of art, which pleases by its ambiguity.

What I also like in the animation film is the power to bring to life the spectator's imagination and senses by that kinship between movement and rhythmic sounds which is at the origin of the dance, and which manifests itself already in our childhood, when at table, we play forbidden games with spoons and forks, games out of which Andersen has made fairy tales.

But what I care for above all in animation is the power to master the tempo of thought and emotions in the audience. It pleases me to construct over a period of four months a synthesis whose presence on the screen will last only one minute, during which the audience cannot withdraw its attention for even a fraction of a second.

I hope that with the progress in motion picture technique, the lovers of moving pictures will be permitted to see them when they wish and *according to their choice*, as one chooses a poem to read or a record to which to listen. If such a day comes, the notion of a film repertory will be definitely established, and with it the new art will be consecrated. It will then be perceived that as in private libraries, the public's preference will go to works of reference and to poetry.

In the meantime, public and private film libraries, and television are preparing, albeit with as yet rudimentary techniques of distribution and transmission, the way to such a future.

(From *Film Culture*, Spring 1964, written in 1956.)

THE SCREEN OF PINS
by Claire Parker

. . . The pinboard is a black and white technique somewhat analogous to the half-tone process: the picture is made up of a very large number of very small black elements on a white ground. The darkness of a tone corresponds to the individual size of each black element on a given portion of the white ground. In the pinboard, the above principle is realized as follows:

The white ground is constituted by a white plate standing upright in a frame, and lighted at an angle to its front surface by a single spotlight. There is an identical lighting on the back surface. This plate is perforated throughout, perpendicularly to its surfaces, by tiny holes in which as many pins slide easily. The pins are somewhat longer than the thickness of the plate, so that when pushed flush with the front surface they protrude at the back, and vice versa. In the former case, the front surface appears as white. If one of the pins is now pushed forward, its shadow appears on the white surface. The further forward the pin is pushed, the longer its shadow becomes. If now a group of pins is pushed forward to the maximum, the shadow of each pin meets that of its neighbor, and the portion of the white surface behind this group of pins will receive no light and appear as black. When this group of pins is pushed, say, half way back again, the shadows will be half as long, tiny white spaces will appear between them, and the effect will be a medium tone of gray.

As there are a million pins in our present pinboard, we never consider the pins individually, but always in groups, like paint on a brush. Instead of brushes we use different sized rollers: for instance, bed casters, ball-bearings, etc., to push the pins toward either surface, thus obtaining the shades or lines of gray, black, or white which we need to compose the picture. As our experience has grown, we have textured surfaces that are very expedient in implanting textures of our choice on the picture.

All that remains as an "original" of a picture made on the pinboard is the photographic negative taken of it before a new picture is drawn.

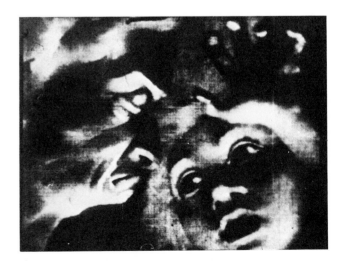

From *Night on Bald Mountain* (1933) by Alexeieff and Parker.

In the motion-picture animation technique, the entire film takes place, frame by frame, on the single pinboard. Instead of making series of separate drawings which are afterwards photographed one after the other, we make the first drawing on the pinboard, photograph it, then modify this first drawing into the second phase of the movement, photograph the second phase, etc. This system, coupled with the ease in shading and modeling which the pinboard provides, makes it possible to work the entire film in chiaroscuro, and thus to escape from the comic or satirical into the poetic and dramatic.

(From *Bryn Mawr Alumnae Bulletin*, Winter 1961.)

ILLUSORY SOLIDS IN THE MOTION PICTURE SYNTHESIS

by Alexander Alexeieff

An Illusory Solid is the course run during a given length of time by a real solid, called a generator or tracer. 1) The existence of Illusory Solids has been known since earliest times through the phenomenon of falling stars. 2) Their existence may also be perceived by touch, as a physical shock. 3) As a general rule, Illusory Solids are perceived by the naked eye when a luminous tracer moves at sufficient speed so that its visible course is accomplished in less than 1/10th of a second (conventionally considered as the duration of the persistent image). 4) But the same Illusory Solid may be examined at leisure with the help of a long photographic exposure of the same, but slower, course of the same, but less luminous, tracer. 5) These photographic records of Illusory Solids are called Totalizations. They are still pictures. 6) The first Totalizations were photographs of the stars. 7) Just as real solids can be endowed with movement by means of motion picture synthesis, so Illusory Solids can be animated. 8) The animation negative of an Illusory Solid will be the result of frame-by-frame shots of a moving tracer; contrary to all the other animation practices, each negative frame is exposed DURING THE MOVEMENT OF THE MODEL. 9) From one frame to the next the tracer's movement is reenacted on a slightly modified course. When the film is projected, this variation in course will be expressed as the movement of the Illusory Solid.

The installation of equipment in an animated Totalization workshop consists of three elements. 1) A frame-by-frame camera whose rotating shutter has been replaced by a still camera shutter of the Compur type, set at B (bulb). The camera brings each frame of the negative to a halt, ready for exposure. The exposure is made by the Compur, operated from a distance by a timer. 2) A tracer: a shining point (or other brightly lit object) in front of a

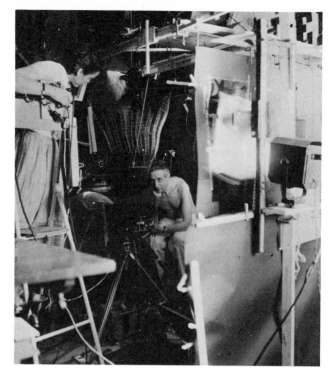

Alexeieff and Parker shooting a sequence in Totalized Animation, in 1960. The striated object between them is an illusory solid which the camera records from above on a single frame made during a long exposure. (Photo by Roger Parry.)

What the camera records in the Totalization technique. The finished film became the logo for Cocinor, a French motion picture company.

black background, capable of executing precise movements which have been determined in advance. These may be varied at will. 3) Electro-magnetic machinery, grouped off-stage, which sets the tracer in motion and directs the timer to open and shut the Compur at precise moments of the tracer's course.

The luminous point can be made easily with a chromium plated ball whose course is in the field of a spotlight. The image of this point, refracted by the lens, will form in the interior of the "dark chamber" a fine ray of light which will repeat the ball's movements, inverting their trace on the negative emulsion. A shining ball will trace a clean line comparable to that of a drawing pen. Any form can be used to trace an Illusory Solid, if it be sufficiently bright or brightly lighted. But the form of the tracer will always be as if "melted" into the Totalized Solid. Our first "totalized" film was 30 meters (1560 images) long. The sum, however, of the photographic exposures, as described above, was 46,800 seconds-780 minutes-13 hours, because each exposure lasted 30 seconds.

From the above paragraph we may conclude that the tracer's movements, which lasted for 13 hours, have become somehow compressed, or condensed, or reduced, into only one minute of projection. Were this a cinematographic acceleration it would be one of 780 times, a very considerable speed-up. (By "cinematographic acceleration" I mean that which occurs, for instance, in the film *Go Slow on the Brighton Line* which records the train trip from London to Brighton in three minutes, that is, the opposite of "slow-motion" author's footnote). But our one-minute film does not resemble a speed-up. What, then, has happened? Something resembling a "solidification," a "congealing" of the tracer's movement—a sort of METAMORPHOSIS OF A MOVEMENT INTO AN OBJECT (in which we recognize quite a few characteristics of a solid, if we except opacity and weight), a transformation of BECOMING (*devenir*) into BECOME (*devenu*). This applies to each frame of the film—to each one of the 1560 Totalizations of which the film is composed.

Taken as a whole, this one-minute film clearly has to do with the animation of an object—of this strange Illusory Solid which is not a normal object, but an object-in-movement. We may say it is a mobile whose speed has been accelerated to INFINITE, thus becoming so great that the duration of the movement has been reduced to NO TIME. The tracing of each totalized image has been reduced from 30 seconds to an instant without duration, since the tracer's start and entire course up to its very end are simultaneously present to the eye in each image of the film. In each of these images the tracer's movement has

become so frozen that it can be looked at for an indefinite length of time—we might say, for all eternity. . .

If I could assert, a moment ago, that the film "clearly" has to do with the animation of an "object", the character of this object is so equivocal that one may with equal force assert that it has to do with the ANIMATION OF A MOVEMENT (as a consequence of sentence 8 above).

There are three ways of observing objects in motion with the naked eye. 1) Stars and moon: From an animator's point of view, the moon might be considered as a tracer, but he would look in vain for its Illusory Solid. Its apparent movement is so slow that it seems immobile. We can do no more than verify its displacement by noting from time to time its position with regard to some fixed point of reference—as a navigator ascertains the drift of his vessel with respect to a lighthouse marked on his chart. Thus, by a mental operation, we conclude that the moon is in continuous motion. 2) Seagull: It flies slowly enough for the eye to be able to appreciate its form and its movement. Here the tracer and its movement are visible—but not its Illusory Solid. 3) Airplane Propeller: As long as it is immobile, one can perceive the number and form of its blades. When it begins to turn, the eye can still follow the blades, but soon begins to lag behind the propeller, stops, and from this instant on, the PROPELLER DISAPPEARS, leaving in its place a translucid and shining disc which is the Illusory Solid generated by its tracer, the propeller.

In the three cases, it is possible to produce Totalizations. But the tracers will not be present in them. Law: ANY SUFFICIENTLY LUMINOUS MOBILE FORM CAN BE TOTALIZED. BUT THE TRACER AND THE ILLUSORY SOLID CAN NEVER BE PRESENT SIMULTANEOUSLY.

(From unpublished material supplied by the author for this volume.)

ALEXEIEFF'S ADVERTISING FILMS
by Derrick Knight

. . . In the late '40s, together with his constant collaborator Claire Parker, he got interested in the visual patterns formed by the slowing down of the weight of a pendulum swinging at different speeds in different planes. Any child knows that by putting a pulse into a slack but elastic cord, you can get different patterns of beat as it slows. Alexeieff set out to explore this kind of phenomenon with a light source, and with the object of being able to control and calculate exactly the swinging pendulum so that repetition could be achieved. Here his problems began. He had first to acquire a knowledge of advanced mathematics and then build a machine that would give the exact result regardless of room temperature and fluctuations in electric current. Only when this had been converted into an apparently effortless mastery of motion was he able to begin to try and make a film.

His first effort, *Fumées* (*Smoke*) took a year and lasted less than a minute. The smoke consisted of hundreds of fine, densely packed, oscillating lines involving many exposures on each frame. Since then he has used the technique for several most beautiful advertising films, notably one for Esso called *La Sève de la Terre* or *The Earth's Sap*. This film combines several forms of complicated object animation as well. The earth lies bare, and from it springs the oil derrick with branches like a tree. From the branches hang fruit, drops of oil. The fruits fall and burst, and more fruit appears and falls. Suddenly one is caught in coloured space and caressed by rings of moving light. The rings of light oscillate and become *Esso*. The earth's sap has been caught and tamed.

From *La Seve de la Terre* (1955) by Alexeieff and Parker, a commercial made for Esso-France.

How do you set about animating a falling drop of fluid? The high speed camera gives you no control. You can't stop the drop in mid-flight, and Alexeieff wanted to do just that. He had a drop photographed by a high speed camera, and gave the resulting 30 or so exposures to an expert glass blower who reproduced each phase of the falling blob accurately in blown glass. Then it is possible to suspend the blobs from the oil derrick tree and have them fall and burst. The next problem is the growth of the oil derrick tree. Since it must be strong and look right, it is not the sort of object which can be constructed before the camera without risk or error. Error has to be avoided like the plague when you have your one and only negative in the camera for weeks or even months at a time. In the case of the tree, it was built and used complete and then cut down gradually before the camera, snip by snip—and reversed in the final film. . . .

In *Pure Beauté*, a publicity film for *Monsavon*, a classical statue of a girl rotates before the camera. At the same time she is caressed by the undulating word *Mon* which spirals slowly over her legs, her bust, her head, until the final plug *Monsavon* is revealed. The result is breathtaking. In *Masques*, a publicity film for a cigarette company, two masks, male and female, engage in a juggling act with cigarettes. It is very witty and a miracle of animation.

There is no question of mass production with Alexeieff and his collaborators. He has found a way of combining experiment with sponsorship and the collaboration means the sponsor gets a little work of art in the artist's own sweet time. The results justify the time and the hours of hard sweat and labor. . . . I have not mentioned the theoretical aspects of Alexeieff's work, though he has, of course, his vision and his rationalization which combine concepts of cybernetics and *total* cinema. For us the eye and the ear are sufficient to enjoy the little gems that come very occasionally from his Paris studios.

(From *Film 22*, published by the British Federation of Film Societies, 1959.)

NOTES ON "PICTURES AT AN EXHIBITION"

by Alexander Alexeieff

The film lasts 11 minutes; it is in three parts. The first and the last parts evolve very fast—in parallel cutting of a special kind—by wipes let us say.

There are two pinboards: the small one in front, the big one behind the small. The small one revolves on a central vertical axis. When its face is turned towards the camera, it hides the big one. At this moment we change the image on the hidden big pinboard. When the small pinboard turns its profile toward us, the image on the big one is fully visible and the image on the small one disappears. It is in this position that we change the image on the small pinboard—and so on.

What I call "image" can be a phase of the action or a new scene. It is an attempt toward a new grammatical link in animation. The resulting passages appear very rapid, and at the first viewing one misses a lot of things, but I made this film with an eye on mini-cassettes.

Doesn't one need to re-read a poem, or rehear a piece of music many times to appreciate them? It is unreasonable of me to try to make poetry for the movies, but it would be even more unreasonable of me to act as if I were different from what I am. My hope is that the film will become up to date 50 years from now.

The second part of *Pictures at an Exhibition* is quite different. It is a ball. There are a great many female dancers (who are white). There are few male dancers (and a few monsters), who are black. Here is the way we made them: 1) First I drew sequences of different dancers in the phases of their dance movement (about 32 phases for each). 2) We filmed each series of 32 frames, white on a black ground, on the small pinboard, while turning it, phase by phase. The result is a loop where the dancer (they waltz) seems to turn like a flat marionette— appearing out of nowhere, then disappearing again, like sail boats when they come about. If you want, this idea is analogous to that of Shakespeare's character called Shadow. Falstaff says he is an excellent soldier for he presents no more surface to enemy fire than the edge of a pen knife. 3) Next we took *one loop* of the ballerina (whom we called "little ballerina"). In front of the camera we stretched a sheet of white paper for a transparent projection screen. Behind this screen, a frame-by-frame projector. In the projection the loop (positive: white on black ground) of the "little ballerina." We panned the projector sidewise until the "little ballerina" was at the right hand edge of the screen. (Our intention was to make a row of 10 ballerinas). We filmed the 32 phases of the "little ballerina" at this precise spot. Then Claire wound the film back to the first frame, and I wound the loop to the first

frame. Then I panned the projector somewhat to the left, and we filmed the same loop, making a second "little ballerina" next to the first. To make the other 8 dancers we proceeded in the same way. We called the new loop thus made a "model," developed and made a print of it. This new "model" loop already had a row of 10 dancers of the same size. 4) So for the different sequences in the ball we could project 10 ballerinas at once, using this "model." But we superimposed the 32 phases of one row on another row, with the camera at different distances,

From *Picture at an Exhibition* (1972) by Alexeieff and Parker.

From the ball sequence of *Pictures at an Exhibition*.

making *two rows* of 10 ballerinas (one row bigger than the other, as if it were closer). Then a 3rd row in the same way, so that our ballet now boasted 30 dancers (which is a lot). 5) On the background of our ballet chorus we superimposed our star-ballerinas, individually. The result—quite lovely—resembles a flight of butterflies. 6) On the background of white ballerinas we superimposed black male dancers and black monsters. Unfortunately, our installation, rather primitive, obliged us to have this last superimposition made in the lab, where the technician

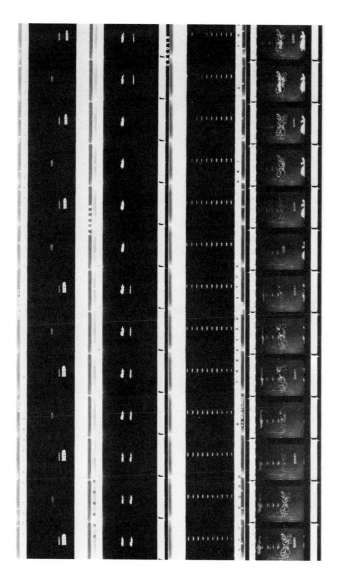

balanced the exposures in happy-go-lucky fashion. (I almost thought he did it on purpose.)

It remains for me to say about this ball the most important things: I have explained how we were able, when superimposing the star-ballerinas or the rows of the ballet chorus, to adjust the distances between camera and projection screen so as to obtain bigger and smaller dancers. But, besides this, we could zoom with the camera and pan with the projector so that our imaginary ballerinas and male dancers moved about in an imaginary ballroom. To sum it up, it became a sort of choreography which we were obliged to understand and direct, to avoid big empty spaces or, on the contrary, chaotic crowds. Given that in the final shooting we were making a dozen superimpositions (without being able to see what was already on the negative in the camera) it all had to be done by calculation. Probably a computer could have helped us, but we had none, and I went almost crazy during the last shooting. Only Claire, who never makes a mistake in calculating, pulled us through. But I didn't always know how to explain to her what my plans consisted of.

During the 6 months of shooting the ball, we would take a half-hour rest after lunch, during which Claire would read aloud—in Russian—Pushkin's poems. I noticed then, with surprise, that the internal and external cutting of our film closely resembled the composition of the poems. (I am thinking particularly of the Tale of King Saltan). But if I give you an example from the English ballads, you will surely understand me (one doesn't even have to understand old English—it is enough to see the typography):

"And twal' and twal' wi' beer and wine,
And twal' and twal' wi' muskadine,
And twal' and twal' wi' bouted flour,
And twal' and twal' wi' paramour."

In other words, I perceived that the use of different dancers at certain moments, of identical dancers at other moments, or the repetition of entire groups of dancers,—was analogous to the use of *words* or entire *phrases*, recurring within a stanza,—or even the repetition of a whole stanza within a poem. Our dancers movements were calculated to fit the measures of the music as the arrangement of a poet's words to suit the meter he has chosen...

(From *ASIFA Information Bulletin*, No. 1, 1972.)

Film loops made for *Pictures at an Exhibition.*

4/Pioneers of Abstract Animation in America

Cecile Starr

INTRODUCTION

New York and California were the two centers around which abstract animation developed in the United States. Mary Ellen Bute seems to have taken the lead on the East Coast, and she was followed by other painters who like herself worked in virtual isolation—Douglass Crockwell, Dwinell Grant, and Francis Lee. Two factors helped create a movement, or the nucleus of a movement, in the years following World War II. One was the growing 16mm market in colleges, museums, and film societies; the other was the availability of grants and subsidies for experimental filmmaking.

In the 1940s, grants for abstract films were given to Oskar Fischinger, Norman McLaren, John and James Whitney [see Chapters 7 and 8] and Dwinell Grant by the Solomon Guggenheim Foundation, under the directorship of the colorful Baroness Hilla Rebay (who was also responsible for collecting the hundreds of paintings by Kandinsky, Klee, and other abstractionists who were little prized at the time). Fellowships in filmmaking were given by the John Simon Guggenheim Memorial Foundation to Francis Lee and to the Whitneys in those same years, as part of a general fellowship program for scholars, scientists, and artists. The monies allotted were fairly small, but the recognition marked a new era for experimental animation. Marie Menken started on her film career when Francis Lee gave her his camera (in the form of a pawn ticket) at the time he left New York to go into the Army. She later filmed most of the works of her husband, Willard Maas, and made a number of her own short films, several of which were animated.

Menken's *Dwightiana* (1959) shows small colored jewel-like objects moving over a painting by Dwight Ripley, in a style considerably reminiscent of Francis Lee's *Le Bijou* (1946).

Sixteen-millimeter distribution brought another kind of recognition, equally important. While it is true that a number of Mary Ellen Bute's films were shown at the palatial Radio City Music Hall in New York City and small art theaters around the country, this was the exception rather than the rule, as it still is today. Most American pioneers in abstract animation had their films shown at special programs in The Museum of Modern Art or at the New York City film society called Cinema 16. Founded by Amos Vogel, the society held monthly programs of experimental and documentary films for nearly 16 years; its success stimulated smaller and shorter-lived film societies in other locations, particularly college towns. On the West Coast a series of programs entitled Art in Cinema was presented at the San Francisco Museum of Art. Organized by Richard Foster and Frank Stauffacher, the influence of the programs was spread primarily through published program notes, under the title *Art in Cinema*. This seems to have been the first book in the United States to deal with the broad range of experimental film.

Perry Miller's Film Advisory Center based in New York City sponsored several Art Film Festivals in the early 1950s, presenting experimental animation by Bute, Crockwell, and Lee, along with films about artists and art. She also recommended films throughout the Center's programming service, calling film "The Artist's

New Canvas." Under this heading she included two animation films of the time that had achieved widespread popularity because of their colorful and imaginative design and their one-world ideology: UPA's *Brotherhood of Man* and Philip Stapp's *Boundary Lines*. With such films, the 16mm market in schools, colleges, public libraries, and museums made huge strides.

The abstract films of Robert Bruce Rogers, who worked first in New York and later on the West Coast, seem no longer to exist, although it is fitting to mention him here as one of the American pioneers. Rogers has described his silent film *Toccata Manhatta* (1949) as "handworking directly on 16mm film by means of inks, dyes, dry point and solvent etching," on lengths of previously exposed color emulsion film as well as on nonphotographed film. His *Motion Painting No. 3—Rhapsody* (1951), based on Liszt's Hungarian Rhapsody No. 6, is described by Rogers as a motion composition in space-form-color-sound, using a "three-dimensional space contrivance of my own, the field of operations being a foreshortened replica of the ultimate projection beam—a pyramided field, roughly 23 inches by 32 inches at the base of background limit, 38 inches from camera aperature as apex." In his selection of the Liszt music and the words "motion painting," Rogers seems to have fallen under the influence of Oskar Fischinger (see Chapter 2).

Fischinger and John and James Whitney (see Chapter 8)—together with Harry Smith (see Chapter 6) who had begun making his own drawn-on-film abstractions between 1939 and 1947—were the major West Coast animators around whom a new generation of experimental animators was developing. Prominent among them were Hy Hirsh and Jordan Belson. Hirsh, who in the late 1930s and early 1940s had been cameraman on a number of experimental films, later made several abstract films using superimposed oscilloscope patterns printed through colored filters. *Come Closer*, made in 1953 for the San Francisco Museum of Art's continuing Art in Cinema festivals, seems to be the first abstract film in 3-D. Even without the two projectors and colored glasses, many spatial effects can easily be sensed. Hirsh died in an automobile accident in Europe in the early 1960s.

Jordan Belson, who directed the visual elements of the Vortex Concerts at the planetarium in San Francisco (1957–59), using as many as seventy projectors to create images that covered the dome or floated somewhere in space, worked earlier in stop-motion animation and fast-editing techniques. His recent films use continual-action photography of luminous abstract shapes and movements created by a form of light manipulation. He photographs the visual and atmospheric ef-

fects created by the light source itself. These films have been widely screened here and abroad.

John and James Whitney span over three decades of important experimental animation, as theorists, technicians, and spokesmen for the field. Aspects of their work, as well as biographical material, are included in the chapters on Sound (Chapter 7) and The New Technology (Chapter 8).

Marie Menken, shown here around 1960.

Mary Ellen Bute

Mary Ellen Bute, around 1954. (Photo by Ted Nemeth.)

Mary Ellen Bute made her first abstract film in the mid-1930s: *Rhythm in Light*, set to Grieg's Anitra's Dance; *Synchromy No. 2*, to Wagner's Evening Star, and *Parabola*, to Milhaud's La Creation du Monde—all in black-and-white. She began using color in the early 1940s; *Escape* was set to Bach's Toccata and Fugue in D Minor, *Tarantella* to piano music composed by Edwin Gershefsky, and *Spook Sport* to Saint-Saens' Danse Macabre (the actual animation work done by Norman McLaren, in his lean years in New York City between England and the National Film Board of Canada [see Chapter 5]).

Mary Ellen Bute, who has been aptly described as a woman of "tremendous enthusiasm and energy," was raised in Texas, where she studied painting, admired Rosa Bonheur, and sent her own sketches and paintings of horses and cattle to competitions in local county fairs. She became interested in the visual study of motion and assisted Thomas Wilfred, who perfected the Clavilux light organ which was used to accompany religious

meditation at St. Mark's-in-the-Bouwerie. Joining the studio of electronics pioneer Leon Theremin, she collaborated with him on his thesis, "The Perimeters of Light and Sound and Their Possible Synchronization," and delivered the paper which he demonstrated electronically before the New York Musicological Society. For a while, Mary Ellen Bute directed the visual department of the Gerald Warburg Studio, headed by musicologist-mathematician-painter Joseph Schillinger; film was included in their visual-aural experiments. Before making her own first film, she supplied the abstract drawings for an experimental film entitled *Synchronization* (1933) by Schillinger and filmmaker Lewis Jacobs; the film, never completed, was possibly the first abstract animation project in the United States.

In his article entitled "Avant-Garde Production in America," (included in Roger Manvell's *Experiments in the Film*), Lewis Jacobs described Bute's first six films as "...all composed upon mathematical formulae depicting in ever-changing lights and shadows, growing lines and forms, deepening colors and tones, the tumbling, racing impressions evoked by the musical accompaniment."

Rhythm in Light, Mary Ellen Bute has written, was made with money she borrowed from a bank as a personal loan, with two friends as co-signers. Another friend, Melville F. Webber (who earlier had collaborated with James Sibley Watson on *The Fall of the House of Usher* and *Lot in Sodom*, pioneer American avant-garde films in the expressionist style), helped in the production of *Rhythm in Light*. Theodore Nemeth photographed the film, as he did several later ones, teaching her enough about photography so that she could film the others herself—a great advantage she explains, as it gives the filmmaker the creative independence of the painter. She and Nemeth, who now heads the Ted Nemeth Studios as producer, were subsequently married and have two sons.

In addition to the frame-by-frame drawings in *Rhythm in Light*, moving objects were photographed in various speeds and lights—ping-pong balls, cellophane, Fourth of July sparklers, barber poles. "It wasn't until I started

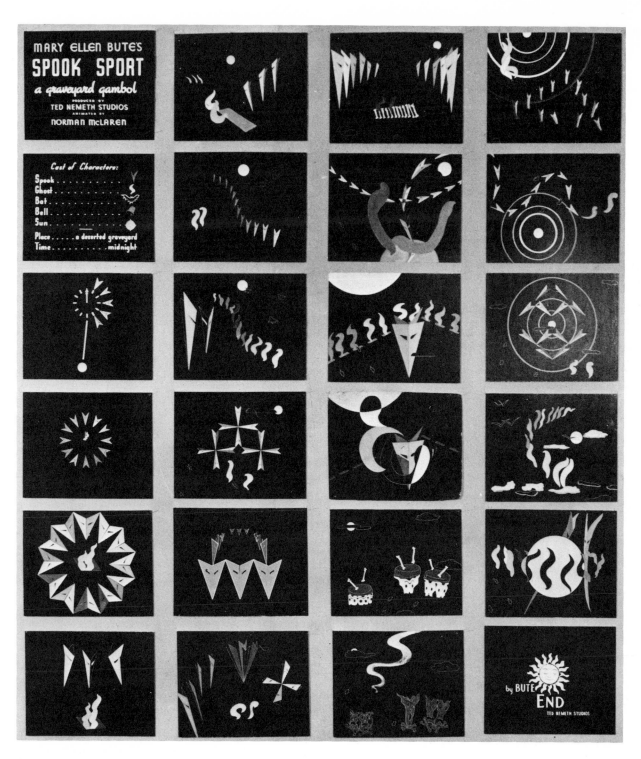

A visual synopsis of the film *Spook Sport* (1939) by Mary Ellen Bute, animated by Norman McLaren.

playing with the camera and using it," Mary Ellen Bute has stated, "that I realized how much you could do with it. Through the wonderful multiple-exposure things you can get very much the effect that you get in thinking—several different levels of activity."

The sketches for *Escape*, according to Mary Ellen Bute, "poured onto paper one evening without much conscious effort or any previous determination to do it." In it, abstraction takes on some dramatic elements as a triangle struggles to escape from behind a gird of horizontal and vertical lines. Bach's Toccata and Fugue in D Minor was added after the film's completion, with visual adjustments being made to fit the music's rhythmic pattern. *Polka Graph* (1952) began as an actual chart of Shostakovich's Polka from The Age of Gold. Some of the graphic patterns pleased her so much that Mary Ellen Bute decided to use them as they were.

Since 1957 she has worked in live-action film, first as producer of a short live-action film called *The Boy Who Saw Through* (which George Stoney directed), and subsequently as director of a feature-length version of James Joyce's *Finnegan's Wake*. She plans to film Thornton Wilder's *The Skin of Our Teeth*. As head of the company called Expanding Cinema, which she organized in the mid-1930s, Mary Ellen Bute says that she finds every aspect of creative and experimental work and research in motion pictures irresistible. Early in 1976, she was awarded an American Film Institute grant to produce a short film on Walt Whitman.

From *Mood Contrasts* (1958) by Mary Ellen Bute, showing elements of the animated background. (Photo by Ted Nemeth Studios).

ABSTRONICS
by Mary Ellen Bute

"Abstronics" is what Lewis Carroll would have called a portmanteau word. It is composed of the first one and a half syllables of "abstractions" and the last one and a half syllables of "electronics." The letter "r," fortuitously, is the hinge of the two parts.

This word, "abstronics," was suggested to me by Albert Tomkins and aptly connotes this important fact: today it is possible for invisible events in the sub-atomic world to be made to have esthetic manifestations which an artist can control, and, via motion pictures, organize into an interesting and meaningful visual experience. . . .

For years I have tried to find a method for controlling a source of light to produce images in rhythm. I wanted to manipulate light to produce visual compositions in time continuity much as a musician manipulates sound to produce music.

It all started while I was a pupil of the remarkable painter and teacher in Houston, Emma Richardson Cherry. Mrs. Cherry then arranged for me to study at the Pennsylvania Academy of Fine Arts under Henry McCarter. At that time everyone was concerned with Cubism, Impressionism and other styles that derive from the desire to obtain the illusion of movement on canvas.

It was particularly while I listened to music that I felt an overwhelming urge to translate my reactions and ideas into a visual form that would have the ordered sequence of music. I worked towards simulating this continuity in my paintings. Painting was not flexible enough and too confined within its frame.

After leaving the Pennsylvania Academy I explored the possibilities of color organs. Most of these used optical devices for the projection of color and images but the end results were disappointing—amorphous shapes far from the creative expression I was seeking.

At about this time Leon Theremin was demonstrating the musical instrument that bears his name and I discussed with him the idea of developing a device for the free control of light and form in movement, synchronized with sound.

I began to work with him and a year later, on January 31, 1932, we gave our first demonstration of "The Perimeters of Light and Sound and Their Possible Synchronization." This was an early use of electronics for drawing. Well begun, this work was short lived because of extreme lack of funds. Theremin's precipitous departure from this country on a Soviet ship killed all hope of resuming this work with him.

At the same time I had been working with Joseph

Schillinger using his theory of mathematical composition as applied to the kinetic arts. I learned to compose paintings using form, line and color, as counterparts to compositions in sound, but I felt keenly the limitations inherent in the plastic and graphic mediums and determined to find a medium in which movement would be the primary design factor. Motion picture sound film seemed to be the answer and I began to make films, most of them abstract in content.

Of the ten films I made, two were not abstract: one, *Escape*, was based on a simple plot set against a musical background, and employed geometric figures for the action; the other was about the parabolic curve. The abstract films were made by the animation technique, that is, by use of countless drawings on paper. In this "cartoon" technique, the spontaneity of the artist's concept and design becomes extremely attenuated.

By good chance, Dr. Ralph Potter, of the Bell Telephone Laboratories, is interested in abstract films and recently asked to see my work. Here again was an opportunity to enlist a scientist in finding means by which to employ a controlled source of light as a drawing instrument. I told him that I had long thought that the oscilloscope (used for testing radio, TV and radar equipment) offered a solution. Dr. Potter said he had thought of it too. He designed an electronic circuit for such an application of the oscilloscope. The equipment based on his design was then engineered and constructed.

By turning knobs and switches on a control board I can "draw" with a beam of light with as much freedom as with a brush. As the figures and forms are produced by light on the oscilloscope screen, they are photographed on motion picture film. By careful conscious repetition and experiment, I have accumulated a "repertoire" of forms. The creative possibilities are limitless. By changing and controlling the electrical inputs in the 'scope an infinite variety of forms can be made to move in predetermined time rhythms, and be combined or altered *at will*.

Beautiful Lissajous curves, (curves resulting from the combination of two harmonic motions, named for French scientist Jules A. Lissajous, 1822–80) e.g., can be put through a choreography that inspires—and startles— the imagination. The resulting beauty and *movement* contains intimations of occurrences in the sub-atomic world that hitherto have been accessible to the human mind merely as mathematical possibilities. I venture to predict that the forms and compositions artists can create on the oscilloscope, and organize and preserve on motion picture film, will not only give esthetic pleasure to all kinds of men and women in all climes and times but will help theoretical physicists and mathematicians to uncover more secrets of the inanimate world.

The figures and forms on the oscilloscope can be made to move on the horizontal and vertical planes, toward or away from the spectator; their shapes can be varied as much and as often as one pleases; the tempo of their movements can be changed at will (the physics of these tempos is a study in itself); luminescence and shadow can be deployed; and the illusion of three dimensional space can be aroused.

And all this can be synchronized with music.

The two abstronic films I have made are based on the music of Hoe Down by Aaron Copeland and Ranch House Party by Don Gillis. Because this music is simple rhythmically, clear and sharp, I thought it suitable for my first experiment in this new art medium. I could not, *as yet*, have dealt with the problems posed by, say, Bach's Sheep May Safely Graze, even though I based one of my abstract films on a recording of it Leopold Stokowski made for me of his own arrangement. Its music is too intricate for a first exploratory venture into an electronic visual interpretation.

I have put my first two abstronic films together into one and called it *Abstronic*. It is a Ted Nemeth Studios production.

The figures and forms in *Abstronic* have been colored by hand. But I have been promised three-color electronic tubes. If these prove successful, the last animation technique I still employ can be eliminated.

(From *Films in Review*, June–July 1954.)

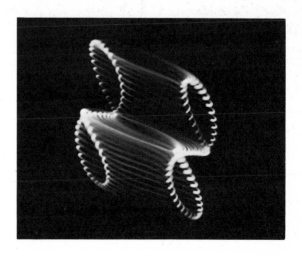

From *Abstronic* (1954) by Mary Ellen Bute, set to the music of Aaron Copeland's Hoe Down. (Photo by Ted Nemeth Studios).

Douglass Crockwell

Douglass Crockwell, around 1948, shown painting at his animation stand.

Douglass Crockwell was born in Ohio in 1904, attended art schools in St. Louis and Chicago, and became a free-lance illustrator-painter in 1931. The following year he moved to Glens Falls, New York, where he lived until his death in 1968.

Crockwell was famous as the creator of covers for the *Saturday Evening Post* and other popular magazines, as well as many advertisements. He painted an estimated 480 or more full-page color illustrations, of which some three billion prints are said to have been made.

In connection with the showing of his film *Glens Falls Sequence* at the Art in Cinema series in San Francisco, 1947, Crockwell wrote: "About eight years ago I set up an animation easel with the camera mounted overhead and the work area arranged much as a draftsman's desk, except that the working area consisted of several movable layers of glass slightly separated. The basic idea was to paint continuing pictures on these various layers with plastic paint, adding at times and removing at times, and to a certain extent these early attempts were successful. This basic process was changed from time to time with varying results and I have still made no attempt yet to stabilize the method. Somewhat as a consequence of this has been the fragmentary character of the work produced."

Crockwell's first films, entitled *Fantasmagoria I*, *II* and *III*, are generally said to have been made in 1938, 1939, and 1940, respectively. In 1944 Crockwell patented an animation system for making abstractions as illustrations to music, and tried the next year to interest Disney and the television networks, with virtually no response—that is to say, here and there a polite letter saying that his proposal would be looked into by someone else at some future time.

For many years Crockwell had collected and restored old hand-cranked Mutoscopes, along with their circular card-frames which turned in rapid succession for peephole viewing. Crockwell also created his own reels for the Mutoscope, including an abstraction of "floating yellows and blues, making patterns in space and time," as one writer described it. Other reels were made from sections of his *Glens Falls Sequence*, which in turn had been a compilation of some of his earlier motion-painting films.

The Long Bodies (1946–7) included a number of earlier films using the sliced-wax technique, described in the following article, which is strikingly similar to the one Fischinger had invented in the early 1920s (see Chapter 2). Crockwell's films, Mutoscope machines, and reels are now owned by the International Museum of Photography (George Eastman House) in Rochester, New York.

ON *Glens Falls Sequence* AND *The Long Bodies*
by Douglass Crockwell

Glens Falls Sequence is a group of short animations bound together chiefly by their position in time. Each has a name of convenience such as: Flower Landscape, Parade, Frustration, etc. These are not mentioned in the film for the sake of greater unity. Generally speaking, the technique has improved the practice. A certain archaic immobilty which characterized some of the earlier films has given way to a greater freedom of action which is pleasing but which may lack some of the former esthetic content. Most of *Glens Falls Sequence* and part of *The Long Bodies* are concerned with pictorial qual-

ities which might more rightly belong to the field of still painting. That it is possible to make an interesting print from almost any single frame gives an indication of this. In these parts the motion and timing have been secondary to the general pictorial scene. Efforts were made later to play down this scenic quality with rather gratifying results. The most simple abstraction was found to take on meaning with motion. Along with others a real question now is how much motion can the observer comprehend and how much immobilty will he accept. The study of these points should prove very interesting.

The Long Bodies is made up of a mixture of old and new material. Practically all of the new film was pro-

From *Glens Falls Sequence* (1946) by Douglass Crockwell, filmed in color.

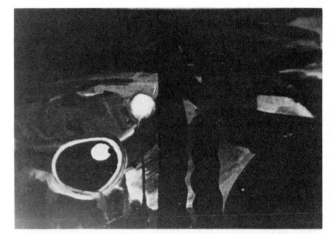

duced by the wax-block method which gives rise to the title. Incidentally, this does not refer to the shapes as they appear on the scene. Rather, the long body of an object is the imaginary four-dimensional path it leaves through space-time during its existence. At any moment of time we see in the real object a three-dimensional cross-section of the long body somewhat analogous to the two-dimensional cross-section obtained when the wax block is sliced. To carry the analogy further, the forms embedded in the block represent the long bodies of the two-dimensional patterns seen on the screen. A rather new and difficult type of visualizing is required to plan the course of a pattern through the block, but as usual the problems seem to fade with experience. In a way, this is a sculptor's art.

(From an unpublished statement to the assistant curator of the Film Department of The Museum of Modern Art, August 26, 1947.)

William Smith, who assisted Crockwell in his filming, added this information in the Spring of 1975: We would squeeze out some non-drying oil paints on a piece of glass. Another piece of glass would be laid on top. By gradually squeezing these two pieces of glass together, we could film the unusual patterns of these colors as they mixed together. Using transparent oils and a light beneath it we could get different effects. Sometimes, with non-drying oil paint, we would remove the bottom layer of glass and finger paint....

The colored wax core was made of a high-melting temperature wax. Around it was poured a low-melting

A BACKGROUND TO FREE ANIMATION
by Douglass Crockwell

In 1934 when I first became interested in the art of comic animation it was already well developed, with a number of studios in operation employing hundreds of artists and craftsmen. Because of the involved technique, thousands of man-hours were required for even a short length of finished film. The inevitable high cost made it necessary that popular themes be executed...

It has always been this high cost that has held back animation experiment. My own first thoughts were of a series of key drawings on a serious theme which could later be activated in a commercial studio. The problem of financing, at first hovering only in the background, soon became dominant. This, along with a growing doubt of the technique, slowed my effort and indicated a need for a new approach....

After a long period of frustration I decided to close

my eyes and do *something*. Any kind of form that moved would be a success. Out went the themes and planned sequences, the complicated symbolism. On my easel I could make a simple form in paint, and I could change its shape gradually by adding to it or taking away from it....

Tentatively I built a simple table with sloping glass surface and camera mounted overhead. Everything was crude. The 16mm camera had no single exposure release. A quick flick of the finger sufficed. Light came from a single bulb. Everything else was comparable. A short sequence was painted, photographed, and developed. The paint itself looked too rough and disturbed the illusion; so afterwards it was applied to the underside of the glass. For a year or so, with this simple animation stand, some quite satisfactory experiments were completed. Subsequent complication of the stand through improved models in a way hampered the actual production of animation footage. The archaic restrictions of the early equipment, I believe, really added to the primitive aesthetic characteristic of my films.

Later footage is more accurately animated, smoother, freer in space, and better planned, but perhaps not more interesting. Facility is a deceptive virtue.

One special animation technique is worth mentioning. A three-dimensional block (3" × 4" × any length) is thoughtfully built up of many pieces of colored wax interlaced and twisted to form a progressive composition. The end of the block is successively sliced off and photographed. The resultant animation is delightfully fluid and unique. If some of the waxes are transparent or translucent, the motion becomes strongly anticipatory and unworldly.

Sometimes the situation is intolerable. The black is resistant, the red too tentative; oppressive indecision muffles the whole. With slight repetitive movements the forms express their frustration. The motion slows. The tension increases. How will this situation develop? What course is inevitable? From moment to moment the artist is confronted with this problem in free animation. And each solution brings its own new set of problems. In a sense this is automatic animation, unplanned, each pause a turning point, each second the father of the next.

While this is but one of the many ways to abstract animation, it is probably one of the most provocative. The dramatic sequence loses its classic form, moving from uncharted point to uncharted point, yet retaining the logic of each minute transition. This is the way I have chosen.

(From *Film Culture*, Spring 1964.)

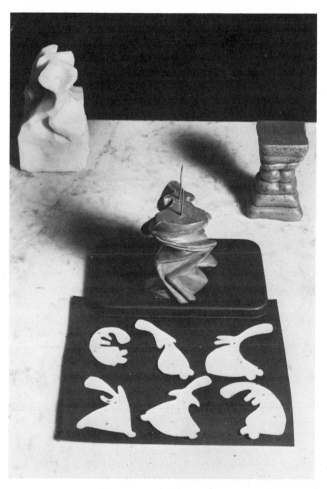

Materials for the wax-block animation technique developed by Crockwell.

temperature wax, to form the background. Sometimes, cut-out pieces of wax were embedded in the background material, instead of a continuous core. The difficult thing in the composition of the wax blocks was the need to remember what they would look like as we sliced through them. The blocks were cut with a meat slicer. About 1/64" was taken for each frame; by varying the number, we could vary the rhythm of the film.

A number of attempts were made to obtain a good black wax. We added various powders and pellets to molten wax, and discovered a wax that changed color at different temperatures. Eventually we found a good black.

The waxes softened under the floodlights, which resulted in smeared colors on each slice. To get a clean cut, we had to freeze the blocks. Then, after 10 or 15 slices, beads of condensed moisture had to be wiped off the face of the wax. Because of these problems, we had to work on many films at once. When the wax core for one film began to soften, it was replaced by the core for another. Upon completion, the film was edited into the separate films.

Douglass Crockwell slicing the wax block.

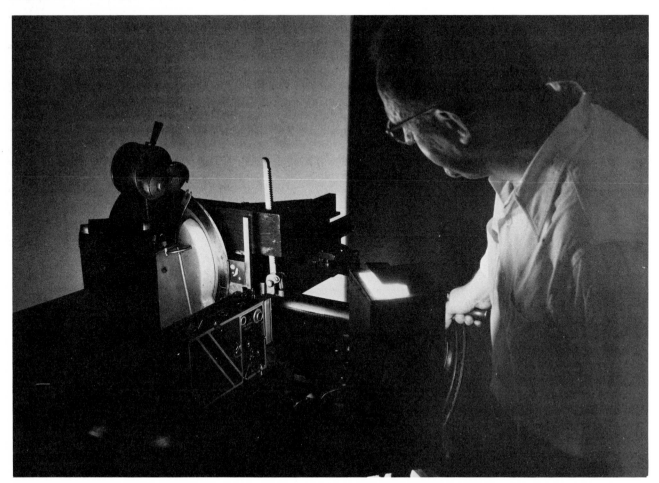

Dwinell Grant

Dwinell Grant was born in Springfield, Ohio, in 1912; he began painting portraits and landscapes in 1923, and studied at the Dayton Art Institute and the National Academy of Design, in New York, in 1932–33. Since 1933 he has been an abstract painter, with several one-man and numerous group shows in the United States and abroad. Between 1935 and 1941 he was an instructor of art and dramatics at Wittenberg University, in Springfield, Ohio.

Grant began making abstract animation films in 1940 and continued for the next ten years with five completed compositions and a number of short experiments. In 1941–42 he was assistant to Hilla Rebay, Director of the Solomon R. Guggenheim Foundation, and was also a member of the American Abstract Artists. Between 1942 and 1947 he was animation director of a New York educational and industrial film company, making training films for the United States Navy.

In 1948 Grant received a grant from the Guggenheim Foundation, for the purpose of developing a theory of abstract film composition roughly on a level with theory of composition for music.

Since 1948, Dwinell Grant has specialized in animation for medical films, first at the company he co-founded in New York City (Sturgis-Grant) and since 1955 as a freelance scriptwriter and animation designer, based in Bucks County, Pennsylvania.

Dwinell Grant, in 1940. (Photo by Ray Whitman.)

FILM NOTES TO *Compositions 1-5*
by Dwinell Grant
Composition 1 (Themis), 1940 (16mm, color, silent, 4 minutes.)
This film was composed after seven years of painting nonobjectively and was a simple attempt to add the elements of time and motion to abstract composition. The animation technique was stop-motion, using wood, glass, and paper forms on several levels. Animated, colored light-forms were also used. Some of the effects were suggested by experience with stage lighting.

Composition 2 (Contrathemis), 1941 (16mm, color, silent, 4 minutes.)
A first attempt to develop abstract visual themes in counterpoint. Animation was accomplished with flat drawings, one per frame. The drawings were kept in register by pushing them into a corner made by two strips of wood at right angles.

Composition 3, 1942 (16mm, black and white, silent, 3 minutes.)
An experiment in stop-motion media, using modeling clay, wire, wooden objects, and a specially constructed light-form projector.

Composition 4 (Stereoscopic Study #1), 1945 (16mm, color, silent, 4 minutes.)
Single-frame, stop-motion animation, using paper cutouts. Two pictures were photographed, side-by-side, on each film frame. The relative positions of the identical forms in the two pictures were determined by a 3-D formula devised by the artist. When the film is projected through a beam-splitter onto a metallic screen and viewed through polaroid glasses, a three-dimensional effect is perceived. In this film, the concepts of thematic development in counterpoint were extended by the added third dimension.

Composition 5, 1959 (16mm, color, silent, 6 minutes.)
First of this series of films designed for and photographed on a standard animation stand. The background, alone, was photographed on a first run. On the second run, double-exposed, the animation consisted of colored under-light projected through cut-out masks. This film was planned as the first part of a four-part composition, based on a more sophisticated concept of thematic development, but the other three parts have not been completed.

(From unpublished technical notes, April 1975.)

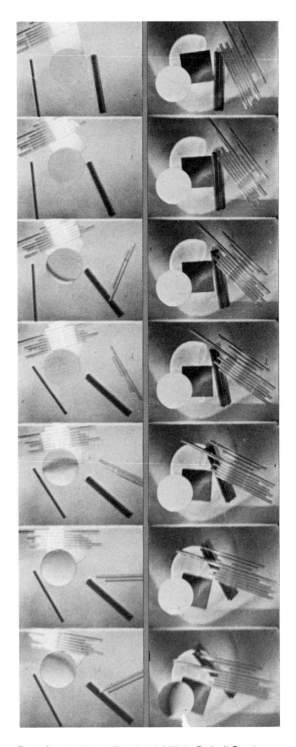

From *Composition 1 (Themis)*, (1940) by Dwinell Grant.

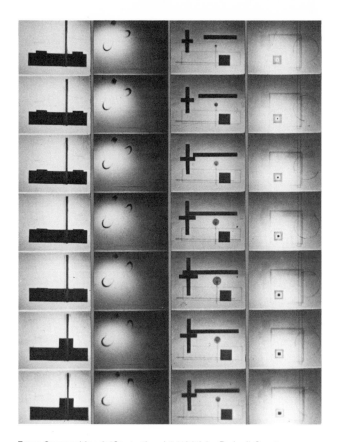

From *Composition 2 (Contrathemis)* (1941) by Dwinell Grant.

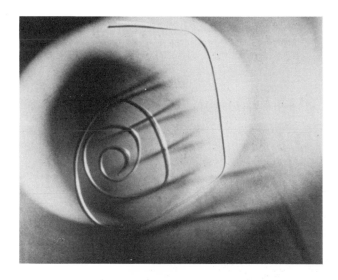

From *Composition 3* (1942) by Dwinell Grant.

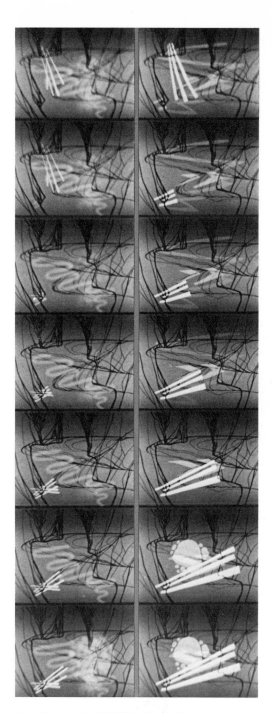

From *Composition 5* (1949) by Dwinell Grant.

Francis Lee

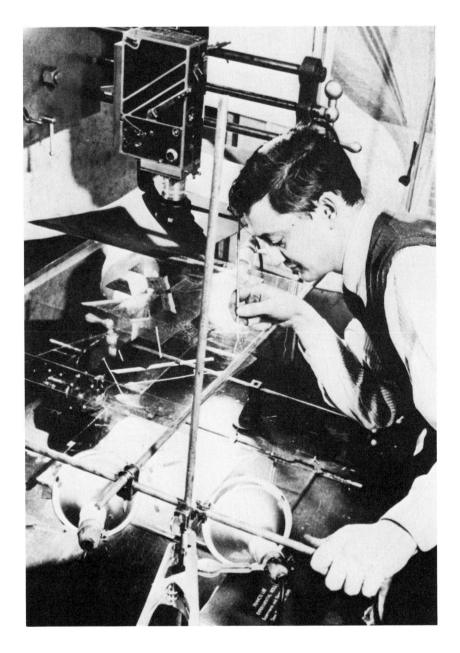

Francis Lee, in 1947.

Francis Lee was born in New York City in 1913. He studied painting at the National Academy of Design and at the Design Laboratory, an off-shoot of the Bauhaus which relocated to New York in the 1930s, and later with Hans Hoffmann.

His first film, *1941*, was his somber interpretation of the Japanese attack on Pearl Harbor. It contrasts an abstract world of greens, blues, and yellows (electric lamp bulbs floating on a sea of colored inks, sprinkled with multi-colored dusts and gilt), shattered by the blood-red of war, ending in a lifeless totality of gray.

Lee spent his next four years as a combat motion picture camera-man in Europe. *Le Bijou*, which he made in 1946, used bits of colored glass, wax, sand, and other materials for design and texture. "When I made this film," Lee later wrote, "I had some feelings about the trials and tribulations of the poet in our society—but that was only a starting point." *Idyll* (1948) is an animated painting of pastels, gouache, and oil backgrounds against which fishlike forms move about in a dreamlike marine world.

Recently Francis Lee has been studying Chinese brush painting and calligraphy, which he has made the subject of one of his latest films, *Sumi-e*. An earlier film has been colorized and video-synthesized by Nam June Paik and John Godfrey; Lee has called it *Synthesis*. After many years of working in film commercials, Lee is now doing mainly animation photography and titles and teaching for a livelihood.

FRANCIS LEE'S FIRST FILMS
by Jonas Mekas

. . . I truly admire Francis Lee's first three films, *1941*, *Le Bijou*, and *Idyll*. Their beauty is unique and real, and their place in the early American avant-garde film is unchallengeable. Of course, they reflect the leading styles and preoccupations in art at that period, and particularly early abstract expressionism and later (American) surrealism. But that is all very fine. One curious thing about Francis Lee's early work is its very special, Chinese-like quality, both in the ink and animation techniques (or styles) and in the feeling, in the special kind of lyricism. . . .

The beauty and the originality of Francis Lee's early three films is in their technique, in their lyrical qualities, and in their unique dramatization of inanimate objects. His three films constitute a world like no other world, where in these subtle, Chinese landscapes there exist these inanimate objects, and they lead these strange lives, mysteriously and gently; and where tensions and suspenses develop and again dissolve, as mysteriously as they came. There are early uses of single-frame techniques in them that are novel for the period (although found in the works of other animators, notably in the work of the Whitney brothers [see Chapters 7 and 8]).

When I see *Le Bijou* or *Idyll*, I am not too sure what I enjoy more, the mysterious travels of the abstract fish-like object, for instance, or the background, the landscape itself (an abstract landscape) in which it all happens and which is subtly colored. I like its reds and its greens, its shades of reds and greens. And there is also something about the pacing in these films that I like. They don't rush. They have a meditative pace. I count Lee's early three films among my favorites of all time. Not that I know why. The only thing I know is that when I watch them, no matter in what mood (or pace) I am, they transform me, they pull me into their own world, and all my resistance disappears. I am there, on the screen, and I feel very very fine in that subtle, personal, lyrical, gentle, and slightly humorous world—it's like nothing else that I know. And it does what all good art does, you want to come back and back to them. . . .

(From *The Village Voice*, February 17, 1972.)

5/Norman McLaren and the National Film Board of Canada

Cecile Starr

INTRODUCTION

Norman McLaren has won worldwide recognition for his work in experimental animation, using direct cameraless animation, stop-motion "pixillation," (see below) hand-drawn sound, three-dimensional films and many other techniques. But it is the quality and quantity of his work—their unique spirit and universality—that have earned this recognition, rather than the techniques themselves.

McLaren was born in Sterling, Scotland, in 1914, and began experimenting with film as a student at the Glasgow School of Art. John Grierson saw in London some of his work and invited him to join the General Post Office (G.P.O.) Film Unit in 1936. There McLaren made films about the London telephone directory, airmail service, and similar informational subjects. In 1939, when World War II was starting, McLaren moved to New York where he worked with Mary Ellen Bute on her *Spook Sport* (see Chapter 4). With grants from the Solomon Guggenheim Foundation, he also made a number of his own hand-drawn films, some with synthetic sound—*Dots*, *Loops*, *Boogie Doodle*, and *Stars and Stripes* (the Scottish McLaren's "patriotic" equivalent to the German Fischinger's *An American March*).

In 1941 McLaren again joined Grierson, this time at his newly formed National Film Board of Canada. McLaren has remained there ever since, except for two year-long furloughs in China (1949) and in India (1952) under UNESCO auspices. This is one of the longest associations any animator (or filmmaker or artist) has ever had with any single sponsor. Canada's solid support of its adopted national artist-animator has been accompanied by an enviable freedom, to which McLaren has responded with a unique sense of responsibility. On his own, and in collaboration with close associates, McLaren has made some fifty short films, in one style after another, for which he has won countless awards in nearly every country on earth. For nearly all his films, McLaren has written information sheets which describes their production techniques in considerable detail.

The animation department which McLaren set up at the Canadian National Film Board—starting with Guy Glover and Evelyn Lambart—soon included as its important mainstays Grant Munro, Jim McKay, Jean-Paul Ladouceur, Réné Jodoin, and George Dunning (the latter best known for the film of *Yellow Submarine*, which he made independently in England). Other well-known NFB animators—Wolf Koenig, Colin Low, Robert Verrall—have worked also in live-action films and in films composed largely of stills.

Here's what some of his colleagues have written about McLaren: "The lesson that McLaren teaches (and which is so hard to remember in the confusion of this world) is that chaos can be made into order only by applying the rules of art." (Wolf Koenig) "In twenty years, I have never heard him speak harshly of another filmmaker, artist, or technician. I have heard him object to a missed opportunity, or an error, or an excess, but always with patience and kindness. It is as if bearing a stern artistic conscience, he is always conscious of the demands and cost of that fierce discipline. He is sympathetic with those who are similarly afflicted and tolerant of those who are not." (Colin Low) "He is a great teacher, constantly alive to exploit the most unlikely leads to a new discovery and has awakened both artists and audiences to the medium." (George Dunning)

Tributes to McLaren have been paid by animators from all over the world, a number of whom have been invited to the National Film Board as resident filmmakers—Alexander Alexeieff, Walerian Boroczyk, Peter Foldes, Lotte Reiniger, among others. McLaren is always the first to praise his predecessors—Cohl and Méliès, Pfenniger and Jack Ellit, Fischinger and Len Lye—whether or not he knew their work before beginning his own similar experiments.

About his early relationship to Len Lye, McLaren has written: "Although I did not work in close proximity to Len Lye when at the G.P.O. Film Unit, and although I started direct drawing on film independently of him, his films have always put me in a state of dithering delight and therefore should be counted as a formative influence." And McLaren adds: "Len Lye was also the first person I know of to make a color film by assembling independent black and white imagery as the separation-negatives of a three-color process, a method which I have subsequently used in films like *Dots* and *Loops*, *Hoppity-Pop*, *Dollar Dance*, *Hen Hop*, etc. I have used indigenously black-and-white material, but Len Lye in his *Rainbow Dance* and *Trade Tattoo* made really exciting and creative use of it, and as far back as the early thirties" (see Chapter 2).

Another generation of filmmakers is now growing up at the NFB—the third or perhaps the fourth—Ryan Larkin, Pierre Hébert, Bernard Longpré, Caroline Leaf, among others. Laurent Coderre attributes his work in animation to his attendance at a short workshop given by Norman McLaren, who also recommended that he be given the opportunity to join the NFB's animation unit. "The National Film Board has permitted me to discover a new means of expression," Coderre has written. "If it is like any other organization submitted to restrictions following administration policies (administrative hierarchies, budgeting), it is nevertheless a unique place. If one is patient enough, the opportunity is there for him to make use of his potential in this creative field... I believe that NFB is, in this respect, rather understanding, recognizing for example that some animators function better in group productions while others prefer to work alone, that some are better equipped for commercial productions and others function to their best in purely creative films."

The kinship between Norman McLaren and the National Film Board of Canada is perhaps best summed up in McLaren's own words: "I'm very lucky, you know. I've been here for 33 years and I had complete freedom as to how I tackled an assigned subject during the war. And afterwards, of course, total freedom for subject and treatment. It's very rare for a creative film person to have the kind of freedom I have had. Yet for an artist it's an absolute must. It doesn't ensure he'll make good art, but it's the only way he'll have a chance."

Norman McLaren, around 1942, shown drawing on film at the animation table that he designed.

The name of John Grierson should be remembered here—founder of both the G.P.O. Film Unit in England and the National Film Board in Canada, who made a place for experimental animation in agencies that were primarily devoted to documentary film production. In recent years the NFB has broadened its animation program by setting up a separate French unit, headed by Réne Jodoin, which, according to McLaren, has tended to explore experimental techniques linked to free-ranging themes. On the other hand the English unit, headed by Wolf Koenig, has tended to harness its technical experience and experimentation to public-service themes in areas of science, education, safety, and the like.

It is difficult, if not impossible, to estimate the effect that Norman McLaren has had upon animators at the NFB. It is equally difficult to estimate the effect that the Film

Board has had on animators all over the world, especially those who work in government-sponsored schools and agencies in middle-European countries, where many young animators are receiving training and support, though not always with the kind of creative freedom McLaren considers essential. (The two Polish animators, Jan Lenica and Walerian Borowczyk, for example, both trained at the Polish Film School, have chosen to work in France.)

That great gift of creative freedom which the National Film Board of Canada has given Norman McLaren has been repaid a thousand-fold. It is not too much to hope that government film agencies in other countries will one day have the same faith in their artist-animators.

THE LOW BUDGET AND EXPERIMENTAL FILM
by Norman McLaren

Perhaps it was because I was born and brought up in Scotland that I have always been interested in small budget films. I certainly admit that I get a distinct pleasure from making a film out of as little as possible in the way of money, equipment, and time.

But there is more to it than that, because in my particular field there is a direct connection between the small budget and the experimental approach. Certainly, for me, limited means (whether budgetory or technical) stimulate the imagination to new directions of thinking and film-making. . . .

All arts need restrictions and limitations. The sonnet form, the fugue, the Roman viaduct, and the suspension bridge, the conventions of ballet, all point to the value of limitations. These of course are technical limitations, but I do think that financial limitations too play a positive role in molding and developing an art; in fact, they often shape technical, stylistic and esthetic ones in fundamental and healthy ways. . . .

But perhaps the most interesting and exhilarating of my experiences with rock-bottom budget and an experimental approach arising from it, was in China and India when, under the auspices of UNESCO, I taught local Chinese and Indian artists how to make simple animated films as part of the UNESCO project's work in public health and social education in the villages. Such films were intended to implant new ideas in the minds of the villagers, such as the need to boil drinking water, the value of children taking physical training, how to make compost from cow dung, the dangers of letting flies tramp around with their dirty feet on your food, etc.

In this kind of basic education work, every penny counts; the usual expensive and elaborate methods of making animated films are out of the question. Contrary to popular opinion, animation need not be a costly process. The very essence of film as a medium comes to the rescue; the saving grace of film is that if you strip it of all its secondary characteristics such as settings, backgrounds, properties, lighting, costuming, and even sound, leaving only the bare skeleton of the action, it is possible to hold firmly the attention of an audience; all that is really essential is that the action be clear, and artfully planned.

In the field of the theater, the great French mime, Marcel Marceau, is a splendid example of action stripped of all its trappings; in fact, of action making a very virtue of this condition.

The animated as against the actuality film lends itself with peculiar aptness to this stripped-down approach, for not only can the background trivia be left out, but the characters themselves can be simplified, stylized, and generalized in such a way as to strengthen and clarify the meaning of the action. Simple matchstick or pictographic figures may behave so vividly, humorously, tragically, or in any other way, that, as the film progresses, they may become enriched, complicated characters in the minds of the audience, though at any one moment they remain extremely simple on the surface of the screen.

And so, if the art of mime and motion is thoroughly understood by the animation artist, he can grip his audience without relying on the overloaded trappings of the usual cartoon. In China and India the first solution to having practically no budget for films was to make the artists realize the importance of silent mime and action expressed through a very simplified form of imagery.

From *Now Is the Time* (1951) by Norman McLaren, originally shown in "3-D."

HOW TO MAKE ANIMATED MOVIES WITHOUT A CAMERA

Norman McLaren

Things needed:

1. *A chair* for the artist to sit on.

2. *A table*  for the artist to sit at.

3. *A board*  fixed securely on the table at an angle to allow the artist comfort while drawing.

4. *A hole*  about 2″ by 10″ (50 mm. × 250 mm.) cut in the board to let light through from behind.

5. *A lamp or mirror or even a wide sheet of white card*  to place on the table behind the hole, to give illumination or to reflect skylight or daylight through the hole.

6. *Two strips of wood*  for fixing vertically onto the board about 3 1/2″ (90 mm.) apart, thus making a channel on the board above the hole.

The film holder:

7. *A piece of wood* about 3 1/2″ by 21″ (90 mm. × 533 mm.), to slide smoothly up and down in the channel.

8. *A row of pegs along one side of the piece of wood* so that the artist's free hand can easily push the wood up the channel a little at a time, while he is drawing frames of film. The pegs should be on the left hand side for the right-handed artist, and on the right hand side for the left-handed artist.

9. *A groove* along the entire length of this piece of wood to hold the 35 mm. film. The groove must be 35 mm. wide and have lips on either side to hold the film securely in place. The lips should overhang about 1/8th of an inch (3 mm.) and should not press on the edges of the film enough to prevent it being pulled through the groove.

10. *A hole* about 1″ by 19″ (25 mm. × 480 mm.) should be cut out of the centre of the groove to let the light through from behind.

11. *A piece of frosted or ground glass, or thick ground celluloid* to be countersunk into this hole, so that the film held in the groove will have a solid but transparent support.

12. *A rod* fixed *below* the table to carry 1000′ (304 metres) roll of blank 35 mm. film for drawing on. The film will feed upwards between the artist's knees and into the groove in the film holder.

13. *A bin* placed on the far side of the table from the artist to catch the film as it drops down from the top end of the channel. The drop should be sufficient to let the wet ink image drawn on the film dry before it hits the bottom of the bin.

"How to Make Animated Movies Without a Camera," a page from the booklet *Cameraless Animation* by Norman McLaren, distributed by the National Film Board of Canada, 1958. The booklet describes the cameraless animation technique developed by McLaren, and includes his designs for the equipment needed. It was originally published by UNESCO in *Fundamental Education: A Quarterly Bulletin*, October 1949.

After that, there was the choice of the technical method by which to make the films. In all, we tried three.

1-DIRECT METHOD The first consisted of drawing directly with pen and ink on black 35mm film without the use of a camera; one small drawing being done on each frame and each one differing slightly from the previous one. This, though serving as a most useful introduction to and exercise in animation, proved on the whole to be too "movie" a method for our education needs, since, by this method, it is very difficult to make a figure or object remain stationary, and so often staticity and slow motion are required in educational films. It is, however, an excellent technique for scenes of boisterous activity.

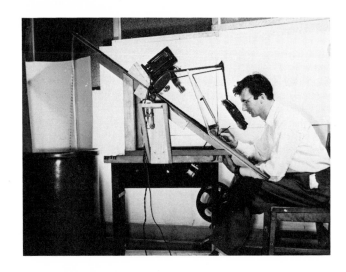

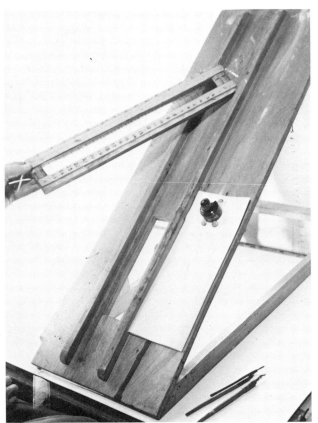

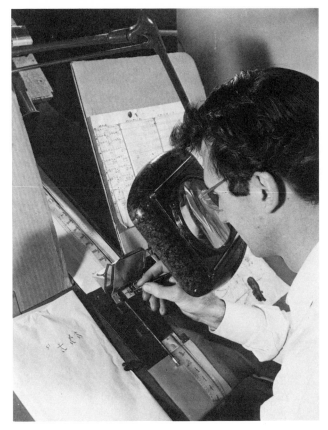

Norman McLaren drawing on film with pen and ink.

120

2-PAPER METHOD Almost everyone knows of the standard method of making cartoons—where thousands of separate drawings (one for each frame of film) are pencilled-in on 10 × 14 inch sheets of paper; these are then traced onto sheets of celluloid with ink outlines, which are then filled in with opaque paint, which are then placed over a background painted on paper or card, and photographed.

Our second method was an extremely simplified version of this standard procedure. It consisted of eliminating the celluloids, the inking, the filling-in, and most of the backgrounds, by doing the final drawings directly on small 4 × 6 inch sheets of semi-transparent typewriter copy paper; when a background or static object was essential to the story, it was drawn on a sheet of celluloid and placed above the paper drawings during the photographic process. The costs of material and labor were thereby cut by about 75%.

Furthermore, we simplified everything down to the absolute minimum necessary for telling a clear story. The outline of the delineated characters was reduced to the fewest number of lines. Backgrounds, settings and static objects were brought in only when and where functionally needed for the story, and removed when their use was over, much like the traditional practice on the Chinese stage. The linear figures were not filled in with opaque paint, but left in simple outline (which is also in keeping with one type of traditional Chinese drawing).

3-FLAT PUPPET METHOD In the third method we adapted the technique that Lotte Reiniger pioneered and made famous in her delightful films, namely, the animated flat-jointed silhouette puppet, usually cut out of paper [see Chapter 3]. It would be equally true to say that in doing so we were also adapting local Chinese and Indian traditions, for manually operated, flat, jointed silhouette (and transparent) puppets are indigenous to the theater of the Far East.

In the use of these three techniques, our guiding idea was always this . . . that any attempt at graphic optical realism was unnecessary in the secondary and static characteristics of the film, so long as the action in itself was realistic.

For example, we thought it better to have a simple matchstick of pictographic figure express grief, joy, or what-have-you, by its gesture and mime, than to have an elaborately drawn human figure, whose facial expression just by its static delineation could convey such emotions. The elimination of static graphic elaboration not only was a great financial saving, but creatively played a positive role in forcing the story content to be expressed by pure

action and movement, which of course makes for better cinema.

To sum up, I would say that I am a firm believer in the creative stimulus of a low budget. I think that the less money there is for a film the more imagination there *has* to be. A small budget, limited technical means and an urgent deadline often act as a catalyst and help to impose the artistic consistency and unity which is an essential part of a well-made work.

(From a statement released by the National Film Board of Canada, September, 1955.)

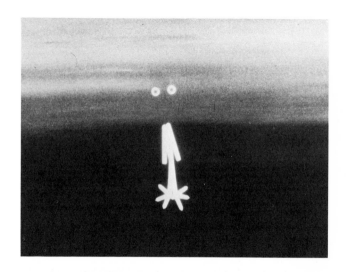

From *Le Merle* (The Crow) (1958) by Norman McLaren.

From *A Phantasy* (1952) by Norman McLaren, combining his pastel method with cutout and object animation.

ANIMATED FILMS
by Norman McLaren

The production method of some of the animated films I have been making for the National Film Board of Canada differs radically from the usual one for animated films and this largely conditions the final result.

I have tried to preserve in my relationship to the film the same closeness and intimacy that exists between a painter and his canvas. This is rather difficult, for in one case only a stick of wood with a tuft of camel hair intervenes between the maker and the finished result, and in the other an elaborate series of optical, chemical, and mechanical processes, which become a perfect breeding ground for lack of intimacy, frustrations, ill feeling, and hostility between the artist and his finished work.

And so my militant philosophy is this: to make with a brush on canvas is a simple and direct delight—to make with a movie should be the same. To illustrate the effect of this philosophy on my technique I will give details of different solutions.

One group of films made for the National Film Board of Canada in the earlier part of the war publicizing the War Savings Campaign were all made by a hand-drawn-cameraless method; they were *Dollar Dance*, *Five For Four*, *V For Victory*, and *Hen Hop*. As *Hen Hop* is the purest example, I will speak about it.

From *Hen Hop* (1942) by Norman McLaren.

In it the camera, shooting, and developing of original negative were completely short-circuited. In one operation, which is the drawing directly onto 35mm clear machine leader with an ordinary pen nib and India ink, a clean jump was made from the ideas in my head to the images on what would normally be called the developed negative. Because these ideas were never thought out in precise detail until the moment of drawing, and because, when drawing, I had a chart of exact footages of the music both beside me and in my head, the equivalents of Scripting, Drawing, Animating, Shooting, Developing of Negative, Positive Cutting, and Negative Cutting were all done in one operation. If a mistake was made, a small amount of water (I use saliva) on cloth would wash the offending images off the frame, and drawing could continue as before. The rectification with one swipe of the damp cloth affected all the traditional processes from script through to negative cutting.

To summarize the technical processes involved: Music is first recorded. Music track is run on a Moviola [editing machine], and each note, phrase and sentence marked with grease pencil. Track is put on a frame counter and the notes measured cumulatively from zero at start. Measurements are put against the notes on a dope sheet, which is usually a simplified musical score, and, by subtraction, the length of each note in terms of frames is written in. The grease-pencilled sound track is run through a two-way winder, along with a roll of clear machine leader, called a "dummy." The notes are copied and identified with India ink on the dummy. The final drawing is done with the aid of an apparatus whose purpose is to hold the film in place, move it on from frame to frame and provide a means of registration from frame to frame. It is actually an adapted camera gate with claw mechanism and an optical system that reflects the image of the frame just drawn on the frame about to be drawn. The dummy is threaded through this apparatus. On top of it and riding along with it is threaded another track of clear machine leader for doing the final drawing on. With a bottle of ink, pen, and dope sheet at hand, drawing can begin.

All drawing is done in natural sequence, starting at the first frame of the film and working straight through to the last. When finished, the drawn track goes into the lab for a couple of prints; one for a checking print to sync up with the sound track, the other for a master for release printing. If color release is desired, various kinds of dupes are made from this master and assembled in parallel to act as the separation negatives for the particular color process used. . . .

The most effortless and easiest thing to produce by

this hand-drawn method is extreme mobility; the most difficult, and almost impossible, is staticity. This is the opposite of most other animation techniques where the static image is the easiest footage to obtain, and the mobile the most difficult. With the standard animation technique, one breathes life into a static world; with hand-drawn technique, one slows down, to observable speed, the world of frantic mobility. (When beginners draw footage by hand and the result is projected at normal speed, the image-flow is so fast that it gives the impression of looking at thought, if thought were visible).

The image must needs be linear; tone value and light and shade cannot be used as they fluctuate too much from frame to frame. For certain types of film this is a severe limitation.

When the National Film Board needed publicity shorts during the war, the above hand-drawn linear technique served quite well, but when the need for animated films on our French-Canadian folk songs came up it was hardly adequate, particularly for the more poetic and slow songs. I had, therefore, to think of maintaining my intimacy with the celluloid in some other way. I felt the need for using chiaroscure and slowness, and solved the problem thus.

In doing oil paintings myself, and in watching other painters at their canvases, it often seemed to me that the evolution or change that many a painting went through from its virgin state to (in my own case) its soiled and battered conclusion, was more interesting than the conclusion itself. Why not, therefore, consciously switch the focus-point of all the effort from the end condition and spread it over the whole process? In other words, do a painting, but put the emphasis upon the doing rather than the painting—on the process rather than the end-product.

And so for *Poulette Grise*, I stuck a bit of cardboard about 18 × 24 inches upon a wall, placed rigidly in front of it a tripod and camera loaded with color film. To avoid reflection and waiting-to-dry trouble, I used chalks and pastel rather than paint.

The picture then grew in the normal way that any still painting grows, being evolved from moment to moment, and each stage being very dependent on the stage before it. About every quarter of an hour the evolution was recorded on the film mainly by short, contiguous dissolves. For three weeks the surface of this one bit of cardboard metamorphosed itself in and out of a series of henly images, and at the end of it, all I had was one much worn bit of cardboard with an unimpressive chalk drawing on it, and 400 feet of exposed film in the camera. In a sense the film was the by-product of doing a painting.

Of course the sound track has to be marked up first and the dope sheet made out in much the same way as for the hand-drawn technique, but once again the creative part of the job happened in one and only one concentrated binge, unhampered by technical headaches and frustrations. Also of importance was the fact that here again the movement evolved in its natural sequence, and as a result I had a chance to improvise everything at the moment of shooting.

As this particular technique lent itself more readily to creating visual change rather than to action (side to side, and to and fro displacement of image on the screen) I intentionally avoided the use of action, partly because it suited the theme, and partly out of curiosity to see if change in itself could be a strong enough cinematic factor to sustain interest.

The technique also invited me to take chiaroscure out of its usual role as a dead element in the decor of animated films, and put it to work as the foremost factor with a life of its own. In this I hope that perhaps I am on the way to bridging the gap that has always existed between painting proper and the animated film. . . .

(From *Documentary Film News*, May 1948.)

From *La Poulette Grise* (1947) by Norman McLaren.

"BEGONE DULL CARE" AND "FIDDLE-DE-DEE"
by Norman McLaren

Fiddle-de-Dee [1947] and *Begone Dull Care* [1949] were made by taking absolutely clear, 35mm motion picture celluloid and painting on it, frequently on both sides with celluloid dyes, inks and transparent prints. Textures were achieved by using brush stroke effects, stippling, scratching off the paint, pressing cloths of various textures into the paint while it was still wet on the film, spraying the paint onto the film, and frequently mixing two chemically different types of paint, such as dyes solvent in alcohol and dyes solvent in cellulose, together; one dye would be painted on the film and the other dye mixed into it, while still wet, to create various textures and patterns in much the same way as mixing oil and water paints on a different surface.

The film, in the process of being painted, was laid out in long lengths on a table in sections. The lengths were metrically organized to fit the music; the sound track having been measured before the painting commenced.

This painted track acted as a master positive for all subsequent color release prints. No shooting with any sort of camera was involved in the making of these films. The process is as direct as an artist using pigment on canvas and subsequently having it reproduced in color.

(From technical notes, March 1961.)

McLaren hand-engraving directly on a section of film for *Begone Dull Care*.

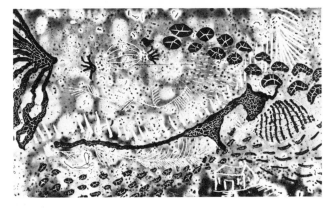

From *Begone Dull Care* (1949) by Norman McLaren.

"NEIGHBOURS" AND "TWO BAGATELLES"
by Norman McLaren

This technique (sometimes referred to as "pixillation") consists of applying the principles normally used in the photographing of animated and cartoon movies to the shooting of actors, that is, instead of placing drawings, cartoons or puppets in front of the animation camera, we place real human beings.

The technique is not new, its origins go back to the early French movies of the Méliès epoch, when the camera was stopped in the middle of shots to produce trick effects, and the same principle has since been used occasionally in films by experimentalists like Hans Richter, Len Lye, Richard Massingham and many others. But on the whole, the technique has never had the exploration it deserves, nor has it had this in the films *Neighbours* or *Two Bagatelles*, where only a few of the possibilities have been applied, and rather crudely at that. Nonetheless, as a result of working with this approach I have jotted down the following observations.

In essence, any technique of animation consists of stopping the camera between the taking of each frame of film, instead of letting it run on relentlessly at normal speed (that is, 24 frames of a second). Once it is assumed that the actor being photographed by a movie camera can stop between any or every 24th of a second, a new range of human behavior becomes possible. The laws of appearance and disappearance can be circumvented as can the laws of momentum, inertia, centrifugal force and gravity; but what is perhaps even more important, the tempo of acting can be infinitely modulated from the slowest speed to the fastest. Apart from the apparently spectacular feats of virtuosity that this makes the actor capable of, it is possible to use the technique in a concealed way behind what appears to be normal acting. Or if used in a less concealed way it can permit to the actor a caricature type of movement. In much the same way as a pictorial caricature can make comment on character and situation by distorting the static form of a drawing, so live-action-animation can create a caricature by tampering with the tempo of human action, by creating hyper-natural exaggerations and distortions of the normal behavior, by manipulating the acceleration and deceleration of any given human movement. This type of caricature is, of course, often found in animated cartoons, but cannot be found in live-action films until an animation technique is applied to them.

It is also possible to devise many new ways for a human being to locomote. Apart from new types of walking and running, a person may get from one place to another by sliding, (while sitting, standing, balancing on one foot, or any other way) by appearing and disappearing, and a host of other ways.

At the outset of shooting *Neighbours* our conception was to get all action by taking a single frame at a time throughout each shot (having the actors move in small amounts, between frames); but after some experimenting

McLaren directing Grant Munro in *Two Bagatelles* (1952).

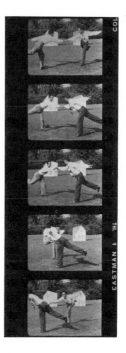

From *Neighbours* (1952) by Norman McLaren.

it became apparent that the single frame approach was best only for certain types of shot.

To meet all our requirements, we decided to use a whole gamut of shooting speeds, from one frame every five minutes to one frame every 1/16th of a second, depending on the nature of the shot, so we would select the most desirable shooting speed. Within one shot we might often vary the shooting speed if different parts of the action demanded it.

The tempo of the actor's movement was also considered a variable factor, ranging from very slight changes of static positions, through very slow movement, up to normal speed.

The tempo of the actor's behavior and the tempo of the camera's shooting were therefore adjusted to any desired ratio, depending on the final desired effect, and the speed at which it would be easiest for the actor to achieve his point. For instance, if the actors moved half as slow as normal and the camera shot half as slow as normal (twelve frames per second), the final screen speed would appear normal but, in the process of shooting, a tempo-control factor of two had entered in and the actor, by performing at speeds between half-normal and normal, had available a range of final screen speeds ranging from normal to twice normal. The concept of a tempo-control factor proved to be a useful one.

Many of the shots in *Neighbours* that appear in fairly normal tempo were shot with camera and actors both moving slowly, sometimes as much as four, six, eight, ten and twelve times slower than normal. In the shots with speeded-up human action the camera often took pictures at eight times slower than normal, while the actors moved about four or three or two times slower than normal.

Another advantage of achieving a final normal speed effect by using a tempo-control factor while shooting was this: to tie in with steady musical beats and phrases of the as yet un-made sound track; we often wished the actions to be of precise metrical lengths, so while shooting at slow speed we would count out the number of each frame as it went by in the camera, thus the actors could arrange to be at such and such a spot on the 60th frame, to have their arms raised on the 80th frame, and their hands touch on the 90th frame, to start rotating on the 100th frame, and to decelerate to a standstill over a period of sixty frames, etc. For purposes of integrating human action with music (in a rather ballet-like way) this method is of considerable value, especially so if the music has already been recorded, and the lengths of beats and phases permanently fixed.

Since both camera tempo and acting tempo are considered as flexible, in order to obtain, for instance, the effect of a man walking, starting at one mile an hour and gradually and almost imperceptibly speeding up until he reaches twenty miles an hour, either the camera may be run at a constant slow speed and the man allowed to accelerate from extremely slow to normal speed, or alternatively the man may walk at a constant speed, and the camera be allowed to decelerate. In either case the overall effect of tempo will be the same, but in the bodily or muscular behavior and center of balance of the figure there will be differences.

We did not use or explore this field of subtle differences, but we did compare the convenience of either varying the actor's or the camera's speed. In many but not all cases it was found better to keep the camera speed constant and let the actor do all the modulating of the movement himself; at times both methods were used, especially if during a take the actors were tending to move either too slowly or too fast, we would compensate by pushing the single frame button slightly more or slightly less frequently.

Obviously a normal effect (a 1 : 1 ratio of camera and acting speeds) can be achieved at any overall tempo, such for instance as the camera running at half normal speed and the actors performing at half normal speed; alternatively, the camera running ten times slower than normal and the actors performing ten times slower as well, etc.

However, apparently normal effects achieved by such means do not appear normal when certain effects of gravity, inertia, certrifugal and centripetal force are involved; for instance if a girl who wears a long full skirt twirls around rapidly, and this is photographed normally, the skirt will fly out in all directions, (the more rapidly she rotates the more the skirt will fly out); but if the camera is made to shoot twelve times slower than normal and the girl to rotate twelve times slower than normal, on the final screening the girl will still twirl at the original fast speed but her skirt will not fly out. The audience will interpret this either as a lack of centrifugal force or more likely as the skirt's being made of lead or some excessively heavy substance. The degree to which the skirt will fly out (or its apparent weight) can thus be controlled by the changes in the overall tempo of the 1 : 1 ratio between shooting speed and acting speed. Many gradual or sudden modifications in the behavior caused by momentum, gravity and other physical forces are possible by this technique.

The creative potentialities of this stop-motion live-action technique are quite considerable—not so much for a straight action movie involving speech and lip synchronization but for a new genre of filmic ballet and mime.

(From technical notes, 1952.)

"BLINKITY BLANK"
by Norman McLaren

This is an animated film done directly on 35mm celluloid, without the use of a camera, by engraving on black emulsion-coated film with a penknife, sewing needle and razor blade, and colored by hand with transparent cellulose dyes, and a sable-hair brush.

Animating directly on opaque black film poses the problem of how to position and register accurately the engraved image from one frame to the next. To bypass this problem *Blinkity Blank* intentionally set out to investigate the possibilities of *intermittent animation and spasmodic imagery.*

This meant that the film was not made in the usual way, one frame of picture following inexorably after the next, each second of time crying out for its pound of visual flesh—its full quota of 24 frames; instead, on the blackness and blankness of the outstretched strip of celluloid on my table top I would engrave a frame here and a frame there, leaving many frames untouched and blank—sprinkling, as it were, the images on the empty band of time; but sprinkling carefully—in relation to each other, to the spaces between, to the music, and to the idea that emerged as I drew.

Optically, most of the film consists of nothing at all. When such a movie is projected at normal speed, the image on a solitary frame is received by the eye for a 48th of a second, but due to after-image and the persistence of vision, the image lingers considerably longer than this on the retina, and in the brain itself it may persist until interrupted by the appearance of a new image.

To make play with these factors was one of the technical interests of producing *Blinkity Blank.* Sometimes, for greater emphasis, I would engrave *two* adjacent frames, or a *frame-cluster,* (that is, a group of 3, 4 or more frames); sometimes a frame-cluster would have related and continuous image within it and would thus solidify some action and movement; at other times the frame-cluster would consist only of a swarm of disconnected, discontinuous images, calculated to build up an overall visual "impression". Here and there, to provide much needed relief from the staccato action of single-frame images and frame-clusters, I introduced longer sections of contiguous frames with a flow of motion in the traditional manner.

During the process of making the film, tests and experiments revealed a number of definite laws relating to persistence of vision, after-image effects and intermittent imagery as it affects both the retina and the mind, especially when organized in sequences and with continuity. If the film does not succeed, it is partly because I have not yet fully understood these laws.

Perhaps the film can be likened to a *sketch,* which uses a kind of *impressionism of action and time,* much like a draftsman when he suggests a scene by leaving most of the page blank and only here and there draws a stroke, a line, or a blob of tone—often to indicate quite a complex subject; this is in contrast to the usual animated film, in which all the frames of celluloid carry images, and which could be likened to a surface of paper which a draftsman has completely covered with a fully rendered drawing.

(From technical notes, 1955.)

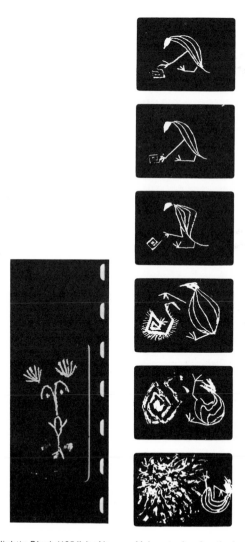

From *Blinkity Blank* (1954) by Norman McLaren, showing the hand-engraving on black film.

127

"PAS DE DEUX"

by Norman McLaren

In the original shooting no attempt was made to get a multiple image. The dancers, dressed in white, were filmed against a completely black background and black floor. The shooting speed was mainly at 48 frames per second, to give a slight slow motion effect.

The multiplication of the image was done at a later stage in an optical printer. In the projector of the optical printer we used high contrast positive (Kodak stock 5362) made from the original negative; in the camera of the optical printer we used stock 5234.

To create the multiple image, we exposed this high contrast many times successively on to our new optical negative. The same shot was exposed on itself, but each time delayed or staggered by a few frames. Thus when the dancers were completely at rest, these successive out-of-step exposures would all be on top of each other, creating the effect of *one* normal image; but when the dancers started to move, each exposure would start moving a little later than the preceding one, thus creating the effect of multiplicity.

The average number of exposures was eleven. The amount of stagger varied from shot to shot, and also within a single shot. A 2-frame stagger created a tightly packed chain of images; a 20-frame stagger made a very widely spaced chain; an average 5-frame stagger gave images that were overlapped, but distinct enough to be separately identified.

Two methods were used to collapse the image-chain into a single image. In the first, as mentioned above, we would have the dancers come to a natural stop and pause. In the second, at a suitable moment in the action, we would optically freeze a frame of the first exposure long enough to let all the other exposures in turn catch up to and freeze on the same frame. When the last exposure was caught up, we would have a single, unified static image, which, by having all the exposures proceed again, this time in step with each other (that is, non-staggered), would continue the action as a single unified image.

If we wished this single image to spread out once again into many images, we would have to optically freeze all exposures except one, allowing only this one to proceed, then allow each of the other exposures in their turn to proceed with, say, a 5-frame delay between each.

In addition to having black backgrounds, it was essential to have back lighting on the dancers. Normal front lighting would have led to visual clutter when the images became multiplied. Delineation of the dancers, by as thin a line of light as possible, gave maximum readability when the multiplied figures were in motion.

(From technical notes, 1969.)

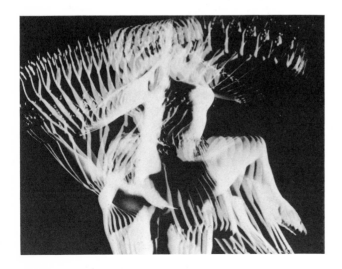

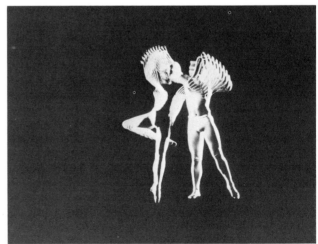

From *Pas de Deux* (1969) by Norman McLaren.

6/Contemporary Imagists

Robert Russett

INTRODUCTION

Until the 1950s, experimental animation and other art-oriented forms of cinema had developed in basically two directions; one approach consisted of a coherent narrative style using figurative or pictorial imagery, the other of a largely perceptual style using abstract shapes and components as subject matter. Although many forms of abstract animation were completely nonobjective, others (however innovative) relied heavily on a predetermined structure such as a musical score or story line. In contrast, the emphasis of the new animation is almost totally on a direct and improvised approach to expression and screen plasticity. Building on the historic and artistic tradition of the early pioneers, experimental animators working in the post-1950s began to create new kinds of content and meaning by investigating the interior logic of nonnarrative and perceptual concepts of cinema.

In addition to new esthetic issues, the change of atmosphere also reflected other important factors: the growing availability of relatively inexpensive 16mm equipment of professional quality, the steady growth of film studies at all levels of education, and an increasing interest in cinema as a serious form of art and communication. In this creative climate, artistic experimentation increased, and animators such as the seven outstanding filmmakers profiled in this chapter began to play a central role in the development of a new and dynamic form of contemporary cinema.

The visual investigations of Carmen D'Avino, Harry Smith, Jerome Hill, and Larry Jordan are basically concerned with the filmic illusion of subject matter. Their animated films, which are essentially kinetic surrealistic paintings, are obviously interdependent with the field of fine arts. On the other hand, film-artists Robert Breer, Tony Conrad, and Paul Sharits are concerned with a more autonomous and reflexive form of cinema. Their animated works, which are basically independent of other art forms, focus primarily on the nature of cinema itself, and evolve their meaning by exploring and amplifying the inherent properties of the filmmaking process. Both of the approaches used by these film-artists avoid programmatic and narrative elements and use the film medium to create emotional experiences which are direct, revolutionary, and totally visual.

Each of the filmmakers in this new generation works in an extremely personal style. The single frame experiments of Robert Breer, for example, have pioneered in expanding the psychology and physiology of perception in contemporary animation. His films, which are produced with inexpensive equipment and minimal graphic techniques, are not composed of realistic movements but of rapidly changing images and optical sensations. In many of his animated works such as *Image By Images I* (1954), *Blazes* (1961), and *66* (1966), Breer gives new meaning to the filmic phenomenon of intermittent movement by constructing his footage with distinctly different images on each frame. The experience created by this frenetic succession of visual sensations does not, of course, have a life-like continuity but instead constitutes an illusory form of collage, which has its own expressive possibilities comparable to other techniques of animation. Although Breer's animated works vary from linear configurations to pure plastic abstraction, his major occupation is with the dynamic temporal activity that can be generated by the single-frame process. His filmic experiments, which make a new order of visual relationships possible, have had an enormous impact on much of the animation of the sixties and seventies.

Harry Smith, who began making films by hand-painting, batiking, and etching nonobjective forms directly onto film stock, has been creating innovative and artistic animated works since about 1939. During the fifties, however, his early abstract approach converged with a surrealistic collage technique, and he began producing his best known and most sophisticated films. Distinguished by their alchemically magical quality, Smith's animated collages rely on an inward stream of consciousness for their original and fascinating imagery.

He is deeply involved with psychological phenomena and employs surrealistic devices to extract the subjective meaning of figures and objects. In his film, *The Magic Feature* (*ca.* 1958), for example, Smith uses the surrealistic principle of "psychic improvisation" to create dream-like effects which are rhythmically structured and transformed. Consequently, the form and content of his complex animated work are determined largely by a subjective process which involves the automatic flow of images and actions. Smith is using the technique of animation, guided by his own uniquely mysterious personality, to probe deeply into human consciousness and to reveal complex facets of inner life.

Like Harry Smith, Carmen D'Avino also creates a form of surrealistic animation; however, his films are composed of more whimsical and lighthearted visions. D'Avino, a painter who uses film as a kinetic extension of his craft, transforms surfaces, objects, and entire environments into a chromatic world of light and motion. In his film, *The Room* (1958–1959), a classic example of this genre, brilliant patterns swarm over every surface with organic vitality. As a result of this painterly process, the walls and fixtures of a drab room are removed bit by bit from the real world and given a new esthetic meaning. By using a fast and furious form of decorative construction, D'Avino has evolved a technique of animation which fuses the act of painting with three-dimensional objects.

Jerome Hill, who for most of his career made documentaries, spent the last five years of his life creating experimental films which employed a specialized form of animation. In these films, among them *Canaries* (1968) and *Film Portrait* (1965–71), Hill creates poetic and dreamlike images by combining hand-painted animated effects with live-action cinematography. Using this confluence of animation and live-action painting and photography, Hill abandoned his experience as a documentary filmmaker and returned, with startling freshness, to the basic resources of film plasticity, color, and animated movement.

The complex animated expressions of Tony Conrad are primarily concerned with the filmic potential of visual perception rather than the subjective content of figurative subject matter. For example, in *The Flicker* (1965), his first and perhaps best-known work, Conrad disregards the normative idea that film must be composed of images and builds his footage entirely with alternating clusters of solid black-and-white frames. The effect is one of pulsating patterns of light which induce various forms of afterimage. These eye-mind generated perceptions artistically explore the photo-chemistry of seeing. Such optical experiments with cinematic light question the form and function of film as a medium of expression, thus creating a new basis for artistic discovery in the field of animation.

Larry Jordan is one of the most prolific experimental animators of the current generation. His animated collages, which are composed of old engravings and illustrations, share with surrealism a fundamental concern for the subconscious. Influenced by the work of artists Max Ernst and Joseph Cornell, Jordan's unsettling films are in direct opposition to conventional logic and the plotted narrative. In his animated works, among them *Duo Concertantes* (1962–64), *Orb* (1973), and *Once Upon A Time* (1974), Jordan uses powerful surrealistic effects such as the dislocation of objects and the distortion of events to produce a poetic and rhythmic vision of reality that appeals directly to our emotions.

Paul Sharits has used the single frame technique extensively in his work to investigate the inherent character and potential of the filmmaking process. Basically, he focuses on the medium itself as the subject of his art and constructs his footage by isolating and exploring the perceptual meaning of filmic phenomena. Although his work is minimal in its stark simplicity of technique and symbolic content, it is complex in terms of its exploration of sensory impressions. In *N:O:T:H:I:N:G* (1968) for example, one of his best-known animated works, Sharits alternates sequences of solid frames and images to create a subliminal barrage of strong sensory impressions, produced with a stroboscopic flicker effect. The film explores the artistic possibilities of intermittent light, temporal color, image sequencing, and other basic facets of filmmaking.

Working outside the mainstream of commercial cinema, these contemporary imagists, like the experimental pioneers before them, have contributed to a rigorous tradition of independence, originality, and esthetic inquiry that has always been the concern of experimental animation. This experimental tradition continues to influence the overall development of the cinema, as well as producing complex and personal forms of animation which must be considered as works of art in their own right. The complete artificiality and boundless possibilities of the single frame technique are more relevant today than ever before to express the multi-faceted nature of reality as we understand it at present. No other art, for example, can so effectively and freely manipulate, condense, reverse, expand, and synthesize the temporal-spatial elements of graphic imagery. Contemporary film-artists, by exploiting this flexible artistic tool, are reaching out for new forms that are contributing to a wider definition of the art of experimental animation.

Robert Breer

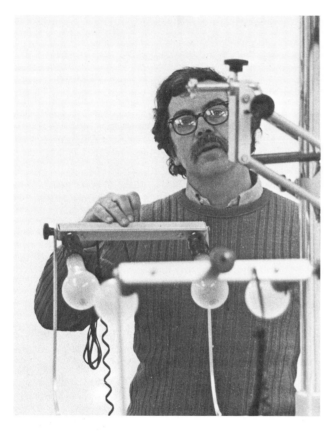

Robert Breer. (Photo by Robert A. Haller.)

footage. His variation of this technique uses stylized drawings from live-action footage to create a synthetic art form that transcends the normal vision of life experience.

Born in Detroit, Michigan, in 1926, Breer studied painting at Stanford University and then moved to Europe, where he lived from 1949–1959. While in Europe he exhibited his paintings in many group shows and became interested in filmmaking. Breer now lives and works in Palisades, New York, not far from New York City. Currently, in addition to his filmmaking activities, he also creates kinetic sculpture and other motion-oriented art forms. His outstanding body of work in the field of experimental animation has won him the Creative Film Foundation Award in 1957 and 1961, the Bergamo Award in 1960, and the Max Ernst *Femmer* Award in 1969.

From *Fuji* (1974) by Robert Breer. Abstract shapes combine with landscape imagery to create an impression of a train moving past Mt. Fuji.

Since his first film, *Form Phases I* (1952), Breer has restlessly investigated the single frame technique, producing more than twenty animated shorts. He has explored new perceptual threshholds with his rapid montage technique, pioneered in the collage film, and experimented with the dynamics of pure abstract animation. In his most recent film, *Fuji* (1974), Breer has experimented with the rotoscope technique in which line drawings are traced one frame at a time from live-action

INTERVIEW WITH ROBERT BREER
by Guy L. Coté

Q: How did you get involved with films in the first place?

Breer: First, I was a painter. In Paris, I was influenced by the geometric abstractions of the neo-plasticians, following Mondrian and Kandinsky. It was big at the time, and I began painting that way. My canvasses were limited to three or four forms, each one hard-edged and having its own definite color. It was a rather severe kind of abstraction, but already in certain ways I had begun to give my work a dynamic element which showed that I was not entirely at home within the strict limits of neo-plasticism. Also, the notion of absolute formal values seemed at odds with the number of variations I could develop around a single theme, and I became interested in change itself and finally in cinema as a means of exploring this further. I wanted to see if I could positively control a range of variations in a single composition. You can see that I sort of backed into cinema since my main concern was with static forms. In fact, I was even a bit annoyed at first when I ran into problems of movement.

My father was an amateur movie-maker from way back; he had even made a stereoscopic camera in the 1940's. I borrowed one of his cameras to film my first tests: a set of cards showing the transformations of forms through various phases. That was in 1952, and I called the film *Form Phases*. For a long time, the films remained incidental to my painting, but I remember a show in Brussels in 1956, at the Palais des Beaux Arts, where the films were received much better than the paintings. They organized a showing of *Form Phases IV* at the cine-club, along with Murnau's *Sunrise*, and I remember feeling a sort of excitement about the dramatic situation of presenting my work to an audience. It's very different from an art show: you never really know if you're making contact with people during an exhibition of paintings.

During that period, I began to consider the problems of free forms floating around. I'd rejected this earlier, trying to get some kind of plastic absolute. That's what had bothered me with the neo-plastic approach to things. In Mondrian, for example, the final absolute is verticals and horizontals. There's no way out, really, and I couldn't accept that. The neo-plasticians said that red was red, that it had a certain wave-length and was meant to be absorbed as a pure sensation. Likewise, blue was blue, and equally a pure sensation. And the two together made for a certain relationship which itself should remain pure. The neo-plasticians felt that the essence of art was in these relationships, and that they had to stay strictly within their own limitations and not take on any other meanings.

Q: Well, you've evolved considerably from that position since then.

Breer: Yes, films have completely liberated me in various ways. You can see it in the subject matter I have treated in my films. The Pope film, for example (*A Miracle*), is a sort of Kafka-like metamorphosis of a human being. Now, I feel that the color red can't be just the color red and have no other meaning. The consecutive fact of film allows for everything! You can mix up symbols and conventions: a red can be a red, or it can be blood, or it can be confused. We deal with metaphors in our experience, and the words we use can have emotional qualities. So can colors and forms. In a sense, I don't entirely believe in abstract films, although I must say that people seem to read into *A Man And His Dog Out For Air* a lot more from its title than what I actually conceived when I made the images. I can describe it as a sort of stew: once in a while something recognizable comes to the surface and disappears again. Finally at the end you see the man and his dog, and it's a kind of joke. The title and the bird songs make you expect to see the man and his dog, and it's the absurdity that makes audiences accept what is basically a free play of lines and pure rhythms.

Q: You have said that your films are constructed like paintings. Is that not self-contradictory?

Breer: In the first place, my films are not literary. The only

From *Jamestown Baloos* (1957) by Robert Breer, a collage film which mixes photographs, newspaper clippings, and painted effects.

literature involved in *A Man And His Dog Out For Air* is its title. That's the whole scenario, and it's almost like the title of a painting which one puts on when the painting is finished. Then, *A Man And His Dog* is constructed from the middle towards both ends. I started with an image which evoked a feeling, and I expanded this feeling in several directions. I work at a painting in very much the same way: you put down a color, which has a relationship to the canvas, and you put down another which alters the relationship, and so forth. The results of this way of working aren't exactly predictable, and in *A Man And His Dog*, for instance, there's a peculiar thing at the end which I don't understand but which obviously tickles the audience. I don't think I could ever find the same spot again, at least not consciously.

I think of a film as a "space image" which is presented for a certain length of time. As with a painting, this image must submit to the subjective projection of the viewer and undergo a certain modification. Even a static painting has a certain time dimension, determined by the viewer to suit his needs and wishes. In film, this period of looking is determined by the artist and imposed on the spectator, his captive audience. A painting can be "taken in" immediately, that is, it is present in its total self at all time. My own approach to film is that of a painter—that is, I try to present the total image right away, and the images following are merely other aspects of and equivalent to the first and final image. Thus the whole work is constantly presented from beginning to end and, though in constant transformation, is at all times its total self. Obviously, then, there is no denouement, no gradual revelation except for the constantly changing aspects of the statement, in the same manner in which a painting is subjectively modified during viewing.

Q: Are you not trying to say the cinematic form and abstract painting form are compatible?

Breer: No, I think they are *in*compatible, at least in my own work. What I've just said is a kind of subjective analysis of the creative processes which I am sometimes conscious of as I make my films. But it's clear to me that the language of painting and the language of cinema have little in common. In my canvasses, I used to make rectangles dance around, like ballet dancers, because of the strict relationships I imposed on them. But as soon as I put them in a fluid medium such as cinema and made them dance, my ballerinas became elephants! Not only that, but the camera had broken up the fixity of the relationships, there was no longer any need for rectangles as such, and I could change my forms completely. I started from scratch all over again.

The only thing I've carried directly from my painting days is a practical discipline which I have observed also in other artists who have transformed to films: that of working alone, at the artisan level. I almost *have* to work that way, and that's why I've had to invent my own shortcuts to making animated films, such as my flip-cards, which make it possible for me to see the action before I actually shoot it on the camera. . . .

I think that the reproduction of the semblance of natural movement is but one of the many possibilities of cinema. For me, the cinema medium is just an arbitrary thing which was invented that way to provide for the reproduction of natural movements. What I'm interested in is to attack the basic material, to tear up film, pick up the pieces and rearrange them. I'm interested in the domain between motion and still pictures. It seems to me that in animation, particularly, the search for the reproduction of natural movements plays far too big a role. Whether stylized or not, I don't think one *needs* to conceive of movements as related directly to those observed in reality. There's more to cinema than creating the illusion of psychologically anthropomorphic movements.

I would rather define a special approach to "abstraction in cinema" by using the word "unrelationship." The initial assumption in unrelationship is that literature is an overrefined and specialized means of expression with only incidental utility in the process of making continuous imagery, or "motion pictures." Words are sophisticated pictures used for the transmission of ideas; "unrelationship," itself a word, indicates a type of cinema built around the art of the non-rational, non-reasonable association of images. There can be no scenario for this type of film, but you must not confuse it with "abstract art"—which pretends to be a world of pure sensations, where red is red. In the new use of cinema, blood is red, and red is red, and the confusion is possible and right. The new imagery I speak of simultaneously appeals to all known and unknown levels of awareness, using the full range of stimuli from primary colors through pictograms to the written and spoken word. The nature of movie film permits the combination in concentrated form of great quantities of diverse materials and interpretations.

Q: One comment heard about experimental films in general is that most of them fall into the category either of trying to reproduce on the screen the subjectivity of mental disorder, or else trying to induce in the audience a kind of mental disorder through the use of unrelated images. It has been said that although such attempts may be occasionally successful, they are a singularly fruitless and unrewarding form of artistic communication.

Breer: Well, the key word you use is disorder, by which I understand formlessness. There are many formless films which have no other purpose than to "épater les badauds," and I agree that these won't last. But you know very well that one cries disorder when one is unable to sense the real order, the esthetic relationships which have in fact been put into the materials. I know it's not easy, but what I constantly try to do in my films is set up what is to be expected of them, even if this is the unexpected, so that audiences will know where they are. My films, if nothing else, are formal: they are concerned with overall form. There are some conventions normal to most films which don't apply in mine, and I've had to forcibly tell the audience that it shouldn't expect the normal notions of continuity. I'm very much concerned with a new kind of continuity; even if it's anti-continuity, it still has a form. Take *Blazes*, for instance. It's a film where notions of continuity are shattered. The succession of abstract pictures follows so quickly and is so different from one to the next that one doesn't accurately see any one picture, but has the impression of thousands. It's a form of visual orgasm. I put the spectator off the track to such a point that he becomes passive and forgets notions of con-

tinuity. He can no longer anticipate the images and is too bombarded to remember the past images. He is forced to just sit there and take the thing in as an actuality: the violence is just a by-product.

Actually, any disruption of normal thought patterns is bound to have an effect, and people often will call that "disorder." Some people stalk out of my films, and are angered. I'd like to think that out of that reaction, people will eventually be brought to see the films as I see them.

Q: But what about boredom? What about the people that are bored by your films?

Breer: Ah, boredom. I'm against boredom. I can work with outrage, but I'm sorry to have to bore anyone. If I had to choose, I'd much rather anger them, though I should say that the eventual goal is pleasure, viz, joy.

(From *Film Culture*, No. 27, 1962.)

A STATEMENT
by Robert Breer

Single images one after another in quick succession fusing into motion . . . this is cinema. For the 60 years of its existence it has been used mainly as a recording instrument, and as an abstract painter I first came to cinema looking for a way to record the myriad form-color relationships I had encountered in painting.

Hoping somehow to preserve the formal purity of the fixed image in this dynamic new medium, I made several attempts to do so by simply imposing movement on the space relationships of my paintings. The resulting breakdown of these relationships and the intrusion of anecdote in these early films forced me to explore deeper into the cinematographic medium itself.

In 1954 I made the following experiment: I exposed six feet of film one frame at a time, as usual in animation, but with this important difference—each image was as unlike the preceding one as possible. The result was 240 distinctly different optical sensations packed into 10 seconds of vision. By cementing together both ends of this film strip to form a loop, I was able to project it over and over for long periods. I was surprised to discover that this repetition did not become monotonous because the eye constantly discovered new images. I am only now beginning to fully appreciate the importance of this experiment which has shown me a way finally to preserve the integrity of compositions in space while modifying them in time. *By simply limiting the viewer of a painting to 1/24th of a second I produce one unit of cinema and by adding several of these units together I produce a motion picture.*

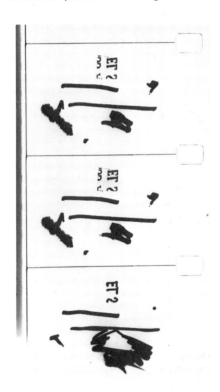

From *Breathing* (1963) by Robert Breer.

Whereas the usual intention in animation has been to represent natural movement and to do this by gradual modification of forms permitting the eye to blend them into fluid motion, I began treating the single images as individual sensations to be experienced separately, more in counterpoint than in harmony. I find myself combining freely very disparate images and finally using continuous motion simply as a means to connect up the various fixed images. This technique tends to destroy dramatic development in the usual sense and a new continuity emerges in the form of a very dense and compact texture. When pushed to extremes the resulting vibration brings about an almost static image on the screen.

(From a statement dated April 1959, and published in *Film Culture*, No. 29, 1963.)

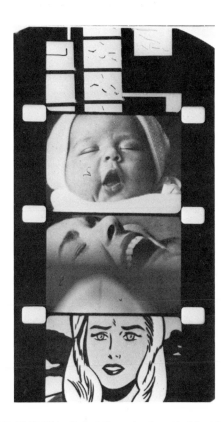

From *Fist Fight* (1964) by Robert Breer. As shown in this strip of frames rapid-fire collage imagery is created by putting a distinctly different image on every frame.

INTERVIEW WITH ROBERT BREER

The animated cartoon is just that—an outgrowth of the newspaper cartoon strip and has stayed pretty close to the stylistic conventions of its antecedents, appealing on the same level to the same audience. While I admire and enjoy the best of these, my own interest is in eliciting deeper responses from myself and others. The animation technique happens to suit my purposes, but as a former painter, I am trained to challenge conventions rather than accept them. Those I have accepted have to do with attitudes to the material itself and this is why I have chosen single frame filmmaking. The single frame is the basic unit of film just as bricks are basic units of brick houses, and blades of grass basic units of lawns. In any case it's because of this special interest plus a love of drawing as such that I can even be included in an inquiry like this. I am really not part of the animation scene as normally defined.

Animation implies making something inaminate appear to be animate; though single frame filmmaking can include that, it isn't necessarily confined to that. A lot of my films don't involve the illusion of motion at all but are constructed out of time intervals and space changes.

Q: How and why did you get into animation?

Breer: My film roots are Richter, Eggeling, Léger, Man Ray, Vigo, Len Lye [see Chapter 2]. I was a painter to begin with. My work certainly came out of a period of innovation in art (i.e., Cubism, Dada and Neoclassicism) and it's in this spirit that I became interested in film. It was a relatively unexplored medium.

I started making films in 1952. The first films were animated—single frame. I was painting simple geometric abstractions at the time, so the first attempts consisted of taking the forms of my paintings and composing them on film. Those first films were really sketches of abstract paintings. It seemed natural at first to treat each frame individually as though it were a painting. In fact, I found I could treat the whole film as if it were a painting. I felt I could deal with movement later, which I did of course. I made an experiment in the middle fifties combining completely unrelated single frames on a loop of film. One frame would be a shot of my hand—the next frame would be the head of my cat that I grabbed (gently) and stuck under the camera—and so forth, as a pure experiment. There was no continuity as such, but there was tremendous visual activity and stimulus. After that, I did everything from continuous line drawings to very, very rapid collage. I'm probably best known for the latter. I guess that I pushed that experience of disparate single frames further than anyone else. My animation is mainly related to art and its conventions, though sometimes cartooning has crept in.

Q: You have also done some work for television, haven't you? For The Electric Company? *Do you like that sort of work?*

Breer: Well, I liked the people I worked with in those cases, but I am really not that adaptable, apparently, and always find that I haven't had enough experience to keep from bending too far in what I assume to be their direction and selling out a little bit. I don't like to start from somebody else's ideas. When I do that I think it diminishes my powers.

Q: What exactly are you trying to accomplish in your animation?

Breer: I am trying to work out my destiny quietly with the least amount of interference between my work and whatever my audience could be. It certainly could be bigger than it is. With this in mind, any help with dissemination would be appreciated.

Q: What are the needs of animation right now?

Breer: I have no idea about needs for animation on a commercial level. I do have a feeling that my own films and others like them could enjoy a much bigger audience if some of the energy used by cartoon factories to corner the market were used in promoting our own efforts, and that the feedback would be beneficial to everyone in the long run. As it is now, the experimenters (and I include myself with a lot of other people) are being quietly ripped off and absorbed into the commercial mainstream. For example, this single-frame collage technique that some other people and myself really developed has been abysmally distorted, stolen and run into the ground, without any benefit to us. There can be an isolation in striking out on your own. It takes such effort to open doors to new things that the easy road is often taken. . . .

(From *The American Film Institute Report*, Vol. 5, No. 2, Summer 1974.)

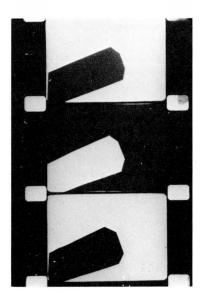

From *69* (1968) by Robert Breer, a color film composed of flickering geometric forms, lines, and movements.

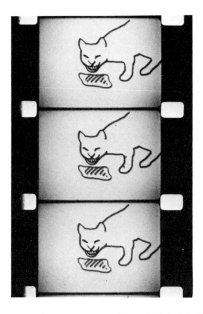

From *Gulls and Buoys* (1972) by Robert Breer. Both in this film and *Fuji*, a variation of the rotoscope technique has been employed. Traditionally it consists of tracing line drawings one frame at a time from live-action footage. Breer, however, graphically simplifies, restructures, and stylizes the original live-action imagery according to his own artistic vision.

Harry Smith

Harry Smith. (Photo by Arthur Cantrill.)

Harry Smith's character, like his films, is complex and surrounded by an element of mystery. Very few details, therefore, are known about his life and artistic career. Since an accurate biography in the conventional sense would be impossible, the following profile by his close friend Jonas Mekas may provide helpful insights into his personality and work.

THE MAGIC CINEMA OF HARRY SMITH
by Jonas Mekas

Does Harry Smith really exist? Is he a black or a white magician? Who will be the next victim of Harry Smith? What horrors is he preparing, and for whom?

For years Harry Smith has been a black and ominous legend and a source of strange rumors. Some even said that he had left this planet long ago—the last alchemist of the Western world, the last magician.

Then one day, last summer, a year ago, Harry Smith gave up the darkness and appeared in the open. He was still full of evil, hate, small curses, and sneers, but he came out. We began looking into him, peeking into Harry Smith. And we were surprised to find, behind the beard and the curses, a sweet, humorous, and completely harmless man. We found that his little curses were only a protective wall, not an attack on others. The black magic was suddenly gone.

But not entirely.

Soon we discovered where Harry Smith's true magic was. Last Monday, at the Cinémathèque, the audience gave Harry Smith a huge ovation. For three hours Harry Smith was pouring across the screen the most beautiful images conceivable. Here was a magician of images, of motion, of rhythms, of color. One of the greatest magicians of cinema alive.

For thirty years Harry Smith worked on these movies, secretly, like an alchemist, and he worked out his own formulas and mixtures to produce these fantastic images. You can watch them for pure color enjoyment; you can

From *No. 1* (ca. 1940) by Harry Smith. Animated shapes were created by drawing directly on 35mm celluloid.

watch them for motion—Harry Smith films never stop moving; or you can watch them for hidden and symbolic meanings, alchemic signs. There are more levels in Harry Smith's work than in any other film animator I know. . . . Harry Smith is the only serious film animator working in cinema today. His untitled work on alchemy and the creation of the world (none of Harry Smith's movies have titles) will remain one of the masterpieces of the animated cinema. But even his smaller works are marked by the same masterful and never-failing sense of movement—the most magic quality of Harry Smith's work.

Not all his work is pleasant and happy. Some of it tastes of horror. But it is always a total expression of a unique personality, a unique world, both evil and kind—open, lyrical, and paranoiac.

(From *Movie Journal*, 1965.)

INTERVIEW WITH HARRY SMITH
by P. Adams Sitney

My first film was made by imprinting off the cork of an ink bottle and all that sort of thing, as I said before. The second one was made with Kum Kleen gum dots, automatic adhesive dots that Dick Foster got for me. It's like a paper dot with gum on the back. The film was painted over with a brush to make it wet, then with a mouth-type spray gun, dye was sprayed onto the film. When that dried the whole film was greased with vaseline. Of course this was in short sections—maybe six foot long sections. Anyway they would be tacked down. With a pair of tweezers, the dots were pulled off. That's where those colored balls drop and that sort of stuff. Being as it was pulled off, it was naturally dry where the dot had been and that part which had been colored was protected by the vaseline coating at this point. Then color was sprayed into where the dot had been. After that dried, the whole film was cleaned with carbon tetrachloride.

The next one was made by putting masking tape onto the film and slitting the tape lightly with a razor blade and a ruler, and then picking off all those little squares that are revolving around. I worked off and on on that film for about five years pretty consistently; I worked on it every day at least. I may have abandoned it at one point for three months or six months at the most. . .

#1 took a very long time. Either a day or a week. Then *#2* which was much longer than the form it is in now: It was actually at least half an hour long—it was cut down to match a recording by Dizzy Gillespie, which I believe is called Guacha Guero. It took maybe a year to make. Then on the next one I worked on about five years, then I gave up that particular style. There were maybe eight years of it. I developed certain really complicated hand-painting techniques of which I made only short versions. For example, painting the whole film a certain color and then smearing vaseline on it; and then taking a stylus and scraping designs off. It is possible to get a lot of spirals and curvilinear designs which I was never able to get by cutting off the masking tape; then spraying bleach into the place where the groove was. I made short samples of that sort of material. As I say, less than half of all that stuff is in my possession at this point. I also made alternate versions of a great number of scenes. Sometimes, in order to demonstrate how it was done, I made up special reels that partially had the masking tape still left on, and partially the first . . . Anyway, there are thousands of feet that were never printed, and several entire very long films. Many of those films are missing totally. I never edited at all, except to cut them down—except that second one, which shows the balls falling. Like I say, it was at least 1,200 feet long originally. It was then cut down to a hundred feet to make it match Guacha Guero. What Jonas Mekas calls *The Magic Feature* (#12) was originally about six hours long, and then it was edited down, first to a two-hour version, and then down to a one-hour version. There was also an enormous amount of material made for that picture. None of the really good material that was constructed for that film was ever photographed. There was a Noah's ark scene with really fantastic animals. I started out with the poorer stuff. The really good things were supposed to be toward the end of the film, but, being as the end of the film was never made . . .

On that Oz film, that expensive one, of course, I had quite a few people working; so that all kinds of special cut-outs were made that were never photographed. I mean really wonderful ones were made! One cut-out might take someone two months to make. They were very elaborate stencils and so forth. All of my later films were never quite completed. Most of the material was never shot, because the film dragged on too long.

Those two optically printed films were made for the Guggenheim Foundation. The three-dimensional one was made from the same batch of stencils as the color one. First, I got a camera from Frank Stauffacher, which is when those two films were made: The first is called *Circular Tensions* (#5); I forgot what the other one is called. The black and white one (#4) precedes that.

Q: The black and white film (#4) begins with a shot of—

Smith: —a painting. It is a painting of a tune by Dizzy Gillespie called Manteca. Each stroke in that painting represents a certain note on the recording. If I had the record, I could project the painting as a slide and point to a certain thing. This is the main theme in there, which is a-doot-doot-dootdoot-doot-doottadootdoot; those curved lines up there. See, ta-doot-doot-doot-doot-dootaloot-dootaloot, and so forth. Each note is on there. The most complex one of these is this one, one of Charlie Parker's records, I don't remember the name of it. That's

From *No. 12* (*The Magic Feature*) (ca. 1958) by Harry Smith, an animated surrealistic collage film.

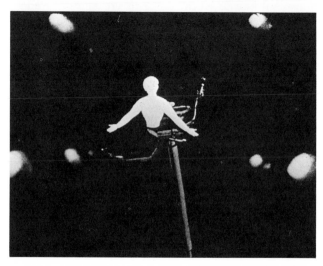

a really complex painting. That took five years. Just like I gave up making films after that last hand-drawn one took a number of years, I gave up painting after that took a number of years to make; it was just too exhausting. There's a dot for each note and the phrases that the notes consist of are colored in a certain way or made in a certain path. The last paintings that I made were realistic things connected with the Tówer of Babel. There was an extraordinary one of the control room of the Tower of Babel, which was built into a railway car leaving it. That painting was derived from a scene in Buster Keaton's film *The General*, where he chops out the end of the box car. A special film was projected onto the painting so that all the machinery operates.

In a number of cases I've made special screens to project films on. All those so-called early abstract films had special painted screens for them. They were made of dots and lines. All those things disappeared. . .

Later I borrowed a camera from Hy Hirsh. He had a pretty good camera, a Bell and Howell model 70-something, and had seen my films. The San Francisco Museum showed that one of the grille works (#4) that precedes *Circular Tensions*, and he came up and spoke. That's when I asked for a camera. I've never owned a camera; I've usually just borrowed one, then pawned it. That's always an embarrassing scene: trying to explain to the person where his or her camera is. I can remember Frank Stauffacher saying to me, "Now you haven't pawned the camera, have you?" He said this jokingly, but it was pawned. Usually, people get their cameras back, eventually. My later films were made with one that belonged to Sheba Ziprin. The *Mysterioso* film (#11) and the

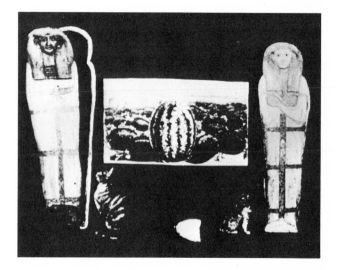

long black and white film (*#12*) were shot with her camera, which is now in a pawn shop in Oklahoma City. The main parts of my film in Oklahoma last year were shot on a camera that belonged to Stuart Reed. That camera is in a barber shop in Anadarko, Oklahoma, where Mr. A's Wollensak also is, unfortunately.

After I first stopped making films, I made those paintings that you point at. Unless you've seen those, it's hard to describe what they really are. They are at least as good as the films. I'd been able to hear Charlie Parker and Thelonious Monk, both of whom had come to San Francisco but wanted to make one final thing, another painting of Thelonious. When I came to N.Y.C., I realized that it would be impossible to make it in the form of a painting, because his music was so complex, and it would be better to make a film. I hadn't made films for at least five years by then. *#10* was a study for the *Mysterioso* film. Generally speaking, those films were made by trying to collect interesting pictures, cutting them out, and then filing them. I had enormous files, possibly only 2 or 3 per cent of which was shot. I had worked on this one thing for twenty years, having collected a lot of that stuff before; but then, when I left San Francisco, I gave it to Broughton, because I felt that he might do something with it; but he obviously never did.

After I came here I started filming again. Toward the end, I had everything filed in glassine envelopes: any kind of vegetable, any kind of animal, any kind of this, that, and the other thing, in all different sizes. Then file cards were made up. For example, everything that was congruent to that black and white film (*#12*) was picked out. All the permutations possible were built up: say, there's a hammer in it, and there's a vase, and there's a woman, and there's a dog. Various things could then be done—hammer hits dog; woman hits dog: dog jumps into vase; so forth. It was possible to build up an enormous number of cross references.

This was all written on little slips of paper, the file cards—the possible combinations between this, that, and the other thing. The file cards were then rearranged, in an effort to make a logical story out of it. Certain things would have to happen before others: Dog-runs-with-watermelon has to occur after dog-steals-watermelon.

I tried as much as possible to make the whole thing automatic, the production automatic rather than any kind of logical process. Though, at this point, Allen Ginsberg denies having said it, about the time I started making those films, he told me that William Burroughs made a change in the Surrealistic process—because, you know, all that stuff comes from the Surrealists—that business of folding a piece of paper: One person draws the head and then folds it over, and somebody else draws the body. What do they call it? The Exquisite Corpse. Somebody later, perhaps Burroughs, realized that something was directing it, that it wasn't arbitrary, and that there was some kind of what you might call God. It wasn't just chance. Some kind of universal process was directing these so-called arbitrary processes; and so I proceeded on that basis: Try to remove things as much as possible from the consciousness or whatever you want to call it so that the manual processes could be employed entirely in moving things around. As much as I was able, I made it automatic.

I must say that I'm amazed, after having seen the black-and-white film (*#12*) last night, at the labor that went into it. It is incredible that I had enough energy to do it. Most of my mind was pushed aside into some sort of theoretical sorting of the pieces, mainly on the basis that I have described: First, I collected the pieces out of old catalogues and books and whatever; then made up file cards of all possible combinations of them; then, I spent maybe a few months trying to sort the cards into logical order. A script was made for that. All the script and the pieces were made for a film at least four times as long. There were wonderful masks and things cut out. Like when the dog pushes the scene away at the end of the film, instead of the title "end" what is really there is a transparent screen that has a candle burning behind it on which a cat fight begins—shadow forms of cats begin fighting. Then, all sorts of complicated effects; I had held these off. The radiations were to begin at this point. Then Noah's ark appears. There were beautiful scratch-board drawings, probably the finest drawings I ever made—really pretty. Maybe 200 were made for that one scene. Then there's a graveyard scene, when the dead are all raised again. What actually happens at the end of the film is everybody's put in a teacup, because all kinds of horrible monsters came out of the graveyard, like animals that folded into one another. Then everyone gets thrown in a teacup, which is made out of a head, and stirred up. This is the Trip to Heaven and the Return, then the Noah's Ark, then The Raising of the Dead, and finally the Stirring of Everyone in a Teacup. It was to be in four parts. The script was made up for the whole works on the basis of sorting pieces. It was exhaustingly long in its original form. When I say that it was cut, mainly what was cut out was, say, instead of the little man bowing and then standing up, he would stay bowed down much longer in the original. The cutting that was done was really a correction of timing. It's better in its original form. . .

(From *Film Culture*, Summer 1965.)

From No. 12 (*The Magic Feature*) by Harry Smith. Originally intended to be projected through a series of masking slides such as the two symmetrical images shown here, *No. 12* was so technically complex that the slides and film have only been shown together once. The slides were projected with specially designed apparatus, and take the form of images that appear on the film itself. The main purpose of these masking slides was to contain the animated movement and transform the outer shape of the screen.

Carmen D'Avino

Carmen D'Avino.

Carmen D'Avino, like many artists in the field of experimental animation, is a painter who has expanded his vision through the medium of film. By means of stop-motion photography, D'Avino has created a delightful form of motion painting in which complex ornamental designs appear to magically paint themselves. Surfaces, objects, and even total environments are whimsically transformed by an endless flow of beautiful and rhythmic patterns.

Born in Waterbury, Connecticut, in 1918, D'Avino began his formal art training at the Art Students' League in New York. During World War II he served as a combat photographer with the Fourth Infantry Division of the United States Army and was on hand to film the invasion of Normandy and the liberation of Paris. After the war he stayed in France to study painting at the Ecole des Beaux

Arts and, following a 1948–49 trip to India, he enrolled in the Ecole Technique de Photographie et Cinématographie. Returning to New York, D'Avino began to experiment seriously with animation and won a Creative Film Foundation award in 1956 with his four-minute color film, *Theme and Transition* (1956). Since then he has continued to receive prizes and grants, including Academy Award nominations for *Pianissimo* (1963) and *Background* (1974). D'Avino, on a selective basis, makes animated shorts for network television and large corporations like IBM, in addition to his personal film work.

INTERVIEW WITH CARMEN D'AVINO

Q: You were a serious painter for many years before you turned to animation. How and why did you make the transition from painting to film?

D'Avino: Photography, as far as I can remember, has always paralleled my interest in painting. I bought my first movie camera when I was 15 years old and since that time I have, in one form or another, continued to work with both still and motion picture photography. However, painting was my serious interest and photography, at first, was more like a hobby to me. It wasn't until after World War II, when I was living in Paris on the G.I. bill, that I became seriously interested in film. I made two documentaries while in Europe and later when I returned to the United States in about 1951, I began to experiment with the techniques of animation. As I worked with the single frame technique I began to realize that painting could be expanded and enlarged by using the filmic elements of time and motion. At this point I began to relate my work in the field of painting to film animation and then it was just a matter of continuing on.

Q: There is a long and rich tradition of painters and sculptors who have turned to film animation as a form of expression. Your work, of course, is part of this tradition along with the work of Hans Richter, Len Lye, Robert Breer, and many others. How do you relate this kind of filmmaking to the overall field of cinema?

D'Avino: Painters and sculptors who have worked seriously and creatively with experimental film animation regard cinema primarily as a visual art form. All of the artists working within this tradition recognize the power and creative potential of the single frame and relate their imagery not to theater, but to the modernist tradition of painting and sculpture. From this unique perspective the artist-turned-animator has made, and is making, an enormous contribution to the visual language and grammar of motion pictures....

My views about animation and the motion picture medium largely stem from my work in the field of painting. As a result of my background and experience in the arts, I approach cinema as a nonnarrative form of expression and tend to think about it in terms of my former craft. For example, I closely associate filmmaking with painting because the single frame has, for me, the same elemental importance as the brush stroke. In both of these arts a personal style can be expressed by structuring an accumulation of basic units. The obvious difference, of course, is that in filmmaking 24 separate pictures make up one second of time on the screen and create the illusion of movement. Nevertheless, in reality each frame is a single static picture or individual component which can be artistically integrated by a process which parallels the technique of painting.

Eisenstein's artistic and visual approach to filmmaking, with his montage technique and regard for each segment of film, came close to expressing the importance of each single frame. Had he approached cinema through the technique of animation, it is probable that the single frame would have loomed quite significantly in his mind. Live action and the running camera have a way of obliterating the true function of film. One tends to break down component scenes, hook them together so as to produce a fluid harmony, and finally tell a story. In this regard the single frame has no particular importance since it is camouflaged by the overall presence of actors and live action. Relating this to painting, one might say that the canvas reveals a story or presents a portrait, but the brush strokes are unimportant. If this were true, personal expression in art would be severely inhibited. In the structural buildup of any work lies the character and individualism of the artist. Unfortunately, in the cinema the value of the single frame has been disregarded by everyone except a small group of animators and experimentalists. Film, up to the present time, has been literal, illustrating its story and largely ignoring other contemporary forms of expression. It has not, for example, paralleled the modern development of painting and is shamefully retarded in this area. As a result of this narrow approach, the single and solitary film frame awaits its discovery. When the realization of its importance coincides with the proper timing, a breakthrough will occur and bring about the first major revolution in the art of film. From that significant step into the future the growth will be frantic and inspiring, and filmmaking will be capable of new meaning and more powerful forms of imagery.

Q: In your animated films painted images grow and evolve so that surfaces and environments appear literally to be painting themselves. Would you discuss the development of this technique and how these beautiful and unusual effects are created?

D'Avino: This technique, which I call dimensional animation by the way, was first used in my film *The Room.* Essentially the technique consists of drawing and paint-

Carmen D'Avino, around 1958, shown at work on *The Room.*

143

ing, in-between frames, on surfaces and objects that exist in space. For example, I add (or brush on) one-quarter of an inch of paint, take one or two frames, and then keep repeating this process. It is a difficult method of filming because it is slow and tedious, yet requires spontaneous decision making. Too much planning, for example, could stifle its exciting, organic possibilities. *The Room*, in terms of its form, was a very strange realization for me. I really can't say how or why it came about because I don't know. However, the films that followed *The Room*, like *Stone Sonata* and *Pianissimo*, for example, were a natural development or continuation of my original idea. After *The Room*, it became a matter of pushing and expanding the artistic possibilities of this technique as far as I could. Although I don't know exactly how dimensional animation originated, the technique and its evolution is obviously in some way a kinetic extension of my earlier work in the plastic arts....

I structure my films very carefully, but improvisation also plays a very important part in their development. The structured aspect of my animation, however, is not verbal like traditional theatrical films, but is a highly visual concept. Within this abstract visual structure I improvise to further develop the form of my films by spontaneously reacting to the animation process itself. The use of structure and improvisation in my animated films is perhaps closer to expressionism in painting than anything I could compare it with in the field of filmmaking.

Q: Your animated films are basically one-man endeavors. Do you feel that you must do everything yourself in order to produce a cohesive and artistic film?

D'Avino: Yes, it is very important for me to have personal control over the art and craft of my films. The myth that motion pictures must rely on groups of many individuals has been with us too long. It is a false premise which grew out of a massive industry. This inflated idea continues to hold sway because we are in an age of specialization and it is presumed that the art of cinema is too complex for a single person. By comparison, it would be amusing to contend that the visual arts, such as painting, sculpture, etching, or lithography were far too complex for any artist to master. In reality, most artists, who are properly trained are proficient in most aspects of their craft, but choose to follow their individual preferences for personal reasons. Just because we are inundated with films that require the unique talents of many people does not mean that films cannot be created by individuals. It would be unfair, on the other hand, to deny that some very significant films have been

produced, and will continue to be produced, by groups of specialists. However, the fact that notable films have been created by a collaborative effort only strengthens my view that the individual approach is capable of generating a greater and more diversified number of films worthy of the name art. Filmmakers, then, should ignore the idea that their expressive powers must rely on an assembly line system, and instead they should depend on their individual initiative just as artists have always done in the past.

Q: You have made one cameraless film called A Trip. *Would you discuss how and why you made this delightful but unusual animated film?*

From *A Talk with Carmen D'Avino* (1972) by Cecile Starr. Samples of D'Avino's technique are included in the filmed interview, for which D'Avino did several short animated sequences.

D'Avino: As I recall I couldn't use my 16mm camera because it had broken down, so I decided to play with the physical properties of some discarded 16mm film that I had on hand. The film that I used was exposed footage with images on it, which had been edited out of another film. Basically, *A Trip* was made by mutilating the film in a variety of ways. I began, for example, by scumbling and scratching the photographic image already on the film; a procedure which formed an overall mottled and pastel pattern. Eventually the image disappeared and in its place a background of unusual color tones became evident. With this start, I began applying ink and drew lines on each frame with the aid of a magnifying glass. A 16mm frame is a very small area in which to work, requiring a great deal of patience and determination. After inking in a number of frames and projecting the results, I began to see the suggested illusion of a train ride. I then began to work earnestly with the concept of a trip by rail. From then on it was a question of giving variation to the theme. I proceeded to put some of the film into dyes which were poured out into the bathtub, and continued to draw on the film after it dried out. I also used a needle to scratch into the film's emulsion and then rubbed colored felt marker pencils into the scratched portions for some more train-track effects. The result was an interesting two-minute film which has been shown in many of the international film festivals. I consider this a good example of how a creative film can be inexpensively molded out of scraps of useless film. The entire production was made without lights, camera, exposure meter, tripod, and all the other assorted paraphernalia usually required to make a motion picture. . . .

Q: Do you experiment with highly specialized equipment of any kind?

D'Avino: No, not really. My techniques are basically simple and direct. I think that highly specialized mechanical and electronic gadgets, coupled with the camera and other motion picture apparatus, tend to limit creative thought. One lazily begins to rely on the function and precision of the so-called practical instruments only to produce the same banal and repetitive solutions. The reason early cinema was exciting and prospered is due primarily to its primitive production methods. One had, out of necessity, to rely on imagination. The equipment lacked those specialized means which so handicap originality today. It is requisite in the film industry today to master machines rather than expressive force. As a result, we have a multitude of technicians but very few creative artists.

Working on his *A Finnish Fable* (1964–65), D'Avino applies a spot of paint to a mannequin.

Q: What new possibilities or directions do you feel should be explored in the field of cinema?

D'Avino: In considering the new possibilities for cinema, I would like to begin by saying that the present and popular form, because of its theatrical origins, has placed severe limitations on the scope and expressive range of the medium. Not that great achievements haven't been produced under this rigid system, but because of its acceptance by the general public and its huge profits, cinema has evolved at a snail's pace. Unfortunately, a strong tradition was established in film before any artistry could intrude. Had the cinema remained more obscure, without the exploitation by business enterprises, we might have had accomplishments beyond what we so readily accept as a triumphant expression of the medium.

Although popularity and profit, in the beginning, made possible certain marvelous technical advancements, I have no doubt that it also stifled the growth and artistic potential of film. If some artistic daring existed then, and continues to exist now, it is only because, thank God, the artist is still with us on every level. Even within limited means of expressions, the creative person finds new ways to explore his medium to the fullest. Despite the inhibiting effects of industry and finance, the infinite possibilities inherent in the art of motion pictures compel the artist to investigate its contagious beauty. The time is ripe and we are due for some courageous and thoughtful pioneering in the field of cinema.

Q: What is your next animation project?

D'Avino: I plan to make a film using a very old, worn, and rusted wicker baby carriage as the central image or theme. This old carriage, with its latent poetic possibilities, will journey through a landscape. I have been thinking about this work for a long time and I hope to start on it this spring. It will probably contain many of the animation techniques that I've used in my other films. Hopefully it will be a beautiful and interesting film to watch, and one that will have a special meaning.

(From a written interview conducted by Robert Russett, November 1974.)

A rich variety of assemblage material and graphic effects was used by D'Avino in creating *Background* (1974).

146

Jerome Hill

In 1968 Jerome Hill produced *Canaries*, a beautiful and poetic fantasy that combines live-action cinematography with hand-painted color and animated effects. Below, Hill discusses how he came to make this unusual four-minute film and describes in detail the demanding physical and artistic task of hand painting "negative" colors and images directly onto processed 35mm film.

Jerome Hill was born in St. Paul, Minnesota, and entered Yale University at the age of seventeen. There he majored in musical composition, designed sets for the "Yale Dramat" and co-directed a feature-length film version of *Tom Jones*. Following his graduation in 1927 he traveled to Europe and studied drawing and painting at the British Academy in Rome and at the Scandinavian Academy in Paris. While in Europe he was drawn more and more to filmmaking as a medium of expression and collaborated with friends on several film projects which were never fully completed. In 1932 he bought his own motion picture camera and after a brief period of pure experimentation with time, space, color, and light he made his first artistically cohesive film, an experimental work called *Fortune Teller*. Two documentary films, *Snow Flight* (1938) and *Seeing Eye* (1940) followed before he entered the service during World War II. After the war he continued to make documentaries, notably *Grandma Moses* (1950) and *Albert Schweitzer* (1950–57). In the early sixties Hill became interested in new forms of experimental cinema that were developing in America and made friends with many film artists associated with this movement, namely Stan Brakhage, James Broughton, Peter Kubelka, and Jonas Mekas. During this period he began a series of hand-painted animated films (among them *Canaries*) which marked his radical departure into more personal techniques and ideas. Other important films that were produced as a result of this extraordinary change of style include *Death In The Forenoon* (1966), *Merry Christmas* (1969) and perhaps his best known artistic work, *Film Portrait* (1965–71), an experimental feature-length autobiography. Jerome Hill died in 1972.

Jerome Hill.

HOW I CAME TO MAKE "CANARIES"
by Jerome Hill

It is always a satisfaction to do something that the authorities say cannot be done. In this case, the authorities were the laboratory workmen. "You can't paint on negative and expect it to last."

This was in 1967.

George Méliès at the beginning of the century had had the copies of several of his delightful films hand-tinted by an assembly line of apprentices. The tremulous effect of these delicate positive tones recalls the petals of flowers and the wings of butterflies. I was lucky enough to see these fantasies in my childhood, and the memory of them is indelible.

Several years ago, in a reckless attempt to emulate this technique with up-to-date overtones, I took an old bullfight film I had made in the 1930s, in 16mm black-and-white, and blew it up to 35mm color. Not really knowing what I was doing, I tried out various dyes and paints on the negative of this blow-up (emulsion side, of course), and using opposite coloration. The matador's cape had to be done in emerald green, to make it come out red. The bull himself was painted robin's egg blue. The results had the unexpected richness of a stained glass window. At the lab I was told it was "terrific," but that it wouldn't last,—said they.

The result of this interchange was a two-minute short called *Anticorrida or Who's Afraid of Ernest Hemingway?*. After running the negative through the printer dozens of times the positives still retained their original freshness (although the lab had assured me the colors wouldn't last).

The true revelation to me, during the making of *Anticorrida*, was that it was not enough to tint the elements that were already there on the exposed film, but that additional elements could be painted in,—a second bull, a lady with a lorgnette, a crowd of costumed revellers. There seemed to be no limit to the plasticity of this technique.

I felt it now imperative to do another picture,—to put color on color this time, and to shoot the material with subsequent negative-painting in mind. The subject was canaries. The terrace of my house in France was an embarrassment of ornithological riches—something like seven cages of various sizes and at least forty birds. The uninterrupted fusillade of song during the mating season was audible as far away as the neighboring beach. In filming we experimented with the stroboscopic effect of the bars of contiguous cages. The rhythms within rhythms set up by their swinging recalled the outpourings of the bird warblings.

The second pictorial element in this film—the pairs of lovers—was another constant. All the rocky shelves that surround the house (I live in an old fort) are covered with even more amorous couples than Antonioni dreamed up for his *Zabriskie Point*. Ours were filmed telescopically from concealed vantage points. Many of the people involved have subsequently assured me that they were not conscious of being spied out.

Next came the sound track. Twelve-tone "serial" music wasn't exactly my cup of tea. Although I loved to listen to it, I couldn't imagine creating it. But here was an opportunity. Why not, again, take a leaf from the canaries' contrapuntal outpourings? Instead of setting it down in an orchestrated score, why not give an atonal, (more or less) melody to each wind instrument, record them one by one on magnetic film, and mix them in the sound lab as one normally mixes the various tapes for a final track? The preliminary studies for this could be done on the moviola (2 tracks) and the sound readers (2 more tracks).

Last came the painting. Vibrant and rapid as the individual brush strokes appear in the finished product, they take an infinity of time to produce. Each tiny frame ends up a miniature painting. Probably three months (certainly many weeks) went into the painting of the four minutes of *Canaries*. The negative on which the miniscule brush strokes are made takes a terrible beating. To insure proper continuity, each element must be done from start to finish. That is to say, from entrance to exit. Each stage of it, luckily, can be sent to the lab, printed, verified, subsequent details added. Imagine the versatility of footage that can be added to *ad infinitum* without reshooting! Imagine the expediency of dropping out frames where the hand has slipped and made a senseless blob! Strangely enough, may I add, the sense of what one is doing takes over almost immediately. I had thought that all movement would have to be plotted out. Not at all! One look at three feet of film, let us say of a flight of birds, held up at arms length is enough to verify the smoothness and naturalness of their motions.

The little animated characters seem to have a life of their own. The foreground figures should be painted first so that later subsidiary figures can pass behind them. The one unsurmountable difficulty is the depicting of an unmovable object. The impossibility of reproducing identical brush strokes on successive frames results in the tremblings and flutterings that seem so natural to canaries.

One effect, subliminal probably, that even the most careful spectator has difficulty in analyzing is the rhythm set up by painting alternating frames in contrasting colors. The eye has probably never had to adjust to such rapid fluctuations. This is the origin of the vibrations that creep up on the girl while she is being kissed.

(From a statement to Cecile Starr, 1972.)

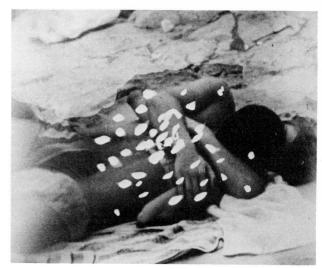

From *Canaries* (1968) by Jerome Hill, in which animated effects and hand coloring were added to live-action footage directly on the film negative.

Tony Conrad

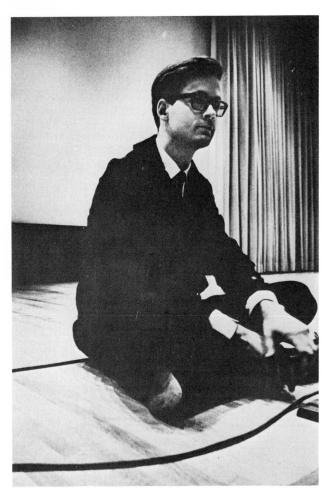

Tony Conrad.

animation to a mental-perceptual plan and explored esthetic possibilities of rhythmic stroboscopic effects. The subject of *The Flicker*, unlike other forms of animation, is not a graphically made configuration or moving image, but the dramatic intensity of pure intermittent light itself.

Presently teaching film at Antioch College, Conrad was born in Concord, New Hampshire, in 1940 and attended Harvard University, where he received a B.A. in Mathematics. After his graduation he moved to New York City and, in 1962, began a long working association with avant-garde musician-composer LaMonte Young. During this period Conrad was playing the "drone violin" and becoming active in underground film circles. He composed the sound track for Jack Smith's *Flaming Creatures*, as well as assisting with Ron Rice's *Chumlum*.

The experience of making *The Flicker* was to form the basis of his film work for the next seven years. Conrad, along with Paul Sharits and Peter Kubelka, is one of the best known of the film-artists who have worked with the flicker-frame effect. Using this technique of animation, Conrad produced *The Eye of Count Flickerstein* (1966), *Straight and Narrow* (1970), and *Four Square* (1971). Between 1968 and 1970 he made *Coming Attractions*, a feature-length narrative film which employs flicker effects and other optical techniques in conjunction with live-action cinematography. The recipient of grants from the Rockefeller Foundation and the American Film Institute, Conrad has had showings at the New York Film Festival, the Whitney Museum, Documenta, an exhibition of contemporary art and media in Germany, and the Museum of Modern Art. Since 1972, he has shifted his approach from perceptual forms of animation to other forms of experimental filmmaking.

The Flicker (1965) by Tony Conrad is a classic among modern experimental films. In this abstract work, Conrad created a new filmic condition by modulating the fundamental energy source of the cinema, projected light. By alternating solid black frames with solid white frames, in various patterns, he reduced the process of

ON "THE FLICKER"
by Tony Conrad
What will be my "first film," which will be incipherably entitled *The Flicker*, will actually consist of an elaborately contrived *tour de force* in a technique that has

interested me considerably for some time. My background in the analytical and physiological sciences has always tended to bend my esthetic inclinations in the direction of the ambiguous outer limits of human sensation, and these boundaries seem to be attracting more and more interest as people begin to discover the richness of the experiences to be had there. I personally think that the whole Op movement is merely a purification of ideas in this direction that started appearing with Impressionism or before. The most hypnotizing beauties in this realm remain undeveloped. Part of the reason for this is that to effectively manipulate creative materials that are initially unfamiliar, it really is necessary to get close to them and then to sit and wait awhile, to let the comfortable, reposeful feelings, that accompany the most cherished esthetic experiences, arise in connection with the new materials. So I always try to give an impression of serenity and repose whenever I work with extreme materials. . . .

The Flicker, conceived as a hallucinatory trip through unplumbed grottoes of pure sensory disruption, naturally has turned into a (superficially) very static flic, both aurally and visually. The soundtrack consists primarily of homemade electronic music composed indissolubly of tones (pitches) bordering closely on the lower range of audibility and of very rapid rhythms, rhythms whose speed is comparable in frequency to the tones. The confusion of pitch and rhythm that occurs in this range gives unexpected birth to a sense of aural vastness and spaciousness. The pitch-rhythm ambiguity has also enabled me to treat the tones as primitive rhythms and vice versa, so that there turns out to be a correlation here with some of the work that La Monte and I (and John Cale and Marian Zazeela) have done in harmony at slightly higher frequencies. This correlation is actually after-the-fact, since the electronic music arose in an independent context, but the advantage of the relationship is the suggestion of a working concept of rhythmic harmony. I do not bring up the sound first because it came first or even comes first in interest or importance, but because I found as I worked on the film that this same concept of rhythmic harmony turns out to be basic in the visual aspect as well. In fact, it seems that *The Flicker* may be interesting primarily as a basic study in the effectiveness of a whole range of operable visual harmonic relationships.

After a lecture La Monte delivered recently in Pittsburgh in conjunction with an appearance of our group there, an art student came up and asked me if there were not harmonic effects manifested visually by colors selected from different ranges of the light spectrum, in a way similar to the harmonic interactions of *sounds* that we had been discussing. I explained that there are two reasons why no such thing occurs with visible light. First, the eye does not respond to colors continuously, as the ear does to pitch, but only to small frequency *bands* (the color primaries). Second, the visible light frequencies fall within a range of less than an octave, to speak in harmonic terms, so that color "harmonies" produce no visible pattern. However, I did go on to say that there is a way to apply harmonic structure to light, and that is to modulate its intensity with time, leaving color momentarily out of the picture. This has to do with the stroboscopic use of light.

Let me cast obscurity aside after all this buildup by explaining that I have not attempted miracles, and that visually *The Flicker* is entirely stroboscopic. I have deliberately avoided any image at all, so that the entire film consists exclusively of black frames and white (clear) frames; nothing at all appears on the screen except the intermittent unobstructed light from the projector.

All this would sound quite improbable, fantasy-like, and apologetic to me, upon rereading, were it not for the fact that *The Flicker* is essentially finished, in the face of what have seemed at times insuperable odds, and were it not that I know well the power of the principles involved. This project has never had quite the stab-in-the-dark, analytically hypothesized quality that my buildup may suggest. In 1962 I first found that I could produce fantastic semi-hallucinatory and hypnotic effects using flicker from an altered 16mm projector. At that time Jack Smith and I spent a lot of time on flicker sessions, turning the rays loose on creatures and sets, and I did some startling experiments with color flicker. . . .

Since those first experiments, many people have begun to exploit flicker, in conjunction with dance, happenings, rock 'n roll shows, etc. etc. And flicker had been widespread before as well, though not nearly so much as during the last year; a tendency which I naturally foresaw in connection with both the Op and Psychedelic movements. In fact, it is widely known that flicker is the standard diagnostic test for epilepsy. It was used in World War I in treatment of battle neuroses. And so on. I devoted a good deal of time to researching the ramifications of these various applications, including my possible legal liability in the event of an unfortunate occurrence of unexpected epileptic seizure. It seems less than .01% of people are in *any* way prone to this. Nevertheless, I have included in the film a waiver of liability, since there are cases of this type on the books (in connection with ordinary silent films, apparently).

Technically, the range of perception of flicker or stroboscopic light is below a frequency of about 40 flashes per second (40 fps), above which the light is seen as continuous. Normal sound projection is at 24 fps. Below about 4 fps, the only real effect is of the light switching on and off. But in the range from 6 to 18 fps, more or less, strange things occur. *The Flicker* moves gradually from 24 fps to 4 fps and then back out of the flicker range again. The first notable effect is usually a whirling and shattered array of intangible and diffused color patterns, probably a retinal after-image type of effect. Vision extends into the peripheral areas and actual images may be hallucinated. Then a hypnotic state commences, and the images become more intense.

Fixing the eyes on one point is helpful or necessary in eliciting the fullest effects. The brain itself is directly involved in all of this; it is not coincidental that one of the principal brain-wave frequencies, the so-called alpha-rhythm, lies in the 8 to 16 cycles per second range. Hence the central nervous system itself must here be considered as a kind of sensory mechanism, though its role is not explicitly understood, to my knowledge. That is, the range of flicker frequencies from 6 to 18 fps corresponds to a unique type of sensory experience, with a continuously variable parameter (frequency), covering a band of effects approximately 1½ octaves wide, plenty wide enough to accommodate harmonic frequency relationships. Since visual perception of flicker extends as high as 40 fps, it should be possible to establish rhythmic harmonic effects over a range of

Exposure timing sheet used by Conrad in making *The Flicker*. (Photo by Robert Adler.)

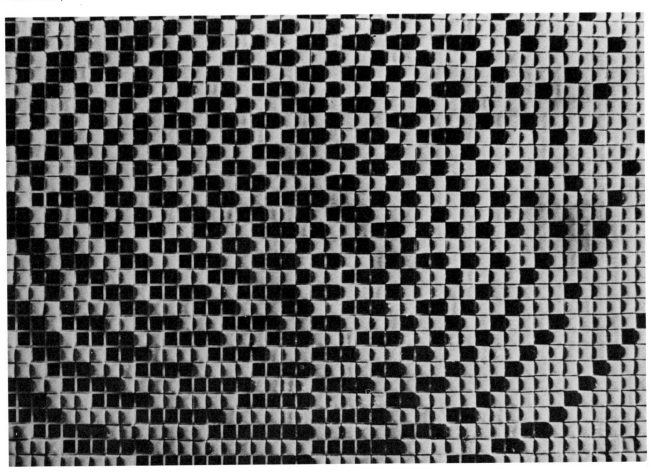

up to 3 octaves. This provides a rational basis for relating the whole flicker experience to a single frequency, corresponding to the tonic or key note in music; in the case of film, a natural tonic is already suggested by the standard projection frequency, 24 fps. Thus all of the patterns of frames I have used are projected at the standard 24 fps, and are so designed as to emphasize each of the chosen frequencies in the flicker range in turn. But due to harmonic rhythmic effects, certain of the patterns suggest more than one frequency, sometimes several, though this is not clear immediately to a viewer experiencing the film for the first time. All in all, I have avoided rhythmic complexity in so far as possible, though I have done a certain amount of investigation of more complex flicker "harmonies." My aim has been to thoroughly develop the basic effects without being pedantically comprehensive.

The absence of contamination with imagery will be the fulcrum which will lever the attention of the audience directly toward full receptiveness to the characteristic flicker effects, which in most presentations are disrupted by eye motions connected with whatever activity is being illuminated by stroboscopic light. I expect to obtain unprecedentedly dramatic results in the audience due to this very lack of subject matter.

The problems I have mentioned so far have been primarily theoretical. After I had worked out the patterns of black and clear frames that I decided to use and had experimentally determined a satisfactory duration for *The Flicker*, I faced a huge practical problem: How to "shoot" upwards of 40,000 frames of essentially alternating black and clear frames. This implies some single-framing technique, as opposed to continuous projection-speed photography. Furthermore, most of the work would have to be done through editing procedures, as I have no 16mm camera. I borrowed a camera from a man who has since gone to prison, and shot a basic 4,000 frames in two days. I was then able to have the remainder done in the lab, but what came back was necessarily hopelessly scrambled. I then faced the main editing job; it amounted to making decisions and almost 600 splices. . . . I decided to use tape splices, which, though they are very primitive, could for this reason be done at home on very inexpensive equipment. Making 600 careful splices turned out to demand about 10 minutes per splice. I have been amazed to find that *The Flicker* has absorbed practically every minute of my spare time for months.

(From a letter to Henry Romney, dated November 11, 1965 and published in *Film Culture*, No. 41, 1966.)

From *The Flicker* (1965) by Tony Conrad, filmstrip showing the alternating solid black-and-white frame clusters.

Audience reaction during a projection of *The Flicker*.

Larry Jordan

Larry Jordan. (Photo by Larry James Huston.)

Animator Larry Jordan uses a wide range of rustic and nostalgic collage material such as old steel engravings and nineteenth-century illustrations to create films which have a magical fluidity of movement. Probing deeply into the interior world of the subconscious, he employs the process of free association to construct his beautiful and dream-like surrealistic imagery.

Born in 1934 in Denver, Colorado, Jordan was introduced to filmmaking by fellow high-school student Stan Brakhage and learned basic techniques as a member of the film club at Harvard University. Following one year of study at Harvard he left school and returned to Colorado where he became involved in summer stock theater. There, heavily influenced by the films of Stan Brakhage, he began a series of live-action films which he describes as "personal psychodramas." The following year he moved to San Francisco, where he continued his film work and became active in film societies and a variety of 16mm theater projects. While in San Francisco he discovered the work of Surrealist artist Max Ernst, which inspired him to begin his experiments with two-dimensional and three-dimensional collage animation.

From 1960–1974, Jordan, a meticulous and inventive craftsman, produced a total of eleven animated films. Outstanding examples of his personal and ritualistic form of symbolism include *Duo Concertantes* (1964), *Our Lady of the Sphere* (1969), *Orb* (1973), and *Once Upon A Time* (1974). Currently, in addition to producing animated films, Jordan is a member of the board of trustees of the American Film Institute and head of the film department at the San Francisco Art Institute.

From *Duo Concertantes* (1962–1964) by Larry Jordan, a surrealistic animated collage.

INTERVIEW WITH LARRY JORDAN

Q: Would you begin this interview by discussing why you are attracted to animation as a form of expression and how, exactly, your collage technique evolved?

Jordan: The technique of animation is natural to me, and has its basis in the love-hate relationship I had with the cartoons and comedies in the magic ritual of childhood. I think in slow-motion when I animate, and know how it will look on the screen. It's something I can't explain. Always there is a theme in each film, and an esthetic game: Weightlessness coupled with improvisation, heaviness coupled with progression, Bardo [see below] coupled with breaking through the flat surface of the image. The progressing from flat collage animations to more three-dimensional works with zooming images stems simply from the acquisition, after 13 years, of a reflex camera with a zoom lens, and a world, or dimension of the same world, that I could never see through an objective viewfinder before. At that point I began to invent new tools to use on the animation bench, various levels of glass through which to shoot, shades for nuances of lighting, colored filters. Color erupted. Just another phase of the eruption which began earlier on the animated flats in black-and-white—the interior world coloring up, starting to dance and sing in a different way. I just followed, like being on a train, looking out the window.

I have completed one phase of the depiction of this world I know so well and am at home in. The animated films which will follow will have a different look to them. That's all I know at present. And that's why I have put all the animated works together on two large reels, running about 90 minutes. The program is called, *Animated Works, 1959-1974.* There are eleven titles in all.

Q: Your imagery has been compared to the work of Salvador Dali, Max Ernst, and Joseph Cornell. Do you see your animated films as a continuation of the Surrealist tradition?

From *Orb* (1973) by Larry Jordan.

Jordan: The imagery in my animated films has always concerned unknown continents and landscapes of the mind. Some call this a real place. Certainly the Egyptians did, so did the Greeks (the underworld), and so do the Tibetans (Bardo). In most cases it is the world of the so-called dead. In this sense it can be a negative world. To me it is not, or has not been. (I may very possibly go to a different dimension entirely next time out, since a new phase is beginning.) To call the images "surreal" is pitifully inadequate, because the term should not be applied to art, but to life. Dali is an idiot; everyone knows that. He's a capitalist with a talent, and was rightfully kicked out of the spiritual brotherhood. Surrealism is a way of life; the works that fall out of that way of life are accidental.

Q: Who has most influenced your work?

Jordan: Influences, looking back, are: Bunuel, Cocteau, Ernst, Jess (Collins), Dreyer, Joseph Cornell.

The Cornell relationship is, was, a personal one, since Joseph is now dead. In 1965 I spent the summer and fall with him in Flushing, working on his films to complete them, and on boxes, the craft of which he taught me, the art of which cannot be taught. This was a close, sometimes difficult relationship, but one that was evidently karmically inevitable. I did not have to go through the grueling process of breaking with the Surrealists, as did Joseph and Cocteau, as Joseph was the only one I knew personally, and he had already broken officially though not spiritually altogether, ever.

Poets and painters, living and dead, were for many years much closer to me and more influential than filmmakers, most of whom (filmmakers) I had nothing in common with, except that our work happened to run through a projector. I considered myself a maker of moving collages. Now I feel like a filmmaker again, because I am concerned with the problems of the medium and with not so much an Audience as with The Viewer, a concern I did not have for many years. . . .

I am the viewer I'm interested in. But being such, I see more and will convey more. At first I was more the *doer*, in the act of making film. That isn't enough anymore. I need a film that is seeable to me over and over again. This kind of film either finds an audience or it doesn't. There's not much I can do about it. If an image honestly excites my eye, it will excite others', as I'm not that different from anyone else.

Q: Duo Concertantes, Hamfat Asar, *and* Our Lady Of The Sphere *are typical examples of your personal and ritualistic form of symbolism. What kinds of ideas and processes are you concerned with in your film imagery?*

Jordan: The basic act in my work is of freeing the objects from the chains of convention and connotation. The whole thing is symbolic of the Surrealist philosophy, which, by definition, is inexplicable. The enigma is quite sacred to the Surrealists like myself who are openly arrogant about symbolism and allegorical inanities. My "characters" don't portray anything in particular, but they still have ties with the mechanics of this world: a flying mushroom represents in no way a psychedelic connotation; it is a new-born giraffe, and moves as such, because *it* wants to be one, not I. And I believe strongly

From *Once Upon a Time* (1974) by Larry Jordan.

156

in the process of free association in combining images, and in constructing them. I find it very embarrassing, for instance, to find in a film that the filmmaker is forcing shots, which of themselves have no real relation to his intentions, into the servitude of fulfilling his intentions. I prefer that the shots (images) construct themselves. This is not a semantic nicety. If one is patient, and sits there with ego subdued, the images come to life on their own. I admit that this is not the *modus operandi* in all my films. Sometimes I do resort to construction and invention, usually when I am struggling with a new technical process. Some of the later films, like *Our Lady Of The Sphere*, *Orb*, and *Once Upon A Time* are combinations of free and constructed imagery. The problem of the three-dimensional aspect, and the treatment of the animation stand as a French Theater with more depth than width has prompted this synthesis.

Q: You employ a wide range of unusual graphic material in your films such as old illustrations from magic, astrology, and anatomy books, nineteenth-century engravings, and turn of the century reproductions of the romantic style. What special significance do these kinds of images have for you?

Jordan: Use of the old engravings is always a question to anyone who has just seen one of my movies: Why? How come? What do they *mean*? Let me invent a few answers, because, aside from the fact that they're good actors, photograph well, and the original artists have paid enough attention to depth-illusion to give me an atmosphere in which to stage my visions, there are no real answers. But let us invent a few more idea-illusions: There is a tension between the old (engravings) and the new (ideas and motifs in the film process). I can't resist the nostalgia of a time when the world was more intact than it is now. There were more distinct delineations, or Spirits of Place, in the nineteenth century than there are now, and I can evoke stronger moods with material from that time, given the assumption that the viewer is susceptible to mood, and not overly demanding of story-content. The engravings are semi-works of art (the commercial art of the nineteenth century) and have an edge on expressionism which contemporary photos don't have. Perhaps there are some real answers, but it's very complicated and boils down to visual preference. Finally, the nineteenth-century imagery is already partly dislodged from mundane connotation, and gives me a head start on the surrealism "freeing" process. Psychological and archetypal questions are games for analysts, not synthesizers (artists). And a parting shot: many of the nineteenth-century engravings are, quite simply,

From *Our Lady of the Sphere* (1969) by Larry Jordan. This sequence of frames shows the effects created by old engravings and other collage material.

beautiful. I love to work out of step, using beautiful things in an age that cannot tolerate beauty.

Q: Your animated films are meticulously crafted, yet have a wonderful organic quality. Do you work from a script or do you basically improvise with collage?

Jordan: Meticulous crafting is an act of love. Sloppiness is an act of sloppiness. Inspiration is 90 percent work. Either you like *all* the processes of making a film or you are in the wrong business. Meticulousness is an act of freedom and thorough seeing and living in timelessness. It is an act of concentration and intense living. To me my films are extremely sloppy sometimes, though not always. I know that not everyone notices the missed stitches. But they are there. In the beginning I didn't notice them either. When I began to, it was a deepening of the living film process to solve the problems of the marred surface. This process of meticulously crafting a work has absolutely nothing to do with whether a script is used or not. In my case half the films are done with scripts (scores, I prefer to call them) and half are done from lists of ideas, executed, then edited first on paper (another score), then cut. Whether or not I use a script depends on 1) my mood, 2) the subject, 3) the techniques I will use, and 4) the length of the film (size of the feeling inside when I begin).

There always being a new esthetic game to each film, that game might include becoming a total slave to a set of verbal indications on paper, executing each direction without the slightest deviation. Another might mean that total improvisation (*Gymnopedies*) was the law. It is these rules or laws that give each film its style, not the use or non-use of a script. Scripts, scores and post-scripts (scripts written after the film is shot) are just part of the game. Organic qualities are a conscious part of my concepts of film, that is the growth of a film around a central unity. The laws and rules of the games I play are the genes of the films. The shapes they fill out into are the ineluctable results of the genes. I do not chop films on the editing table. Like music, which they are in essence, they are scored either before the visions are captured in the camera or after, and then performed for the printer at the lab. At times I know all the backgrounds and all the characters that will be in a film. At other times the introduction of material is openended. Sometimes the mood is to sit calmly before a table and compose; at other times it is to sit at the piano and improvise; and sometimes it is to step into the dark naked and fall until wings sprout. There is order in any mood if you look for it. If I have produced a number of short visions (shots) with only a vague idea of the theme, and must resort to the post-script, I start writing without stopping to think or judge, letting the first image lead to the second, the second to the third, freely associating, until I have used up all the images. I make a silent print and construct a sound track for the film afterwards. There is a great deal of trust that goes on in this kind of process. To say where the order or the rightness of the ordered images comes from is an insoluble mystery, leading out of art and into philosophy. One thing I try never to do is force an image to perform a superficial (intellectual) role in the work, such as a quick shot of an eye which is not really angry to stand in for anger at a given moment where I think there 'should' be anger. I like to believe that is in my films. We hear a lot about film being the work of illusionists. True. But only *part* of the mind can be fooled. Whatever the visual process is, it is no dummy. Subliminal images register as surely as ten second shots. Therefore, artificially constructed montage sequences are nothing more than artificially constructed montage sequences that are dear to the hearts of intellectuals, fool one level of the consciousness, and leave the spirit, which knows truth instantly, high and dry. If intuition is a dubious or feared process to an artist, that artist is in trouble and will have to talk his way out of it or get a good press agent.

Q: Do you use any specialized equipment or unusual techniques to create your films?

Jordan: As the process of image-making deepens, the mechanics of the image-making broaden. Often a theoretical technical problem will spark a period of photographic invention. I will be off to my favorite machinist with drawings and plans, which he will straighten out for me and construct the needed part, motor, lens, or whatever. You can buy only a very small percentage of the equipment needed for individual efforts in films and must rely on a mechanic, if you are not one yourself, to make up the equipment to order. Over the years my stand has acquired some peculiar devices, most of which I decline to discuss, not because they are secret processes so much as that it is boring to discuss them. Anyone who is seriously interested in doing a thing will eventually figure out how to do it. So far I have not resorted to optical printing in the animation films, although some of the effects are identical to results obtainable on the optical printer. My interest in optical printing is theoretical. I have been instrumental in inventing a type of optical printing never before used in the industry— a front-projection system. Several of the machines were built and one is used commercially now. But I have never used it, preferring to matte images on the stand, exposing and re-exposing each frame—hand-making each frame, so to speak. There is more immediacy, more bounce, better color, and resolution to the image when it is first generation.

Q: Your animated films are an important part of the artistic tradition of personal film. What do you think that animators, working in this tradition, can contribute to cinema that is not already present in other areas of filmmaking?

Jordan: The contributions this kind of film can make to the body of cinema are far more extensive than the contributions it has made. Very few people are willing to devote themselves to experimentation. This goes without saying. However, if the material incentives were there, as say in experimental medicine, with huge grants and great prestige, you would have just as many animation experimenters. The contributions that are made by the few working in this area are hard to evaluate from the inside—by the doer. A 'contribution' is really only valuable to the user—the seer. But I will try: Time-slippage and visual-musical manipulation is the forte of nonconventional animation. In nonconventional animation the irrational, explosive force of vision is condensed to the limits, far beyond any other form of cinema. If, as in one of McLaren's films, little bursts of images occur only every ten frames, the manipulation of time and vision are being conducted at an intensity not to be found in other forms of cinema.

Experimental animation approaches the essence of music, without intruding into the territory of music. The reason is simple: they both happen in time, and they are essentially both nonrational, conforming to inner laws and to mathematics.

Conventional animation—animation with little stories—will not enter the realm of the subliminal, or even approach it, for instance. Instantaneous shifts and dislocations of objects in the frames are not tolerated. Sometimes grace notes are needed for the visual rhythm. However, if the expectations of the viewer of animated cinema are insolubly linked with rational progression, "story" in a literary sense, or even with recognizable mood, then the acceptance of animation as visual music is denied and the experimental is deemed esoteric. In fact it is no more esoteric than Bartok's music, or the music of Erik Satie.

The real contribution of experimental animated cinema may explode on the consciousness of the cinema public quite unexpectedly at some time in the future, when, through unforeseen circumstances, the need (more than the understanding) for irrational vision becomes manifested in a large segment of the population. Then the contributions of the meager productions in this area of cinema would loom suddenly much larger than they do today. It would be seen that visual musicians had broken the ground, but that traditions in visual, nonrational music had not yet been established. At the point where those traditions grew up, "experimental animation" would cease.

On a less speculative level, the contributions I have made are primarily on a one-to-one basis, where a student or a viewer of one of my films will 'connect' and a whole new range of esthetic possibilities will be opened up to them, and they will go off and start constructing their own personal visions in their own way. That kind of contribution is very rewarding, because it carries the "freeing" surreal quality over into life, where it ought to be.

If one understands "contribution" (through experimentation) to be that process whereby the dedicated amateur makes amazing but rough discoveries, which can then be converted, sanitized, and used by the professionals in more conventional movies, then we could say that the professionals have mercifully ignored experimental animation, and I wouldn't want it otherwise. I'd rather have the experimental animation left intact, rough but with full integrity, because I don't in the least think any process of creation is experimental—a term which denotes tentativeness. One merely looks for whatever means are necessary to produce the vision. If this is experimental, the difficulty is semantic.

(From a written interview conducted by Robert Russett, October 1974.)

Paul Sharits

Paul Sharits.

In a burst of work from 1966 to 1968 Paul Sharits used the single frame process to produce six outstanding films including one of his best known works *N:O:T:H:I:N:G*, a frenetically animated montage of flickering color frames and images, which expresses his deep interest in the imagistic power of intuitive symbolism. Although filmmaker Sharits does not regard himself strictly as an animator he has perhaps more than any other contemporary filmmaker questioned the primary meaning of cinema in an attempt to redefine the basic element of filmic analysis, the single frame unit.

Born in 1943 in Denver, Colorado, Sharits received a B.F.A. in painting from the University of Denver and an M.F.A. in visual design from Indiana University. In 1966, while still a graduate student at Indiana, he made *Ray Gun Virus*, his first attempt at creating rhythmic sensory impressions by using alternating frame struc-

tures. This initial work served as a base for the more complex optical strategies which were to follow in other animated films such as *Razor Blades*, *N:O:T:H:I:N:G* and *T,O,U,C,H,I,N,G*, all completed in 1968. Clearly a new and vital force in the field of experimental cinema, Sharits has screened his films extensively in museums, galleries, and avant-garde film festivals and in addition he has received production grants from the American Film Institute and the Ford Foundation. Currently, Sharits is, in his phrase, "administering" filmmaking courses at the State University of New York at Buffalo and, with a public media grant from the National Endowment for the Arts, is producing a six-screen environmental film piece which was scheduled to be installed on special screening equipment in Washington, D.C. in 1975.

N:O:T:H:I:N:G
by Paul Sharits
The film will strip away anything (all present definitions of "something") standing in the way of the film being its own reality, anything which would prevent the viewer from entering totally new levels of awareness. The theme of the work, if it can be called a theme, is to deal with the nonunderstandable, the impossible, in a tightly and precisely structured way. The film will not "mean" *some*thing—it will "mean," in a very concrete way, *no*thing.

The film focuses and concentrates on two images and their highly linear but illogical and/or inverted development. The major image is that of a light bulb which first retracts its light rays; upon retracting its light, the bulb becomes black and, impossibly, lights up the space around it. The bulb emits one burst of black light and begins melting; at the end of the film the bulb is a black puddle at the bottom of the screen. The other image (notice that the film is composed, on all levels, of dualities) is that of a chair, seen against a graph-like background, falling backwards onto the floor (actually, it falls against and affirms the edge of the picture frame); this image sequence occurs in the center, *thig le* section of *N:O:T:H:I:N:G*. The mass of the film is highly vibratory color-energy rhythms; the color development is partially based on the Tibetan Mandala of the Five Dhyani Buddhas which is used in meditation to reach the highest level of inner consciousness—infinite, transcendental wisdom (symbolized by Vairocana being embraced by the Divine Mother of Infinite Blue Space). This formal-psychological composition moves progressively into more intense vibration (through the symbolic colors white, yellow, red, and green) until the center of the mandala is reached (the center being the *thig le*, or void point, containing all forms, both the beginning and end of consciousness). The second half of the film is, in a sense, the inverse of the first; that is, after one has passed through the center of the void, he may return to a normative state retaining the richness of the revelatory *thig le* experience. The virtual shapes I have been working with (created by rapid alternations and patterns of blank color frames) are quite relevant in this work as is indicated by this passage from the Svetasvatara Upanishad: "As you practice meditation, you may see in vision forms resembling snow, crystals, smoke, fire, lightening, fireflies, the sun, the moon. These are signs that you are on your way to the relevation of Brahman."

I am not at all interested in the mystical symbolism of Buddhism, only in its strong, intuitively developed imagistic power. In a sense, I am more interested in the mantra because unlike the mandala and yantra forms which are full of such symbols, the mantra is often nearly pure nonsense—yet it has intense potency psychologically, esthetically, and physiologically. The mantra used upon reaching the *thig le* of the Mandala of the Five Dhyani Buddhas is the simple Om—a steady vibrational hum. I've tried to compose the center of *N:O:T:H:I:N:G*, on one level, to visualize this auditory effect.

From a letter to Stan Brakhage, late spring 1968: "The film is 'about' (it is) gradation-progression on many different levels; for years I had been thinking that if a fade is directional in that it is a hierarchical progression, and that that exists in and implies forward moving 'time', then why couldn't one construct inverse time patterns, why couldn't one structure a felt awareness of really going through negative time? During the final shooting sessions these past few months I've had Vermeer's *Lady Standing at the Virginals* hanging above my animation stand and have had the most peculiar experience with that work in relation to *N:O:T:H:I:N:G* (the colons "meant" to create somewhat the sense of the real yet paradoxical concreteness of "nothing"... as Wittgenstein so beautifully reveals). As I began to recognize the complex interweaving of levels of 'gradation' (conceptually, sensually, rhythmically, proportionately...even the metaphoric level of subject making music, etc.) in the Vermeer I began to see what I was doing in the film in a more conscious way. I allowed the feelings I was getting from this silent dialogue between process of seeing and process of structuring to further clarify the footage I was shooting. I can't get over the intense

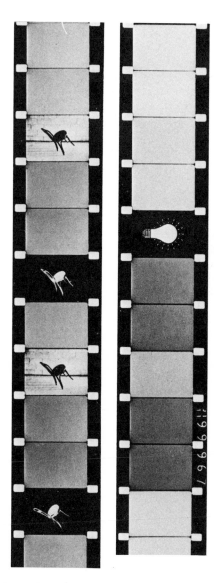

From *N:O:T:H:I:N:G* (1968) by Paul Sharits. These strips show the solid frames and minimal imagery used in his flickering animated film.

mental-emotional journeys I got into with this work and hope that the film is powerful enough to allow others to travel along those networks.

Light comes through the window on the left and not only illuminates the *Lady at the Virginals* but illuminates the subjects in the two paintings (which are staggered in a forward-reverse simultaneous progression-creating a sense of forward and backward time) hanging on the wall and the one painting on the inside lid of the virginal! The whole composition is circular, folds in on itself but implies that part of that circle exists out in front of the surface. What really moved me was the realization that the light falling across the woman's face compounded the light-gradation-time theme by forcing one back on the awareness of (the paradox of) awareness. That is, one eye, itself dark, is half covered with light while the other eye is in shadow; both eyes are gazing directly at the viewer as if the woman is projecting music at the viewer through her gaze (as if reversing the 'normal' role of 'perception') . . . I mean the whole point is that the instrument by which light-perception is made possible is itself in the dark.") . . .

(From an application for a grant published in *Film Culture*, No. 47, 1969.)

A page of preliminary notes and diagrams made by Sharits for *N:O:T:H:I:N:G*, shown on his improvised animation stand.

7/Experimenters in Animated Sound

Robert Russett

INTRODUCTION

A form of filmic sound has been explored and developed within the realm of experimental animation which is unlike any other auditory experience in motion pictures. Basically, the technique consists of creating sound, not from conventional musical instruments or other sonic sources, but by inscribing graphic patterns directly onto the soundtrack of film. This unique form of sound production is a totally synthetic process which closely resembles the technique of animation itself and is sometimes called synthetic sound or animated sound. Although experimenters in various areas of art and science have contributed to the technical development of synthetic sound, the best known artistic works in this medium have been created by experimental animators, most notably, John and James Whitney, Norman McLaren, and Barry Spinello.

Attempts at creating sound tracks directly from visual patterns have been in progress since the development of the sound film and the photoelectric cell; tentative proposals for graphic sound were formulated as early as 1922. During those early years this new medium was investigated in both Russia and Western Europe by technically oriented experimenters such as Moholy-Nagy, Avzaamov, Yankovsky, Voinov, Scholpo, Pfenninger, and Fischinger (see Chapter 3). As a result of their experiments with sound production and their search for modern forms of artistic expression, a wide range of synthetic concepts were developed and codified.

Among the first to theorize about the artistic potential of a totally synthetic approach to the sound film was Lazlo Moholy-Nagy, a visionary Bauhaus artist and teacher. Even before sound on film was widely used, Moholy-Nagy published several articles about the possibilities of creating original compositions directly in film. In 1933 he demonstrated his theories by making *The Sound ABC*, an experimental optical soundtrack on which he recorded letters of the alphabet, profiles, fingerprints, and all types of signs and symbols. Each of these visual forms produced a distinct and audible result. To complete his experiment Moholy-Nagy rephotographed the soundtrack so that the images could be simultaneously projected onto the screen and viewed. Sound and image, then, were cinematically generated in this dual presentation from the same visual patterns. This relatively simple film, which Moholy-Nagy termed "a lighthearted experiment," effectively demonstrated his acoustic theories and suggested a new and graphically unified approach to structuring the sound film.

About the same time that Moholy-Nagy made *The Sound ABC*, animator Oskar Fischinger was also experimenting with synthetic sound on film. Fischinger's approach to the medium, however, was quite different than the theoretical exercises of Moholy-Nagy. Working with a holistic concept of film, Fischinger was attempting to create a new audio-visual language by using nonobjective animation as a vehicle of expression. Since the late 1920's he had been producing abstract animated films in which visual patterns were tightly synchronized to music recorded on discs. Fischinger's basic aim, then, was to artistically interrelate the sensory modes of sight and sound into a totally synesthetic film experience. This concrete concept of animation led him to experiment with synthetic sound techniques.

His first sound studies were concerned with converting the characteristic elements of sound into a vocabulary of geometric shapes, a form of "opto-acoustic notation." These shapes were drawn on paper scrolls and photographed onto the soundtrack. He quickly developed this technique and was able to produce and compose a range of complicated musical effects. Fischinger also tried drawing different kinds of symbolic designs and ornamental configurations which produced unusual or "a-musical" sounds. This aspect of his research predates electronic and concrete music by many years and its artistic implications were almost immediately recognized in the field of music by composers Edgar Varèse and John Cage. Fischinger's sound research was interrupted by World War II and his experiments never fully developed into a cohesive artistic form that could be employed in his animated films. It should be noted, however, that the synthetic soundtracks of both Fischinger and Moholy-Nagy were widely shown in Europe and England and helped prepare the groundwork for new artistic concepts of animation which were to follow.

During the late 1930s, for example, Norman McLaren began to use the principles established by these early experimenters and was the first to create a significant body of artistic work employing synthetic sound techniques. In his early films such as *Allegro* and the brilliantly conceived *Dots* and *Loops*, McLaren drew both sounds and images directly onto film celluloid without the intervention of a camera. With this totally graphic approach to sound and image, McLaren created beautiful and refreshing animated films by experimenting with colorful abstract designs and a whole range of delightful auditory effects. Later, using a technique similar to Oskar Fischinger's, he began to carefully draw and index graphic patterns or wave forms which were later photographed onto a soundtrack one frame at a time. With this photographic technique McLaren could create and control a wider range of synthetic effects including chords, counterpoint, and harmony. This form of animated sound, which he occasionally combined with conventional musical instruments, is demonstrated in films such as *Now Is The Time* and *Phantasy*, for example. Although McLaren has used animation techniques to produce both sound and image, he never resorts to mere parallelism of track and picture. Instead, he orchestrates his films with a freer and more artistic approach, allowing each of these compositional elements to make a distinct contribution to the final effect. Over the years, Norman McLaren has done more than any other single animator to develop and popularize the art and craft of synthetic sound.

In 1941, John Whitney, a filmmaker and technical innovator, and his brother James Whitney, a painter, began working with yet another form of synthetic sound on film. The purpose of their experiments was to develop a unified bi-sensory relationship between film and music. The Whitneys, however, felt that music produced by conventional instruments, because of certain past associations and preconceptions, would be inappropriate for the abstract kinetic imagery of their films. Therefore, to create original auditory effects that would directly relate to the quality and character of their thematic animated patterns, they designed and built a highly specialized sound-producing apparatus.

As a result of their mechanical approach to sound as well as image, their early films were totally machine-realized art forms. Their visual designs, which consisted of hard-edged geometric shapes, were manipulated by virtue of an optical printer, pantograph, and color filters. Multiple exposures, magnifications, reductions, and inversions enabled them to create an astounding variety of compositions in time and space. Their sound, which was produced with their specifically designed infrasonic instrument, consisted of a series of pendulums that created light patterns on a soundtrack of normal specifications. The instrument did not produce an audible sound but instead made an optical soundtrack from a purely visual source. Their soundtrack, which was a graphic record of oscillating light waves, was entirely synthetic and abstract, as was their imagery. Together the Whitneys demonstrated that the apparently cold world of machines and mathematics can be effectively channelled to meet human and esthetic needs. These early films, which they termed "exercises," were not only important artistic accomplishments, but also helped bridge the gap between film animation and the more advanced forms of modern technology.

More recently, Barry Spinello, a young animator working in the tradition of Norman McLaren, has produced a series of abstract sound films using a new vocabulary of graphic techniques. To create his synthetic sounds and images, Spinello, in addition to drawing and painting directly on clear celluloid, also creates patterns by using a variety of self-adhesive materials such as micotape, zip-a-tone shading sheets and press-apply lettering. These techniques are combined and used on both the soundtrack and in the picture area to create geometric patterns that undergo complex evolutionary changes. His overall intention is to shape and compress the tremendous kinetic energy of handmade images into a harmonious audio-visual unit. Two outstanding examples of this unique approach to animation are *Six Loop-Painting* and *Soundtrack*. During some of the more frenetic moments of these abstract films, sight and sound relationships change 24 times a second, and the patterns on the screen are frequently those that are heard. As a result, this audiovisual form of animation supersedes synchronization and becomes a conceptually unified approach to filmmaking which stresses the synthesis and interdependence of sight and sound.

Over the years, many beautiful animated films have been produced with forms of synthetic sound and, although this approach has never been widely used, interest in the concepts and techniques of this medium continue today. Not only can synchronization of visual and sound images be precisely obtained, but animators who are not musicians can easily relate to this visual technique for creating sound, and produce what is, in effect, a unique form of electronic music. In addition to the various manual and mechanical approaches used by McLaren, Whitney, and Spinello, some of the most promising new research in this area involves electronic computer technology. Currently, computer engineers like Ken Knowlton (see Chapter 8) at Bell Laboratories, for example, are working with the problem of generating animated film images and synthetic sound from the same computer program. In order to create a unified theory of animation, efforts are being made to analyze electronic music and its numerical relationship to computer generated images. Although there are many technical and artistic problems to be resolved, preliminary tests show that computerized sound-image relationships will be feasible in the future. The computer, then, could be one of the most effective tools yet for synthetically producing audio-visual effects on film.

Fischinger with sound scrolls, 1932.

Norman McLaren

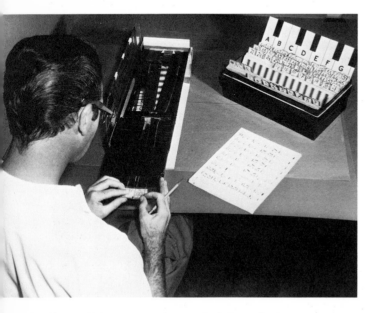

Norman McLaren, composing an animated soundtrack.

Throughout his career, Norman McLaren has experimented with the graphic technique of creating sound on film. He has used a number of synthetic sound techniques, which are little known but important, to significantly enlarge the process of animation and to produce a whole range of new and expressive auditory effects. In his early years of experimentation with animated sound, beginning about 1940, he produced delightful and rhythmic audio patterns by drawing and scratching directly on film. *Dots* and *Loops*, two animated works produced without a camera or tape recorder, are highly successful examples of this graphic approach. Later, McLaren devised a single frame photographic technique to record and control more complicated hand-drawn sound waves. This technique, which has been used in a number of outstanding films such as *Now Is The Time* and *Phantasy*, was developed and refined during the 1950s at the National Film Board of Canada. During this period of re-

search and production, McLaren wrote *Animated Sound on Film* (see below), a detailed account of the concepts and methods used in creating artificial, or synthetic, sound on film.

ANIMATED SOUND ON FILM
by Norman McLaren

THE TERM ANIMATED AS APPLIED TO SOUND-TRACK
The term "synthetic sound" is generally used to cover a wide variety of new, non-traditional methods of making noise, sound effects, music, and speech, by electronic, magnetic, mechanical, optical, and other means; and it is not necessarily connected with the use of motion picture film. The term "animated sound" as used here has a much more restricted meaning and refers to a way of producing sound on film which parallels closely the production of animated pictures.

Since the technique as developed at the National Film Board of Canada bears the closest possible resemblance to the standard method of making animated cartoons, a brief description of it at the outset might be in order.

Black and white drawings, or patterns of light and shade, representing sound waves are prepared. These drawings are photographed with the same kind of motion picture camera as is normally used in the shooting of animated cartoons. In fact, they are shot in precisely the same way as the drawings of a cartoon; that is, one drawing is placed in front of the camera and one frame of film is taken, and then the first drawing is removed, replaced with another drawing and the second frame of film taken, the second drawing is changed again and the third frame taken, and so on.

The only difference from normal cartoon picture shooting is that the drawings are not of scenes from the visible world around us but of sound waves, and they are not done on cards of a screen-shaped proportion but on long narrow cards. These cards are photographed not on the area of the film occupied by the picture, but to the left of it, on the narrow vertical strip normally reserved for the sound-track. When the film is developed and printed, and run on a sound projector the photographed images of these black and white drawings are heard as either noise, sound effects, or music.

It is therefore logical to call the kind of sound produced in this way "animated," for not only is it made by the same method as animated pictures, but from a creative and artistic point of view it shares many of the peculiarities and possibilities of animated visuals.

But just as there are many techniques of animating visuals, so there are of animating sound. Some of these combine with or shade off imperceptibly into other methods differing in principle. In attempting to trace the history, I shall refer only to techniques that are a close parallel to visual animation.

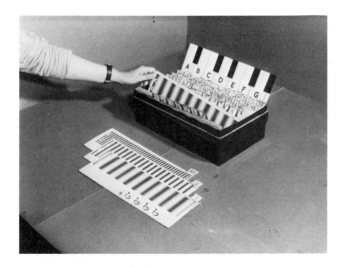

One system of McLaren's animated, or synthetic, sound is produced by photographing graphic patterns, one frame at a time, directly onto the film's soundtrack. His patterns are assembled in a box, in which they range systematically from highest to lowest pitch. As the bands of tones widen on each successive card, the pitch becomes correspondingly lower. There are five parallel rows of cards in the box, each row containing twelve cards and thus covering an octave.

HISTORY Before the general adoption of the sound film in 1927, the possibility of the synthetic production of sound on film was already foreseen. In 1922, for instance, L. Moholy-Nagy discussed some of its potentialities in articles published in Holland and Germany. Later, Ernest Toch, the German theoretician suggested the direct writing of sound without traditional performers.

The first body of investigation and practical work seems to have been done in Russia at the Scientific Experimental Film Institute in Leningrad, where in 1930 A. M. Avzaamov,

a musical theorist and mathematician, worked with the animators N. Y. Zhelinsky and N. V. Voinov on "ornamental animation in sound." Later this work was carried on at the Leningrad Conservatory by G. M. Rimski-Korsakov and E. A. Scholpo.

From a study of the available papers, their work appears to have been fairly extensive and along a number of different lines.

Avzaamov used a frame-by-frame method with a standard animation camera. Geometric figures such as rectangles, triangles, trapezes, ovals, parabolas, ellipses, etc., were the basic units for his sound waves. Pitch was controlled either by bringing the camera closer to or farther away from drawings of these shapes, or by preparing separate drawings for each pitch.

Volume was controlled by varying the exposure; harmony or counterpoint by multiple exposures, or by subdividing the sound-track lengthwise into sections, or by the very rapid alternation of several tones; portamento by a rapid series of micro-tones.

Avzaamov, who had set as his goal the freeing of his music from the restrictions of the twelve-tone tempered scale, and the creation of new tonal systems assimilating many of the scales of the traditional folk music of the Eastern and Southern Republics, achieved very adequate control over pitch and volume; his range of timbres was more limited; the fact that he used geometric forms like triangles and rectangles indicates he was using an empirical approach to tone-quality. He was not searching for complete flexibility in timbre, but rather for a limited number of new tone qualities, arising naturally from simple graphic shapes.

Soon afterwards, Scholpo and Rimski-Korsakov began the oscillographic analysis of natural sounds, and this in turn led to the building up of the music for a film by the assembling of small units of film, each bearing separate tones, into an edited whole of music and sound effects.

At about the same time, in Moscow, B. A. Yankovsky developed a system of animated sound in which he abandoned the frame-by-frame shooting of drawings on a standard animation camera in favour of continuously moving patterns (obtained from rotating wheels with cog patterns).

Animator N. Voinov's system was said to be the most practical of all the Soviet animated sound techniques. He had a library of eighty-seven drawings, graded in semitones covering slightly over seven octaves of the twelve-tone equally-tempered chromatic scale, with a fixed tone quality of great purity. With this he produced an interpretation of Rachmaninoff's *Prelude in C Sharp Minor*, and Schubert's *Moment Musical*.

Almost simultaneously with the Soviet experiments, a Munich electrical engineer, Rudolph Pfenninger, began to work on his own system of animated sound. His researches seem to have been done quite independently of the Russians.

Pfenninger's method was rather similar to Voinov's and Avzaamov's. He had a library of cards each bearing the drawing of a single pitch, graded in semitones over a wide pitch range. In these drawings the basic units for sound waves were sine-curves and saw-tooth forms (using variable area); they were therefore not so arbitrarily chosen but were related to natural sound wave forms. To control volume he used variations in the amount of exposure (variable density).

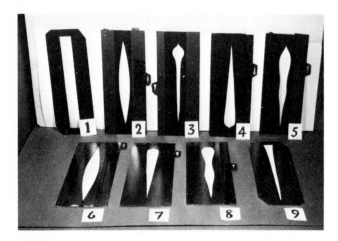

Some of the different types of envelopes, or masks, used by McLaren for contouring the pitch within a single frame.

About 1932 he produced an interpretation of Handel's *Largo*, a series of musical compositions as played by various musicians, and the musical sound-track for an animated cartoon film. He achieved great control over dynamic nuances. His method of making animated sound was clearly shown in a documentary film made in the early thirties called *Tönende Handschrift*.

About this same time, also in Germany, the Fischinger Brothers in Berlin were photographing geometric shapes on the sound-track, and L. Moholy-Nagy was boldly using alphabetical letters, fingerprints, and people's profiles as the basic graphic material for sound waves.

In England the New Zealand musician, Jack Ellit, experimented along lines similar to Pfenninger, and in 1933 pioneered in drawing sound directly on the celluloid without the use of a camera.

In the U.S.A. there has never been, either on the part of the government or film industry at large, any interest in the possibility of this kind of sound. It was only during the later forties that private individuals seem to have taken it up.

In California, the Whitney Brothers have developed a system differing in principle from European systems. It depends on the building up of the basic sound waves by the sine-wave motion of pendulums. The movements of several pendulums may be added together to produce the fundamental and overtones of a note. They can be made to operate a shutter in front of a light source, the fluctuations of which are recorded on continuously moving film. Their approach is therefore more radical. It has been applied in a number of their abstract films.

The sound-track is made by linking together mechanically twelve pendulums of various lengths by means of a fine steel wire attached to an optical wedge. This optical wedge is caused to oscillate over a light slit by the motion of the pendulums, producing a variable-area type of sound-track. The pendulums can be operated together in any combination, or separately. The frequency of each can be adjusted or tuned to conform to any kind of scale by moving a sliding weight. Through the choice of pendulum lengths and driven speeds the full range of audio frequencies can be recorded. No actual sound is involved in recording the wave patterns generated by the pendulums. Only when the resultant film is projected at regular sound-projection speed is sound produced.

It is said that in recent years, the Englishman, C. E. Buckle, has worked out a system of synthetic sound.

In Ottawa, under Canadian Government sponsorship, the writer, with the assistance of Evelyn Lambart, has developed a system of animated sound, in general principle very little different from the Voinov and Pfenninger system, with a library of cards each bearing the representation of sound waves. However, a number of refinements have been incorporated, especially in relation to the contouring of tones, and the method has been streamlined to a point where it has become a simple and economic operation.

Love your Neighbour, *Now is the Time*, *Two Bagatelles*, *Twirligig* and *Phantasy* are successful examples of the use of the technique. Music for the first three was composed and photographed by the author, with the exception of the old-fashioned calliope section in *Two Bagatelles*. The music for the last two was composed and photographed by Maurice Blackburn, that for *Phantasy* being written for a combination of animated sound and saxophones. . . .

(From a pamphlet published by the National Film Board of Canada, 1950.)

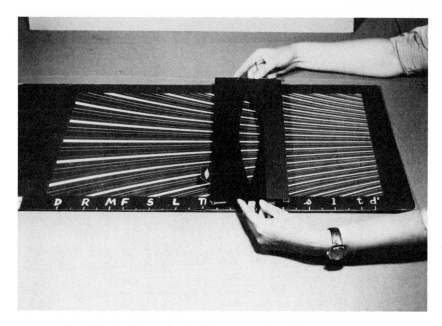

In addition to his box of cards, McLaren uses other methods to synthetically produce pitch so that portamento, glissando, vibrato, and microtones are possible. These effects are achieved by using long cards with converging lines which slide under the tone envelopes, or masks.

Different kinds of striated lines on the sliding cards produce different tone qualities. The near card, for example, produces a rich, complex tone quality, and the distant card produces a much simpler timbre.

John Whitney

John Whitney (at left) and his brother James Whitney, shown with their
optical printer and pendulum sound recorder.

John Whitney, since the early days of his career, has been one of the foremost artist-technicians working in the field of experimental animation. Following his studies at Pomona College in California, Whitney spent a year in Europe, where he studied photography and musical composition. In 1940 he began his experiments with the filmic relationship of sound and image, working with his brother James on a related series of abstract animated films which won first prize at the 1949 Experimental Film Festival in Belgium. During this period of collaboration, the Whitneys devised a unique method of graphically composing and recording synthetic sound for their kinetic, geometric films.

MOVING PICTURES AND ELECTRONIC MUSIC
by John Whitney

The year 1940 marks the beginning of this short history. It might be called a piece of Western frontier history for there are signs of a frontier in it—in one sense—and there is a note of isolation.

Stimulated by the avant-garde filmmakers of France and Germany of the early twenties, I began alone and was soon joined by my brother James, making what were then called abstract films. My point of view was that of a composer; my brother was a painter. I had been casually introduced to the Schoenberg twelve-tone principals by friends in Paris a year earlier. Other than this brief exposure to a modern trend of music composition, we had Ernst Krenek's pamphlet, *Studies in Counterpart*, plus recorded music to listen to, including Pierrot Lunaire; the pieces for piano Opus 19 and the Opus 37 String Quartet of Arnold Schoenberg; also Alban Berg's Lyric Suite and violin concerto. It may be said that we were more broadly acquainted with the temper and spirit of modern art, including the Bauhaus in Germany.

As unprecedented comparatively as our art was, the tools were also new or actually awaiting invention. We looked upon toolmaking as a natural aspect of our creative occupation. We treated this facet of endeavor with respect, designing with care even the appearance of an instrument, for example. We accepted, of course, the probability that formal considerations would somehow evolve as a result of an interactive play between ourselves and the character of these tools. And to bear this out, it will be seen that certain formal ideas did come directly from the subsonic approach that we found for producing the sound of our films.

Our subsonic sound instrument consisted of a series of pendulums linked mechanically to an optical wedge. The function of the optical wedge was the same as that of the typical light valve of standard optical motion picture sound recorders. No audible sound was generated by the instrument. Instead an optical sound track of standard dimensions was synthetically exposed onto film which after processing could be played back with a standard motion picture projector.

The pendulum, whose natural sinusoidal oscillation is fixed by the location and size of its weight, constituted our limited source of tone generation. Though the frequency range of our set of pendulums extended only somewhat over four octaves, from a base frequency of one second, the extremely slow drive mechanism which passed the raw film over the light slit at the recording optics was also variable over a range of several octaves. By changing the drive speed the pendulums as a group could be shifted up or down the frequency spectrum.

The pendulum sound recorder was specially designed to produce synthetic music for a series of experimental abstract animated films made by John Whitney and his brother James Whitney.

The pendulums were individually tunable. We soon found that we could watch the comparatively slow swing of these pendulums and adjust their weights to any of the common interval relationships. For example, it was easy to count two strokes of one pendulum and adjust another to make exactly three strokes in the same period; both pendulums swinging past a nodal point in unison every 2nd and 3rd oscillation respectively. This tuning would sound the interval of the 5th. Due to the design of the mechanical linkage any number of pendulums could be played simultaneously. The linkage in effect "mixes" sinusoidal oscillations without undue distortion.

Composing for an instrument with the thinness of tone spectra as ours had determined a need to exploit our resources with ingenuity and to their fullest. There were other reasons, of course, but this sense of a need for extreme economy motivated avoiding any tuning of the pendulum set to a "scale" that would not be used in its entirety.

As a formal point, then, we chose to tune the instrument to a serial row that would be different with each composition. This serial row might be played out sequentially depending upon horizontal considerations of the music structure. Also, all or any part of the row could be played simultaneously. This way a vertical note mixture (not a chord) would be produced, the timbre or components of which could be continuously varied by bringing in and out different groupings of frequencies. The attack and decay of the tones of the instrument could be controlled by literally starting and stopping the pendulums either abruptly or slowly. Vertical or horizontal aspects of a composition were thus structurally interrelated in a peculiarly meaningful way.

Furthermore, since the drive speed was so slow (sometimes as slow as one motion picture frame in sixty seconds) it was possible to start and stop a sequence of perhaps 20 pendulums within one frame; that is, within one twenty-fourth part of a second at playback speed. It was even possible to play a small pendulum or to correlate in different ways various (literally counted by eye) numerical orderings of cycles. We soon observed that microclusters of transient tone sequences produced this way presented very rewarding compositional possibilities. These tight clusters produced distinctive timbres; yet if the elements of the groups were progressively lengthened in duration they became audible as discrete note sequences of rhythmic order. We found that here was established a continuum from rhythm to pitch. Our instrument could encompass the range. It became a structural foundation of our music compositions.

There is one other aspect of the sound techniques that deserves mention before proceeding to a discussion of image and space concepts. At an early point in our filmmaking a method was devised to record four channels of sound. This was done primarily to facilitate recordings of structures of a degree of complexity otherwise physically impossible to perform even at the extremely slow recording rate we employed. Second, third, and fourth records were exposed on the sound track at different recording speeds according to our notational system.

In this way it became possible to conceive still another facet of the interrelationship of time and pitch. The act of performing on this instrument—essentially starting and stopping the pendulums and controlling their amplitude—could be governed by the instrument time (i.e., frame speed) or by the constant clock time. Assuming a given clock-time interval, then pitch and duration became a function of the drive speed of the machine, i.e., the recording rate. Thus pitch ratios and time ratios were drawn still closer together and became more accessible as compositional elements. (Indeed the continuum of pitch, timbre, and rhythm relationships of this machine was unprecedented in Western musical resources and anticipates the application of computer technology to musical composition. Our *Five Abstract Film Exercises* were made under these auspices—note added in 1973 by John Whitney.)

Our activities were not alone musical since our first interest had been to compose abstract graphic compositions with a time structure as in music. Before the above musical researches were begun, we had made several silent abstract films.

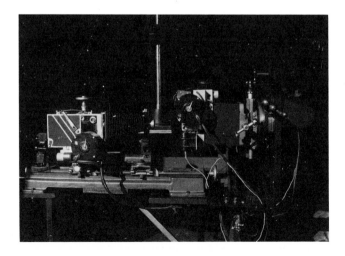

The Whitneys' optical printer was used to rephotograph and artistically manipulate previously filmed images.

Figure 1.

Figure 2.

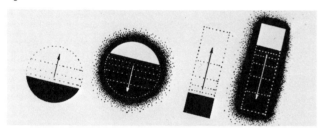

Figure 3.

The earliest film to be completed consisted of 24 variations upon a graphic matrix. This matrix was given action potential by an extremely simple animation idea. The illustration (fig. 1) shows a diagram of the complex matrix which was actually never revealed on film in this static configuration. This matrix was broken down as shown in fig. 2 and produced with an air brush. The forms of the matrix served as a simple positive and negative stencil as shown in fig. 3. The resulting animation cards with phases of movement were then photographed in sequence onto black-and-white film.

This film strip was in fact one of perhaps many possible serial permutations from the original total static matrix. We devised an optical printer in which this film strip could be rephotographed onto color film using color filters; either in normal direction or retrogression, right side up or inverted, or mirrored. Graphically here was a parallel to the transpositions and inversions and retrogressions of the twelve-tone technique.

Seeing this short film back from the laboratory for the

first time, my brother and I experienced the most gratifying stimulation of our entire filmmaking activities. Within its extreme limitations, here was a generous confirmation of our compositional principles; the permutability of the simple graphic material permitted a great variety of compositional structure. We were soon engaged in elaborations upon the matrix ideas which presupposed some form of serial permutation to be juxtaposed dynamically against itself by retrogression, inversion, and mirroring.

The following years were a time of continuous discovery of steps toward a more fundamental graphic element. The static matrix ideas were modified then supplanted by other discoveries.

(From *die Reihe*, 1960.)

NOTES ON THE "FIVE ABSTRACT FILM EXERCISES"
by John and James Whitney

FIRST SOUND FILM, COMPLETED FALL 1943: Begins with a three-beat announcement, drawn out in time, which thereafter serves as an imageless transition figure dividing the sections of the film. Each new return of this figure is condensed more and more in time. Finally it is used in reverse to conclude the film. There are four sections constructed from the same three thematic ideas. They depend upon subtle alterations of color and juxtaposition of these three distinct themes for contrast.

This film was produced entirely by manipulation of paper cutouts and shot at regular motion picture camera speed instead of hand-animating one frame at a time. The entire film, two hundred feet in length, was constructed from an economical twelve feet of original image material.

FRAGMENTS, SPRING 1944: These two very short fragments were also made from paper cutouts. At this time we were developing a means of controlling this procedure with the use of pantographs. While we were satisfied with the correlation of sound and image, progress with the material had begun to lag far behind our ideas. These two were left unfinished in order to begin the films which follow.

FOURTH FILM, COMPLETED SPRING 1944: Entire film divided into four consecutive chosen approaches, the fourth being a section partially devoted to a reiteration and extension of the material of the first and second sections.
Section one: Movement used primarily to achieve spatial depth. An attempt is made to delay sound in a proportional relationship to the depth or distance of its cor-

responding image in the screen space, that is, a near image is heard sooner than one in the distance. Having determined the distant and near extremes of the visual image, this screen space is assigned a tonal interval. The sound then moves along a melodic line in continuous glissando back and forth, slowing down as it approaches its point of alteration in direction. The line would resemble slightly a diminishing spiral as viewed on a flat plane from the side. This section concludes with a frontal assault of all imagery with an interacting tonal accent.

Section two: Consists of four short subjects in natural sequence. They are treated to a development in terms alternately of contraction and expansion or halving and doubling of their rhythm. Sound and visual elements are held in strict synchronization. Color is directed through a blue to green dynamic organization.

The Whitneys' animation stand, equipped with pantographs to animate sequences of abstract images.

Section three: A 15-second visual sequence is begun every five seconds, after the fashion of canon form in music. This constitutes the leading idea, a development of which is extended into three different repetitions. This section is built upon the establishment of complex tonal masses which oppose complex image masses. The durations of each are progressively shortened. The image masses are progressively simplified and their spatial movement increasingly rapid.

Section four: Begins with a statement in sound and image which at its conclusion is inverted and retrogresses to its beginning. An enlarged repetition of this leads to the reiterative conclusion of the film.

FIFTH FILM, COMPLETED SPRING 1944: Opens with a short canonical statement of a theme upon which the entire film is constructed. Followed by a rhythmical treatment of the beginning and ending images of this theme in alternation. This passage progresses by a quickening of rhythm, increasing in complexity and color fluctuation. After a complete repeat of this, there follows a deliberate use of the original theme in a canon form, slow and with a sound counterpart also in canon. The sound thereafter is entirely constructed upon the material derived from this section. The canon is repeated in contrasting variation by means of color and leads into a further development of the early rhythmical ideas on beginning and ending images.

A second section begins after a brief pause. Here an attempt is made to pose the same image theme of the first section in deep film-screen space. As the ending image recedes after an accented frontal flash onto the screen it unfolds itself repeatedly, leaving the receding image to continue on smaller and smaller. The entire section consists of variations on this idea and further development of the rhythmical ending image ideas which recur in the first section.

(From technical notes, written in 1947, which were also published in *Art in Cinema*, 1947.)

Barry Spinello

Barry Spinello.

Barry Spinello, born in 1941, comes to animation as a capable painter, with degrees in English and music, and two years of graduate work in architecture at Columbia University. Following his formal studies he began to seriously explore the techniques of drawing and painting sounds and images directly on film. Experimenting with various kinds of ink, pens, and other materials, Spinello was soon spending fifty or sixty hours a week determined to make in his own words, "a film that was intense, joyous and audio-visual, with sound and image functioning as a unit on a frame-by-frame basis." Between 1967 and 1971 Spinello developed and refined a personal form of abstract imagery and synthetic sound, producing a series of outstanding films which include *Sonata For Pen*, *Brush And Ruler*, *Soundtrack*, and *Six Loop-Painting*. His films have been shown in the New American Filmmakers Series at the Whitney Museum of Art and in film festivals throughout the country and abroad, winning numerous awards. Presently Barry Spinello is teaching animation at the University of California at Berkeley where he recently conducted a workshop on "visual thinking" with Harvard psychologist Rudolf Arnheim.

NOTES ON "SOUNDTRACK"
by Barry Spinello

I have recently completed an 11-minute film-painting entitled *Soundtrack*, made without camera or sound equipment of any sort and using a variety of audio-visual film-painting techniques. These notes concern the relationship between sound and sight in film. John Cage wrote, in 1938, of a "new electronic music" to be developed out of the photoelectric cell optical-sound process used in films. Any image—his example is a picture of Beethoven—or mark on the sound track successfully repeated will produce a distinct pitch and timbre. This new music, he said, would be built along the lines of film, with the basic unit of rhythm logically being the frame. How-

Spinello creating abstract patterns directly on 16mm film celluloid.

175

ever, with the subsequent development of magnetic tape a few years later (and the advantages it has in convenience, speed, capacity to record, erase and play back live sound), the filmic development of electronic music initially envisioned by Cage was obscured. Had magnetic recording tape never been invented, undoubtedly a rich new music would have developed via optical sound means, and composers would have found ways to work with film.

We are now at the point where film and music have gone their separate ways, so that the only conciliation of the two seems to be some form of "synchronization"; that is, music will be composed for an existing film sequence, or vice versa. This is really choreography of one art form (technology, or thought sequence) to another; but to my mind, it's not what true audio-visuality can be. The synchronization process is analogous to two people collaborating on one story, one person providing the verbs and the other the nouns. Why not produce an audio-visual mix that is conceptually a unit?

In 1947 L. Moholy-Nagy wrote: "Only the interrelated use of both sight and sound as mutually interdependent components of a purposeful entity can result in a qualitative enrichment or lead to an entirely new vehicle of expression...To develop creative possibilities of the sound film, the acoustic alphabet of sound writing will have to be mastered; in other words, we must learn to write acoustic sequences on the sound track without having to record real sound. The sound-film composer must be able to compose music from a counterpoint of unheard or even non-existent sound values, merely by means of opto-acoustic notation." (Moholy-Nagy, *Vision in Motion*, N.Y., 1947). My film-painting, *Soundtrack*, is a descriptive record and anthology of several techniques of doing just this.

During the first half of *Soundtrack*, the "sound-painting"—*drawn on the sound track*—is magnified and redrawn, frame by frame, on the image track so that the viewer literally sees what he hears. The images, primarily compounds of dot and line, are drawn with black ink (*Pelican Ink*, series K; *Grumbacher Masking Ink*) against the clear leader with mechanical drawing pens (*Rapidograph, Acetograph, Leroy*, sizes *000* through *8*). High

frequencies, for instance, are made by scribing very close, thin, evenly spaced lines into a previously opaqued section of the sound track. A *Linex* crosshatching tool helps produce these lines rapidly. Pitch is controlled by relating drawn symbols to the time-constant of the frame. For example, a size five *Leroy* drawing pen consistently will fit five dots in the space of a frame, thus giving a constant, predictable pitch. A size six pen will consistently draw four dots per frame, thus giving a different pitch. Rhythms are built by spacing sound particles on multiples of the two-frame series (2-4-8-16-32 frames), the three-frame series (3-6-12-24 frames) and combinations of both. One passage in the film counterpoints these two series directly against each other.

The symbol necessary to produce a given sound becomes clear to the viewer after subsequent screenings. As it happens, the visual images in this section are very reminiscent of one of the most familiar (but seldom realized) images of the mid-20th century—the broken line down the center of the highway. With practice in image-sound interpretation, certain visual experience (kinetic-sequential-rhythmic-visual) can be interpreted through imagination as sound experience. Fences, trees, posts, and the dots and lines of the highway divider, take on rhythmic sounds. When seen from a moving car, one imagines what they would sound like if they were passed through the photo-electric cell of the projector.

The closing section of *Soundtrack* makes use of acetate self-adhesive screens and tapes (*Zip-o-tone* and *Mico-tape* being two brand names). These screens and tapes, cut to fit the sound track, yield controlled pitch for any duration in as many different timbres as there are patterns. Sound density is controlled by arranging multiple layers of tape. In addition, these tapes produce extraordinary images in black and white, as well as solid colors, when also used on the image track.

With acetate tapes and the direct-drawn methods described above, a vital, inexpensive, readily accessible array of building materials is available to the composer who wishes to explore audio-visual compositional techniques.

(From *Source*, Music of the Avant Garde, No. 6, 1970.)

From *Soundtrack* (1970) by Barry Spinello, a black-and-white film with some hand-painted color applied to each print. Both sound and image are produced with handmade graphic effects.

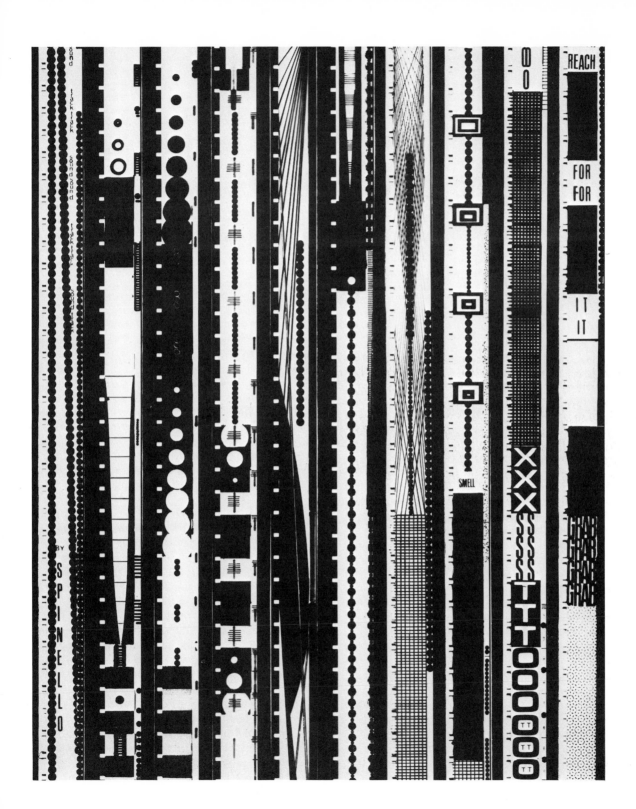

177

8/Animation and the New Technology

Robert Russett

INTRODUCTION

The use of high, that is, complicated, technology in the field of animation, as well as in other contemporary art forms, is the predictable outgrowth of our scientifically oriented society. As modern technology develops, its image-making potential is being examined and explored by a new breed of animator who is a technician as well as an artist. The visual vocabulary of animation is being enriched by such fundamental new provisions as computers, video tape, synthesizers, and intermedia-projection systems. However, as impressive as these new tools and techniques are, the art of animation still depends basically on the individual's imagination, creative insight, and sensitivity toward relevant esthetic issues.

Among the pioneers who are establishing this new frontier in animation are John Whitney and his brother James Whitney (see Chapter 7), Ken Knowlton, Stan VanDerBeek, and Ed Emshwiller. A growing number of others, including Lillian Schwartz, Peter Foldes, and John Stehura (see Chapter 1), are also beginning to make substantial contributions to the fusion of animation and technology. Although these artist-technicians employ similar electronic techniques and instruments, their work does not have a common style, but rather takes a wide variety of interesting forms and directions. For example, John Whitney, perhaps the best known experimenter and technical innovator in the field of computer-generated films, photographs the evolution of programmed abstract patterns with the aid of either a digital or analog computer. He has designed and built much of the specialized equipment that he uses to produce his animated films.

Working in another direction in the field of computer animation is Ken Knowlton, a research engineer at Bell Telephone Laboratories. Knowlton has designed and developed several ingenious computer languages and is continually looking for new ways to make digital computers more responsive to graphic concepts. The animated films that have been produced with his programs and technical assistance range from visually rich abstract patterns to highly stylized human figures in motion. Knowlton's work with computer graphics deserves close examination for what it may indicate about the future of kinetic imagery.

Stan VanDerBeek, a prolific and technically oriented filmmaker, has been involved in a multiplicity of innovative media projects. He has worked simultaneously with animated films, single and multiple projection formats, movie murals, and intermedia events. More recently, he has turned to computer-generated films and video art. Although VanDerBeek's motion pictures and media installations are fundamentally visual and poetic, they frequently contain underlying social themes and political content. Clearly a vital force in the convergence of art and technology, Stan VanDerBeek has displayed a visionary's insight into the esthetic and cultural problems of contemporary image-making.

Ed Emshwiller is currently working with the artistic and kinetic possibilities of scanimate, a real-time form of video animation. This new technique, unlike stop-motion film animation, uses computers to completely calculate, update, and electronically manipulate the graphic artwork during the actual taping process. His animated tapes, which are recorded continuously, incorporate and often fuse a wide range of interests including dance, abstract drawing, cinematography, and symbolism. While exploring this hybrid form of image processing, which expands our concept of motion graphics, Emshwiller has produced a series of video tapes which are among the most complex and sophisticated art works yet created with high technology.

These animators, along with other experimenters concerned with the artistic potential of technology, are working with tools and techniques that are patently different from other forms of animation. They have introduced into the field of motion pictures not only a fresh vocabulary of visual images and structures, but also new levels of consciousness and intelligence. However, despite their important contributions, this technological approach is still in its infancy, and its creative possibilities have only begun to be realized. Presently the emphasis is on computer graphics, video-electronic production, and multi-media events, but there are new technological concepts on the horizon: film and video cassettes, holography, and quadraphonic sound, among others. No one can foresee the future, but judging from current trends, the process, structure, and intention of experimental animation will be increasingly affected by modern electro-technology. A Glossary, which includes the definitions of some of the technical terms used in this chapter, may be found at the back of the book.

From *Scape-Mates*, by Ed Emshwiller.

John Whitney

John Whitney.

John Whitney, who is deeply engaged in a comprehensive study of graphics in motion, regards the computer as the ultimate instrument for his visual research. His abstract computer films, which consist of intense color and movement, are not only sophisticated technical accomplishments, but are also complex artistic statements which operate on a subjective and emotional level. Following the early years of collaboration with his brother James (see Chapter 7), he began to experiment with the production of various kinds of 16mm commercial films. In 1952 he wrote, produced, and directed engineering films on guided missile projects for Douglas Aircraft. The animated title sequence for Alfred Hitchcock's *Vertigo* was among the works he produced in association with designer Saul Bass during this period. Following these projects, he directed several short musical films for CBS, and in 1957 he worked with Charles Eames as a film specialist as-sembling a seven-screen presentation for the Buck-minster Fuller Dome in Moscow.

In 1960, Whitney founded Motion Graphics Inc., to produce motion picture and television title sequences and commercials. Much of this work was done with his own invention, a mechanical analog computer designed for animating typography and various forms of abstract designs. The full range of his analog work is demonstrated in his film *Catalog*, a collection of brilliantly colored, ever-changing line, dot, and typographical patterns. In 1962, he was named Fellow of the Graham Foundation for Advanced Study in the Fine Arts, and, after ten years of working on commercial projects, he was once again free to experiment with the purely esthetic aspects of motion graphics.

With his advanced artistic work in computer animation, Whitney soon gained a worldwide reputation, and other honors followed, including a Guggenheim Fellowship and a residency at the Center For Advanced Visual Studies at MIT. In 1966, IBM awarded Whitney a three-year research grant which enabled him to embark on an extensive study of motion design using the IBM System 360, a digital computer. The first artistically cohesive film that he produced with this system was *Permutations*, a beautifully composed abstract animated work in which he employs complicated forms of visual counterpoint. In 1971 Whitney, under the Arts and Humanities Program and IBM sponsorship, continued his computer animation studies with graduate student seminars at Cal Tech. Presently, he is conducting proseminars in design for the art department at UCLA and continuing his work with computer-generated films.

AN INTERVIEW WITH JOHN WHITNEY
by Austin Lamont

To begin really far back, I had a couple of years at Pomona College, and at that time was interested in music and thought that I would possibly become a composer. Simultaneously, I was also intrigued in a technical way with film and with cameras. I had played with cameras when I was very young. After two years at Pomona, I went to Europe and spent a year in Paris. And at that time, two things happened. I was a neighbor of René Liebowitz, who's a conductor, known for his position with the French National Symphony Orchestra. But at that time he was best known as one of the outstanding pupils of Arnold Schöenberg; so he was writing and teaching Schöenberg music composition techniques. It was a very new thing, he was really of the radical avant-garde in Paris at that time, 1939, before the war. I had a very close association with him. I saw him two or three times a week over a period of several months. And so, though I had no formal training, I gained quite an extensive background in serial music composition that long ago. But also, the second thing that was happening was, that I was there with an 8mm camera and intrigued with the idea of using it creatively. I had never heard of this kind of a film. I thought I had invented the concept of an abstract film. I began playing around with making abstract films. I thought of them as a kind of visual musical experience. It was only when I returned to California in the following years that I learned about Oskar Fischinger and the avant-garde filmmakers of the early twenties in Paris [see Chapter 3].

Q: You were in Paris and . . .

Whitney: . . . knew nothing about any of that. I met Man Ray in Pasadena after I came back, though he was there in Paris when I was there. So really, when I came back, then I began seriously to experiment with little abstract designs with an 8mm camera, and by about 1940, my brother and I were working together. Those are still, to my way of thinking, very interesting little films. They're hard to show, they're silent. I was working on file cards and animating with an air brush, cutouts, stencils. The first film consisted of a simple circle and a rectangle. The two were juxtaposed over each other in a certain way. I cut a stencil that represented the circle, and another stencil that represented the rectangle, overlapping. And then I made a stencil of that clean circle, and a stencil of the rectangle. And then I made a stencil of the negative shape created by the circle and the rectangle and so on.

Q: Then you air-brushed cards through the stencils.

Whitney: Laying a card against two edges, and laying the stencil against the same edges, spraying a corner of each card lightly with the air brush, you just start to fill in one little corner on one card. Then I take the stencil away and replace the card with a fresh one: and this next one will be filled in this much more, and the third more and more; and in ten steps. I fill out the shape. Then there was a possibility of using the negative, so I would put down the negative stencil of that shape and I would blow just a little bit around one corner and then air brush all around, until it completely enveloped that shape. So I had the shape in a positive form and a negative form, and the motion generated by these cards was quite a lively motion with a front edge that would fade out characteristic of air brush. So, just from that simple technique, I had a whole

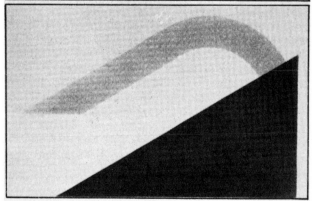

Three airbrushed cards used by John and James Whitney to make an animated 8mm film.

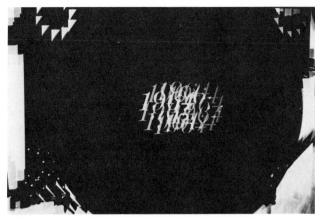

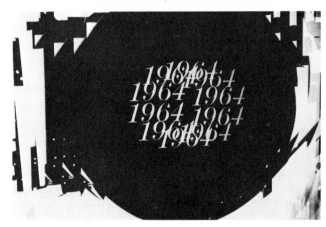

The date, 1964, is graphically manipulated by Whitney's analog computer to create a graduated sequence of form changes as shown in these demonstration photos.

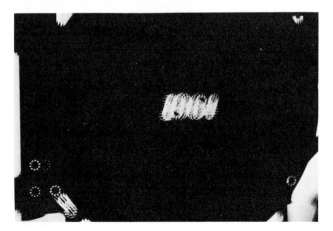

library of all these different air brush sequences. They added up to about one hundred fifty to two hundred cards.

And at that point then, I conceived of the idea of using the optical printer, and having made these cards, I photographed the cards onto 8mm black and white film. I built an 8mm optical printer, so that I could rephotograph those sequences according to a carefully worked out script, introducing color filters into the light source and photographing the sequences onto color film. And so I developed the technique that I am still using here with the optical printer now, with the computer-graphic material. [*Indicates optical printer nearby.*] Here's a light source, then a mirror goes here, and the filters rest on top of this condenser lens. Up above I have a lens tube extension and bellows arrangement, and the lens is normally at one-to-one; the field travels east and west and it rotates on its own dead center and another rotational point. It rotates down here, as well as at this level, so I can locate a rotational center that's off the center of the field.

Moreover, the camera goes up or down, so I can enlarge or reduce the field. Now the first 8mm optical printer had none of these complications. It was straight one-to-one, and I had no power to reframe the image. The film was built entirely within a very strict set of limitations. But completion of the 8mm films was one of the peculiarly rewarding experiences in making film, because despite the limitations, I had control of all the possible permutations of that original material; and it was amazing how many effects could be worked out, how many little variations could be made. They were quite interesting complex rhythmical actions all determined by the way these sequences were combined. The other point is that there's always more than one superimposure. I'd back the film up in the camera and then run through a second time with a second color, some other element, working in a different way. The final thing is that the film strips could be threaded into the projector in such a way that you could mirror them, turn them over, or you could invert them. So, you had four different positions for each of the ten shapes. And there were still some other variations.

It was truly gratifying, and it was stimulating enough so that we went on and made a 16mm optical printer. My brother and I felt very strongly that we wanted to be able to compose music as well as the picture. I invented a pendulum machine for making a variable-area sound track; and with that my brother and I together made the five abstract film exercises, through about 1944. Those are the films that got many showings. They won a first prize at the first experimental film competition in Belgium, and the Museum of Modern Art took prints, and Amos Vogel started distributing them through Cinema 16 . . . .

The *Five Abstract Film Exercises* take me up into the late forties; I had a Guggenheim Fellowship for two years and during that time developed some spontaneous real-time animation techniques. I could manipulate paper cutouts to music. I was working with jazz—music that had no pretensions or none of the complexity and subtlety of structure of traditional western music. I was finding ways of generating a visual motion by ways that avoided the tedium and the restrictions that you get by any cel animation or any conventional techniques. I was manipulating cutouts and working with fluids, very much as they are used in the light shows. I had an oil bath on a level tray with the light below. I put dye into the oil until it was deep red, and then used red-blind film in the camera. With my finger or with a stylus, I could draw on this thin bath of oil; and that would push the oil away and the light would shine through so I could draw linear sequences very freely; and by selecting the weight and thickness of the oil, I could control the rate at which the line would erase itself, so that it was constantly erasing with a constantly fresh surface to draw on. I was doing that and manipulating paper cutouts, and then doing a lot of direct etching on film as McLaren had done. I made, during that time, half a dozen little films to classic jazz such as Will Bradley.

Q: *You mean, you put the jazz on, and as it was playing you would draw.*

Whitney: I would do these things, yes, real time. I was building all of my own equipment all the time. I had a Selsun interlock system. The sound track would have been previously recorded, and it could be run backward and forward in interlock with the camera. The only cue I had was what I could hear; so I'd rehearse two or three riffs of a piece, plan it more or less spontaneously right there and then shoot it, then back the film up and work on another section or over the same section, a superimposure over that, and then shoot it. I'd shoot a whole three-minute film in one afternoon's work. Those things were shown around a lot. They were shown in Belgium at the Universal and International Exhibition of Brussels in 1958.

Q: *Did you run them through the optical printer?*

Whitney: No, those were all generated in the camera. I was experimenting a lot with contact printing ideas; I would combine positives and negatives. I would do one sequence and then print it in one color and a different sequence with entirely different kinds of action and print it with a second color and possibly a third color. The film, *Celery Stalks At Midnight*, I made that way in two or three colors. And another film, *Dizzy Gillespie Hothouse*, I did that way.

Q: Then did you go back to working more with an optical printer system?

Whitney: No. That work pointed to a kind of spontaneous performance—real-time performance. It pointed to something else, to give up film techniques entirely and go into video techniques. I made a proposal in the early fifties at UCLA that we set up an arrangement with six or eight video cameras and six or eight performers using these various manipulation techniques, and the cameras were to be mixed electronically—then you'd perform a real-time graphic experience as an ensemble: and it seemed to me that it had great validity, and I still think very highly of that kind of a possibility. And I'm surprised that the people working with the light shows haven't really ever done anything like this in that way. Their work is so totally unrehearsed and spontaneous. Even if they do rehearse—and some of them do—few of them have really thought of a kind of structuring of graphics. They're more concerned with a kind of story-telling, as far as I can see.

A commercial venture could never put up the money to pay a whole orchestra. But at a school, it could have been set up, and maybe it will be. A group might work together, and develop the same rehearsed dexterity and professional skill as an ensemble that you find in music. This goes on all the time with music groups. They all work together to develop great sensitivity, and spend a tremendous amount of time rehearsing and developing interactive responses.

Q: The proposal was turned down?

Whitney: Yes. The communications part of UCLA, just as it is at any other university, is pretty much oriented toward either educational television or training for the television profession, training directors and so on, and they stay pretty close to the standards. They follow instead of lead.

Q: What did you do then?

Whitney: Well, by that time, the late fifties, I was becoming concerned with the concept that the whole media of motion pictures was not the media that I thought it was, that actually what the motion picture camera would see to record is the thing that's important. I began to give my attention to mechanical design machines. It coincided with a growing skill that I was developing with the technology of the surplus junk yard.

And so, by 1957 or 1958 I was on to these analog computing devices that were used as anti-aircraft gun directors, and aware of the fact that I was able, for pennies, to buy mechanical equipment that's unbelievably costly, and involved fantastic skill in engineering design and production. And I began to see these things as containing within

them, somehow, the possibilities for a very flexible design tool, which should be the thing of my interest, instead of trying to improve cameras or develop other camera techniques. And that led me into developing my animation machine. The film *Catalogue* was made on it.

Q: It looked like a lot of oscilloscope images very carefully controlled and moving in a very precise fashion.

Whitney: It actually is doing mechanically what an oscilloscope would do; and that's when I began to realize that what I was doing mechanically could be done on the cathode ray tube computer terminal. In about 1966 I made a proposal to IBM, and I began operating under an IBM research grant. That's where I am now. But between 1958 and 1966, I used the mechanical-optical machine primarily to make a living. It became quite successful. I did a number of commercials and feature film titles, and titles for television shows, using that equipment.

Q: Did you make any of your own films with it?

Whitney: The Museum of Modern Art is distributing *Catalogue* now, but I never thought of it as a film. I didn't enter it in competitions and never thought of it as a work of art. It was what it was—a catalogue. I used it as a sample reel.

John Whitney, shown at work with his mechanical analog computer.

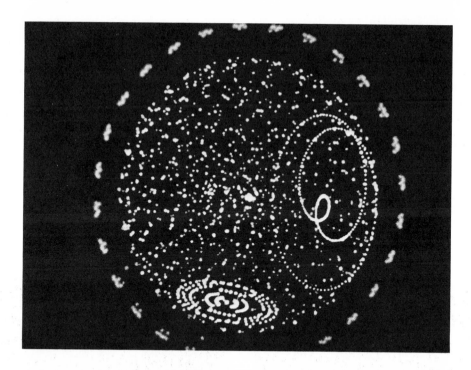

From *Permutations* (1967) by John Whitney, produced with the aid of a
digital computer under an IBM research grant.

Q: How was the film Lapis *made?*

Whitney: Jim made that, my brother. He continued to make films, he was not so much hardware-minded as I was, and he worked patiently by himself. He lived over in the valley out in California. The fact that he lives in the valley and we live in the Pacific Palisade means we're in two different worlds practically. We kept in touch and had quite amiable contact with each other. And in fact, after I got this cam machine built, Jim finished a film titled

Yantra, by the same technique that we had used from the very beginning. He much more carefully, much more patiently, made elaborate cards of hand-drawn dots— thousands of dots, and then subjected these to optical printing procedures where patterns of dots were piled upon patterns upon patterns—one level after another, then solarizing all of those sequences, and then printed them in different colors. When he finished *Yantra* it was shown around extensively. I think it was finished in the

From *Lapis* (1963–1966) by James Whitney. A mandala image is transformed by computerized particles of light, as shown in this sequence of frames. This film was animated with the aid of technical machinery developed by John Whitney.

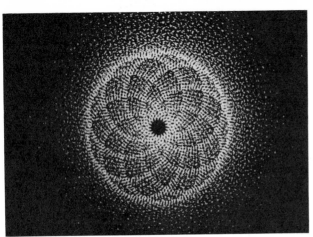

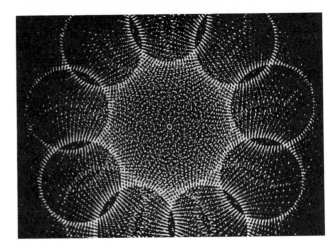

late fifties. And then I had my cam machine operating, and I helped him construct a similar machine for himself. He started working on *Lapis*. The year 1943, when I went to the Belgium experimental film competition, he finally reached that absolute end point, terminus point. He was having such frustrations with his machine. It was getting at him so strongly that he finally decided that he was not going to go on and work with film at all. He became interested in ceramics. And so *Lapis* sat around in cans for two or three years, Jordan Belson persuaded him to put it together in its present form. He's not been making films since then.

Q: Did you do anything between the cam machine and the IBM computer?

Whitney: No, but during that time, actually, my sons and Jackie [his wife] were beginning to get involved in making films. And when I became a consultant for IBM, that left the cam machine free for them to work with. And each of them has done things with it. Jackie's getting more and more involved. My oldest son John has been making very significant refinements of that machine this year, changing it over—adding another level that was beyond me, working with servo systems, the most sophisticated of electrical engineering technology. Servo systems are not like Selsun systems, they are motors that run according to computerized information that you give them. They'll run fast or slow and under absolute control. What's actually shaping up is the probability that that machine is going to become a functioning optical system under computer control. This we're expecting. We may very well finance this next year and, if we do, I'll have a system with almost the same potentials as the programming system that I have with the IBM equipment in my own machine.

Q: What else are you doing? As if that wasn't enough?

Whitney: Well, that's about where it is. The thing to emphasize beyond that is that I think this kind of film is starving for want of much more creative imagination in the area of formal esthetic creativity.

Q: The hardware is so dominant in the whole process.

Whitney: That's so. And there are periods all the way along when they screwed around with all kinds of machines and then finally they learned to fly, in all that time no real flying was taking place. But we are, I feel, approaching a time when we'll have something that flies and with that, the really important emphasis should fall completely away from the technology and the hardware and we'll be face to face with the real problems. And I am quite gratified in these last two years because, in a way,

that's exactly what I've done in my relationship with IBM, I have not had to worry about hardware there. I have a system here which I described to you, but it's an established system; I haven't had to be innovating or messing around with inventing new technical problems. Nor have I with the program that I've had. The program that I've had has had a few refinements made during the time I've used it, but essentially it's the same one that I started out with. And so, I've really had three years of the most rewarding creative study . . . And I think that's been enormously valuable: I think that I'm getting insights into structural solutions to learn how to make a graphic experience with some impact and done with some feeling and not just as a mechanism. I think, in that sense, *Permutations* is suggestive and points in that direction.

Q: I think you've been doing this in the films. You're very strongly taken and gripped by this thing you're looking at and you don't care how it is made when you watch it. You just want to watch it.

Whitney: Well, that's what I hope is the response.

(From *Film Comment*, Vol. 6, No. 3, Fall 1970.)

A COMPUTER ART FOR THE VIDEO PICTURE WALL
by John H. Whitney

It is noted that computer graphic systems, like the microscope and telescope, can reveal a new world to our vision. This new world includes periodic mathematics which has now become directly visible. Here is the possibility for a new art form of pattern structured movement not unlike the structured pattern of music. George Santayana, John Dewey and Buckminster Fuller are cited as having remarked about this possibility in their reflections upon the nature of art and science. My own studies of computer graphics reflect this background. It is proposed that my films deal in this domain of visualization of periodic mathematical phenomena.

It has already been suggested by Ivan Sutherland that computer graphic visual displays, like the telescope and microscope beforehand, have begun to open to our vision an heretofore invisible world. We can say that the computer has the power to bring about visual enlightenment with regard to much in the world that was formerly abstruse mathematical data. For example, periodic phenomena of nature, that could be understood in mathematical terms only have failed often to have meaning outside the society of mathematicians and scientists in general till the present when computer displays are beginning to present new real-time visualizations of these phenomena.

One domain of periodic phenomena however has had its impact upon our sense of hearing. This domain has been a matter of deep interest and feeling and even considerable understanding to artists. The immediacy of impact upon the audio sense is unequivocal here. The artists to whom I refer are the musicians and composers of the world's diverse musical cultures. This periodic domain is of course the audio spectrum of music with its tones and rhythms, its harmonic inter-relationships.

It is interesting to speculate how early in pre-history it was that man stumbled onto a system of ordering the audio spectrum. Here was a continuum, a chaos, of infinite frequencies existing between the lowest tone, roughly 18 or 20 cycles per second, to the highest, say eighteen thousand hertz. Yet surely long before Pythagoras the simple intervals of the octave, the fifth, and fourth were extracted, you might say, from that chaos by musicians and chanters and used constructively. Addison in his journal *The Spectator*, in the year 1711, assigns to Pythagoras his traditional claim, an anachronism of music history which was a common error of the 17th and 18th centuries: Pythagoras, wrote Addison, ". . . reduced what was only before noise, to one of the most delightful of all sciences, by marrying it to mathematics; and by that means caused it to be one of the most abstract and demonstrative of arts" [1].

We know very little about the music of earlier civilizations (music was so perishable) but the music of Western European culture since about the 14th century has been held in great esteem, often honored as the very highest intellectual achievement of Western civilization. And one further point is that, at least until the beginnings of our present era, music and science progressed hand in hand, with considerable interest shared by scientists and artists interchangeably over the mystery of the mathematical verities underlying the structure of music and their relation in turn to the "rhythms" of the cosmos. In a way all of this has been obscured by modern preoccupations, and yet the relation between mathematics and music has not been discredited. Although Jean Philippe Rameau and many others did not succeed in their efforts to discover a comprehensive mathematical foundation for music, we can state with certainty that there is an implicit and very complex order of periodic structures behind most of the musical art of all times.

Let us say it is one of the fortuitous happenings of nature that a vibrating string of fixed length and tension sounds a characteristic pitch of tone consistently. But to embellish this tone to esthetic perfection violin makers devoted several centuries of exacting sound box experiment. They were engaged, without ever calling it that, in research upon a harrowingly complex periodic wave form study designed to satisfy a particular human sensitivity.

Today the computer offers a means to deal analytically with periodic phenomena of such subtle complexity— suggesting that we may come to an understanding of some of the profusion of quandries that permeate musical analysis. John R. Pierce, discussing the computer's powers to synthesize music, confirms the complexity of these problems [2]:

We are faced with an intriguing challenge. In principle, the computer *can* become the universal musical instrument. All that stands between us and all that was previously unattainable is an adequate grasp, scientific and intuitional, of the relevant knowledge of psychoacoustics. Both by experimentation, and by careful measurement and analysis of musical sounds, we must find among the bewildering complexity of the world of sound what factors, what parameters are important, and in what degree, in achieving the effects at which we aim: all the variations of sound that we hear from a skilled instrumentalist, all the characteristic sounds of instruments, the rich massed sound of the orchestra, and everything that can possibly lie beyond these familiar elements of music.

But more to the point of this presentation, I wish to stress new visual powers of the computer. Computer graphic displays offer an entirely unique method of dealing with *visual* periodic phenomena. The computer can manipulate visual patterns in a way that closely corresponds with the manner in which musical instrumentation has dealt with the audio spectrum since the first strings, skins, metal and reeds were used to make music. In saying this one is confronted with an instantaneous assumption by most people that I am comparing the audio spectrum to the spectrum of light with its colors. No such thing is the case.

The similarity of tones to colors has caught the imagination of many composers and painters and philosophers since as long ago as Leonardo. Yet today we may look upon this viewpoint as being rather too simplistic. Here is a typical expression of this viewpoint in a quotation from George Santayana [3]:

There are certain effects of colour which give all men pleasure, and others which jar, almost like a musical discord. A more general development of this sensibility would make possible a new abstract art, an art that should deal with colours as music does with sound.

To come nearer to the truth of this matter one may turn to John Dewey [4]: for another prediction of a future art that is astonishingly like Santayana's in some ways but also significantly different:

Today rhythms which physical science celebrates are obvious only to thought, not to perception in immediate experience. They are presented in symbols which signify nothing in sense-perception. They make natural rhythms manifest only to those who have undergone long and severe discipline. Yet a common interest in rhythm is still the tie which holds science and art in kinship. *Because of this kinship, it is possible that there may come a day in which subject-matter that now exists only for laborious reflection, . . . will become the substance of . . . (art) . . . and thereby be the matter of enjoyed perception.*

This idea, written well before computers were born is exactly the point I wish to make. Let me repeat, the computer graphic display can make perceptible to the sense that which was heretofore invisible except to the educated discerning mind. Certain phenomena, especially periodic aspects of the world of mathematics, has so intrigued the specialist as to evoke in some a sense of wonder as with music itself.

Those very qualities can now be made accessible to direct visual experience.

R. Buckminster Fuller has talked about this matter of direct experience in another way. He places emphasis upon the function of the artist to humanize and communicate a modern world vision. He reminds us that this century's science and technology has discovered and put to use practically the entire electromagnetic spectrum. Yet this periodic field is still, to the senses, invisible and quite incomprehensible to individuals whose lives are transformed daily by new technology. This makes for a large part of the chasms of misunderstanding, he says, that characterize the latter part of the 20th century. Fuller rightfully comprehends the possibilities for new arts in these freshly discovered domains and the cultural imperatives of a restoration of kinship between science and art.

Now neither Buckminster Fuller nor John Dewey nor Santayana has the last word on the overlapping domains of art and science. But their words tell you much in the way of background to the field that I have been involved with throughout the last five years. I have been using the computer as if it were a new kind of piano. Using the computer to generate periodic visual action with a mind to reveal harmonic, juxtaposed against enharmonic, phenomena. To create tensions and resolution and to form rhythmic structures out of ongoing repetitive and serial patterns. To create ordered variation of changes. To create harmonies in motion that the human eye might perceive and enjoy.

I do not pretend to have advanced far beyond elementary exercises with the few films I have to show. In fact as I listen to some of the earliest known ensemble compositions of anonymous 13th century composers of Europe, I envy their skill and sophistication with their young art. Yet it is historic fact that the evolutionary process, underway that long ago, somehow foretold the achievements of Bach and Mozart. Was it not a kind of collective learning process? Learning to manipulate and construct such an enormous variety of periodic phenomena of pitch, rhythm, tonal relationships and dynamics. At least we do know that learning and invention progressed hand in hand with the refinement of a great variety of instrumentation capable of satisfying the musical discoveries of composers by providing hardware with which to realize their compositional software.

The marvel of the modern computer need not obscure the probability that even smaller and more versatile graphic systems lie ahead. Nor the probability that future generations of artists will know better how to use these systems.

I have tried thus far to present a different, hopefully an unexpected, introduction to my work in order to stress that it is not a film art like any of the forms of film art that are established and well-known today. I could say that what I am doing is more akin to music than to film art, but that too evokes preconceptions that I wish to avoid. All that my work has in common with music is, let us say, this patterning of various periodic phenomena in time.

With the computer as an animation tool, however, its mathematical determinants have led directly into a new world of integer ratios and algebraic functions—harmonic phenomena which express themselves graphically.

First of all, since the computer positions and shapes any graphic object by *x-y* coordinates, it becomes the most natural way to position and move objects by way of some dynamic numerical functions of *x* and *y*. Immediately harmonic functions come to mind with regard to moving objects relative to each other. Thinking of graphic form, since it all must be expressed in *x-y* or polar coordinates anyway, impels one toward number functions.

It is ironic, to say the least, that most artist experimenters with computer graphics thus far have sought ways to circumvent the imposing fact that all their graphic conceptions must be translated into number functions. After resisting this rather tedious reality for some time myself, I have come to welcome the mathematical basis of computer graphics because of the structural advantages I have discovered thereby. I have come to accept the numerical problems which are natural procedure with my computerized tool. Now I find that this very acceptance has opened the door to a new world of visual design in motion whose true essence is digital periodicity. But for some details that are not important, this is much the same world that the composer has known for at least a thousand years, composing audio design periodicity.

The first illustration (fig. 1) is a series of frames from the computer generated film, *Permutations*. These frames were selected from much longer sequences in the film in order to illustrate what might be termed periodic visual harmonics. In each frame, there are 281 points which move about the motion picture field according to a set of instructions in a graphic program which were input to the computer. The program instructions say, in effect: Starting at the center of the screen, step to the right a computed distance and move in an arc around counter clockwise so many computed angular degrees and place one point. From there, compute a new radius distance outward and a new theta arc around and place another point. Now repeat this procedure again and again to locate a total of 281 points. This takes about a second or two computation time on the computer to produce only one frame of the motion picture. Each frame is slightly different because some of the parameters of the instruction equation are changing with each new computed picture.

If you were to watch the picture on the screen 24 new pictures a second are displayed and you can see changes taking place sometimes very rapidly and sometimes quite slowly. This rate is determined by the size of the incremental steps, or the parametric changes, as they are written into the basic equation. Points seem to be scattered around in a circular area randomly at one moment. But at certain moments they all seem to fall in line to make up some simple rose curve, symmetrical figure; sometimes it is a three-lobed figure, or ten or four or two-lobed figure.

These action sequences proceeding from order to disorder and back to ordered patterning, suggest a parallel to harmonic phenomena of the musical scale. In an esthetic sense, they have the same effect; the tensional effects of consonance and dissonance. The scattered points fall into some ordered symmetrical figure when all the numerical values of the equation reach some integer or whole number set of ratios. The effect is to subtly generate and resolve tension which is similar to the primary emotional power of music composition. Incidentally, the link between mathematics and music having been remarked, it is particularly the whole number harmonic ratios which support such suppositions.

It is unfortunate that the static illustrations to this text do not begin to show what is already a rather subtle and fleeting experience in the motion picture film. Musical illustrations to any text on that subject usually presume that the reader may perform the illustration if need be. That is, of course, impossible here. Yet this is the best and simplest illustration I have so far. This may suggest how a motion graphic parallel to the harmonic phenomena of music is beginning to take shape. It is a clue as to how visual form may be shaped into periodic elements for the construction in time and space of moving visual elements of nascent time-oriented abstract art.

As a second illustration of periodic visual harmonic structure, a few frames have been selected (in the same manner as fig. 1) from the film *Matrix*.

Instead of the simple circular pathway of *Permutations*, now, in *Matrix*, the pathway is a more complex orbit which folds around and back on itself and extends in three dimensional *x, y, z*, space. (See first frame of fig. 2.) All action moves along this path and the visual harmonic principle has become more sophisticated. Lines and cubes move around this orbit path in the film, but in this example, I will show what happens to the cluster of squares. Each square moves independently of its neighbor. The lead square has the fastest rate. Each following square is moving slightly slower. So the squares spread out along their orbit. The lead square "laps" the slowest moving square, like cars on a race track. However, chance is not the controlling factor. The factor of whole number ratios is at work here as in the previous illustration. Harmonic phenomena dictate that sooner or later this apparent randomness will be punctuated by an orderly arrangement of these squares just as the random array of points in *Permutations* fall into rose-curve patterns. (See last three frames of fig. 2.)

So *Matrix* too is another exercise in visual harmonic composition. It too, I think, is rather clumsy, as you would expect from beginning exercises of a youthful composer's first notebook. I am not that young, but I hope you can share with me what promise I see in all this.

REFERENCES

[1] W. D. Allen, Philosophies of Music History, A study of general histories of music 1600–1960 (Dover Publications, Inc., New York, 1962).

[2] Cybernetic Serendipity, The computer and the arts, Studio International Special Issue, Reichardt (ed.), (Studio International, London, July, 1968).

[3] George Santayana, The sense of beauty (Modern Library and Collier-MacMillan, 1896).

[4] John Dewey, Art as experience (Minton, Balch & Company, New York, 1934).

(From a statement delivered by John Whitney at the 1971 conference for the International Federation of Information Processing Society, held in Lubliana, Yugoslavia.)

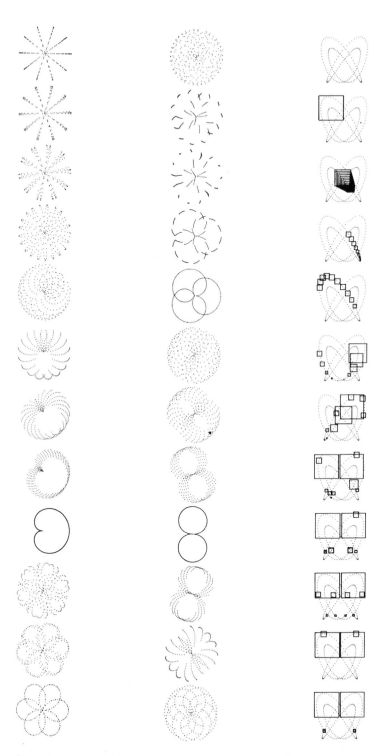

Figure 1. From *Permutations*.

Figure 2. From *Matrix* (1971).

A WORD ABOUT "MATRIX"

by John Whitney

I prepared this once again to try to discourage reviews that go: "kaleidoscopic patterns that swish and swirl and scintillate."

Matrix is a short film consisting of horizontal and vertical lines, squares and cubes. All motion is along a closed invisible pathway (the matrix) which is a classical Lissajous figure positioned symmetrically within the motion picture field. The motion of the entire film is simply a sequence of events of clustering and dispersal of the lines, squares, and cubes. These three sets of figures divide the film sharply into three sections, and each is characterized by different qualities of action-events and color.

The horizontal and vertical lines of the first section gather and separate frequently. These lines define, by their terminus points, segments of the matrix while a solitary white square travels the orbit of the matrix.

After an interlude of many squares orbiting the matrix, a single square in yellow begins a long evolution in which that square becomes a cluster of dispersing squares whose relative positions continue to separate throughout their entire orbital voyage. At three moments in this separating progression, after some squares have begun to lap slower ones advancing around the closed orbit, the complete set arrives at positions of perfect symmetry relative to each other. To coincide with these significant moments the exact identical sequence of squares, by double exposure, is juxtaposed over itself. But this second set is caused to rotate so as to reach horizontal and vertical consonance exactly at these symmetrical events, that is, either 90 or 180 or 270 degrees between one set and the other. This departure from and return to horizontals and verticals echoes Piet Mondrian. The horizontal and vertical denote a state of "expansion, rest unity of nature"—dynamic equilibrium of repose, a pause in the action, caesura.

Toward the conclusion of this middle section, the solitary white square of the opening section reappears, this time juxtaposed symmetrically against itself. Inconspicuously, the final action of the squares gives way to a cube set accompanied by a single cube that moves along the matrix orbit in opposed direction and in contrasting color to the others. The set of cubes, in contradiction to the squares, are gathering instead of dispersing. Since the cubes rotate in three dimensional space, their final clustering forms a circle pattern.

The film ends with a cascade of cubes suggesting perhaps that the entire film was a series of entropic events in which the matrix functioned as an ordering force until its dissolution at the end by the gathering of cubes into a decidedly noncubic and discordant figure such as the circle.

The sonata segments by Padre Antonio Soler were selected to accompany this film after the film was nearly in final form. Very little stretching or shortening of picture or sound was required.

(From technical notes, 1970).

Ken Knowlton

Ken Knowlton.

An explorer in the art-technology interface, Dr. Kenneth C. Knowlton, born in 1931, is a member of the Computing Techniques Research Department at the Bell Telephone Laboratories. With degrees in Engineering Physics from Cornell and a Ph.D. in Communication Sciences from MIT, Dr. Knowlton is the developer of BEFLIX, a language for computer production of still pictures and film, and EXPLOR, a computer language for making designs from Explicit Patterns, Local Operations, and Randomness. His work in the area of programming has made it feasible to create various kinds of graphic motion pictures which heretofore would have been prohibitively intricate, time-consuming, and expensive. Knowlton, however, is not only interested in the technical performance of his machines, but he is also concerned with the human and esthetic aspects of computer graphics. Between 1964 and 1970, for example, he assisted Stan VanDerBeek in producing nine computer-generated films and, more recently, he has collaborated on numerous computer film projects with artist Lillian Schwartz. Films programmed by Knowlton, such as *Pixillation* (1970), *Olympiad* (1971), and *Apotheosis* (1972), have won many festival awards and have had retrospective showings at the Whitney Museum of Art and the International Animation Festival in New York.

COMPUTER FILMS
by Kenneth Knowlton

It is becoming increasingly feasible to monitor and ultimately to control a person's formerly private patterns of spending, travel, and communication. We face a future, in the words of Erik H. Erikson, "which will pit naked humanity against the cold power of super machineries."

However, we are obliged to try to use at least a part of the new machinery deliberately to make our environment more beautiful and inspiring through new forms of design, the possibilities of which are greatly augmented by the computer blending of detail, symmetries, regularities, randomness, textures, and richness heretofore impossible to achieve.

We are further obliged, I think, to try to extend the use of computers into the area of more profound art—that which helps us to appreciate, understand, and enhance our humanity. If we are successful in this pursuit, then the computer will have been helpful not only directly, but it will have helped us psychologically to perceive it as a friend—as an instrument not necessarily of regimentation but one which can significantly help us to experience and assert our humanity.

From *Pixillation* (1970) by Ken Knowlton and Lillian Schwartz. A broad range of visual effects is produced by combining geometric computer images and liquidly flowing organic forms produced by other animation techniques.

A computer equipped with a graphic output device is potentially a very powerful tool for making drawings: it can draw straight lines and true circles, can copy, reflect, or mathematically distort images; it can create textures and combinatoric images of great complexity. The computer can be used to develop elaborate and hierarchically-organized structures, and it can manipulate them by a hierarchically arranged repertoire of operations. In short, the computer can be used for creating and manipulating a wide variety of images which are logically easy to define, but which might be too difficult, if not impossible, to render by hand. The computer will be, I believe, a tool of great power for artistic expression if appropriate software techniques and languages can be devised.

But there are serious problems in the creation and interpretation of computer "art." First of all, just what languages should one adopt? At one extreme we can imagine a machine governed almost entirely by its own random number generator, requiring very little human participation except culling of the results; at the other extreme we can devise a system where the artist has complete spot-by-spot control over the output picture but where it requires far too much human effort to achieve an interesting result. In between, there are areas where the machine utilizes a great deal of its own computational powers, but still leaves a large number of parameters to be specified by the programmer-artist.

There is such a thoroughly bewildering array of conceivable languages and tools that it is difficult to know where to start, or to know what it means if the first few attempts are not very successful.

A second problem is deciding who we should expect to be the "artists" in these new media—people traditionally called artists, or computer programmers? These two groups are, I think, quite different bunches of people. I would describe both groups as creative, imaginative, intelligent, energetic, industrious, competitive, and driven. But programmers, in my experience—and myself included—tend to be constricted, painstaking, logical, precise, inhibited, cautious, restrained, defensive, methodical, ritualistic, cold and inscrutable in human terms. Their exterior actions are separated from their emotions by several layers of logical defenses, so they can always say "why" they did something, without in the least revealing their ultimate motives. Artists, in my experience, are free, alogical, intuitive, impulsive, implicit, confused, bewildered, bewildering, experimentative, perceptive, honest, frustrated, sensitive, and vulnerable. They do things without being able to say why they do them nor what they were trying to accomplish: the rules of the game are that one doesn't ask. In view of these considerations, I expect art to come from artists or artists working closely with programmers—I do not expect much art to come from programmers alone, solely by virtue of their clever gimmicks for do-

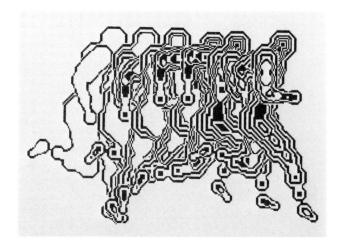

From *Olympiad* (1971) by Ken Knowlton and Lilliam Schwartz, a composition of computer-stylized athletes.

194

ing cute things. What this means in practical terms, then, is that we need to develop a great deal of collaboration between artists and programmers in order to develop meaningful, understandable, and useful sets of tools and ways of using them. A by-product of this collaboration, of course, will be better-organized artists and more human programmers—who can complain about that?

Finally, there is, I think, a fairly serious problem in the interpretation of computer art. The machinery which intervenes between artist and viewer precludes a great deal of normal communication. Even at the first stage—the punched card—one cannot tell whether the card was punched tenderly or in fury. In addition, the medium itself is so new that the viewer is apt to be completely disoriented—he does not know or understand the contortions that either the artist or the machine went through to yield the visible result, nor does he perceive the parameters of control available to the artist and the way they map into result space. He has little feeling for how the result relates to nearby pictures which the artist could have produced but didn't, or what sort of search, if any, the artist made in settling upon and preserving this particular result. This difficulty is linked closely with the philosophy of information theory, which says that a message has little meaning unless the recipient knows something about the total set of possible messages.

Lillian Schwartz, an accomplished artist and filmmaker, who has collaborated on a series of film projects with Ken Knowlton, shown at work in a computer research lab.

From *Googolplex* (1972) by Knowlton and Schwartz. Stroboscopic patterns are employed to create persistent and vibrant optical effects.

Because of these difficulties, I see no short-cut to the very large amount of experimenting which has already begun, but which has hardly touched the phenomenal number of things to be tried. The outcome, hopefully, will be a number of relatively stable languages, each for a distinctly recognizable medium of expression. Such a medium should become sufficiently established that the artist can use it to "say something," without the medium itself arousing such curiosity, acclaim, or disdain as to severely distract from the artistic content of the work.

(From an article in *Filmmakers Newsletter*, Vol. 4, No. 2, 1970, based on a lecture given at Experiments in Art and Technology in 1968.)

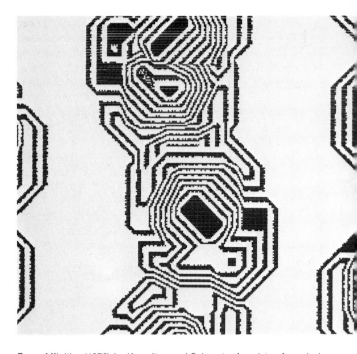

From *Apotheosis* (1972) by Knowlton and Schwartz. The film is composed of complex textural forms which were developed from images produced in the radiation treatment of cancer.

From *Affinities* (1972) by Knowlton and Schwartz. A variety of precisely formed squares and octagons was programmed to move rhythmically in a series of geometric and sensuous interactions.

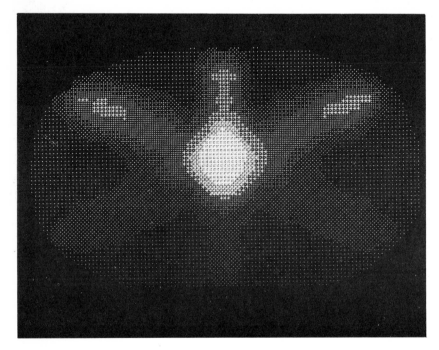

Stan VanDerBeek

Stan VanDerBeek, perhaps more than other contemporary filmmakers, is infatuated with modern technology. He has, in a wide variety of experimental projects, attempted to bring the computer, television, and all the essential communications media within the range of the creative film artist. Born in 1931, VanDerBeek studied architecture for a year at Cooper Union and then attended Black Mountain College, where he first became interested in filmmaking. Following his studies, he took a job designing sets at a New York television station and, with professional facilities at his fingertips, he began making animated films. *What Who How* (1957) was his first, an animated collage that won a bronze medal at the 1958 Brussels World Fair Film Competition. Several dozen highly successful animated, live-action, and documentary films quickly followed. Dissatisfied with the limitations of conventional film recording and projection techniques, VanDerBeek began to pioneer enthusiastically in the areas of computer animation, experimental video art, and multi-media theater. In 1964 he received a Ford Foundation grant for his work in film and in 1970 he was an Artist/Fellow at MIT, working with computer graphics and video tape at the Center For Advanced Visual Research. In addition to his creative work in the fields of film and video art, VanDerBeek has been a faculty member and artist-in-residence at a number of major universities.

Stan VanDerBeek. (Photo by Ken Feil).

STAN VANDERBEEK: TECHNOLOGY'S MIGRANT FRUITPICKER

by Janet Vrchota

For nearly 20 years, filmmaker Stan VanDerBeek has been exploring ways to harness the technological means at the artist's disposal—photography, television, computers, videotape; he even speaks of making realistic three-dimensional films with lasers to create the illusion of form and mass. At the least, VanDerBeek has established that merely staying abreast of today's information tools and media can be a life's work in itself. At most, he has demonstrated that turning these tools and media into art involves much more than technical proficiency— that by adding emotional and expressive content, the artist can humanize the products of technology and infuse them with a creative potential that is circumscribed only by the limits of his imagination.

Always a very technically-oriented artist, VanDerBeek, after studying at Cooper Union and at Black Mountain College, N.C., in the early 1950s, was teaching himself to make movies by the mid-'50s.... Early films such as *A La Mode*, 1958, a montage of women's appearances; *A Dam Rib Bed*, 1959, which combined animation and trick photography on two screens; and *Wheeels #2*, 1959, a fantasy farce on the automotive mania display his technique of combining his own ink drawings with previously photographed pictures into visually surprising and delightfully effective animation. Perhaps the most graceful example of this technique is a 1962 film, *See Saw Seems*, shown at both the 1967 London and Lincoln Center Film Festivals. Surrealistic transformation of a footbridge into an eye that opens to a path that leads to a glowing flower that becomes a body that becomes a landscape, have the effect, in VanDerBeek's words, of "an experiment in animation in which the eye of the viewer travels deeper and deeper into each scene, finding new relationships and visual metaphors in what appears, at first sight, a simple scene.... Juxtaposed with what we see is what we think we saw.... The memory of the dream is as real as the dream itself, but it is completely different from the dream."

Improvising on the technique of collage animation, VanDerBeek, in 1963, produced *Summit*, which combined live actors with animation. The film depicts a comic shuffling of world leaders at the crossroads in their endless negotiations and re-negotiations to ban the bomb. Last year, VanDerBeek pursued this technique on a more technologically sophisticated level by combining videotaped dancers with computer animation. Yet another animation method developed by VanDerBeek was that of drawing films *right under the camera*. VanDerBeek draws a bit, takes a picture, draws a bit more, takes another picture, and the film gradually shapes itself. *Mankinda*, 1957, was painted under the camera utilizing this method, as were *Days and Nights in Blacks and Whites*, 1960, a film with limericks by Anita Steckel containing "images of landscapes that keep escaping, traces of faces, where everything is almost what it is but never stays that way"; *Night Eating*, 1963, with drawings that evoke the illusion of endless space; and *One*, 1958–59, a film combining drawn and animated graphics and live-action video graphics, with colors added to black-and-white film electronically— described by VanDerBeek as "a fusion of electric/ collage graphics and the painted image."

Computers were added to VanDerBeek's technological arsenal when they developed the capacity for making graphics in 1963. A year later he began using them for his own filmmaking. Having determined that the computer was a tool he needed to say what he wanted to say, VanDerBeek has subsequently proven that so formidably expensive and complicated a tool can be obtained and used by someone who's not even particularly trained for it.

What, precisely, could computers offer a graphic/ film artist? By 1970, three technical innovations had enabled the artist to produce in an hour computer-animated movies that previously would have taken weeks—even years—to produce, by a procedure VanDerBeek likens to "driving by looking in a mirror instead

From *Days and Nights in Blacks and Whites* (1960) by Stan VanDerBeek. Constantly changing black and white images were drawn under the animation camera.

of at the road." One of these innovations was the electric microfilm recorder that, together with the computer that controls it, draws 100,000 points, lines or characters or several frames of simple line drawings per second (a million times faster than a human draftsman). Consisting of a display tube and a camera, the microfilm recorder understands simple instructions, e.g., for advancing film, displaying an alphabetic character at specified coordinates, or drawing a line from one point to another. A second technical innovation was an automation computer program developed by Ron Becker, of Lincoln Labs, that allows the artist to erase, add details, cull and move in on detail. And a third innovation was a special computer language called BEFLIX, developed by Ken Knowlton of Bell Telephone Laboratories: VanDerBeek produced nine computer-generated films between 1964–1970 using an IBM 7094 computer loaded with instructions written in BEFLIX.

From *Mankinda* (1957) by Stan VanDerBeek. This ink drawing was made frame by frame, directly under the animation camera.

In the January/February, 1970, issue of *Art in America*, VanDerBeek suggests a way for the novice to visualize the entire process of making computer-animated films. "Imagine a mosaic-like screen with 252 by 184 points of light; each point of light can be turned on or off from instructions on the program. Pictures can be thought of as an array of spots of different shades of gray. The computer keeps a complete map of the picture as the spots are turned on and off. The programmer instructs the system to draw lines, arcs, lettering. He can also invoke operations on entire areas with instructions for copying, shifting, transliterating, zooming, and dissolving and filling areas. The coded tape is then put into another machine that reads the tape and instructs a graphic display device (a Stromberg-Carlson 4020), which is a sophisticated cathode-tube system similar to a TV picture tube. Each point of light turns on/off according to the computerized instructions on the tape. A camera over the tube, also instructed when to take a picture by information from the computer, then records on film that particular movie frame. After much trial and error—during which time the computer often informs you that you have not written your instructions properly—you have a black-and-white movie. This is edited in traditional movie techniques, and color is added by a special color-printing process developed by artists Bob Brown and Frank Olvey."

VanDerBeek produced his computer art series, *Poem:Fields*, by means of the above procedure. This group of eight computer-animated graphic films explores variations of abstract geometric forms and words—among them the mandala—and each is fast-moving and in color.

Since 1970, VanDerBeek has taken advantage of two more recent innovations to produce his latest films. *Symmetriks*, symmetrical variations of infinite form, and *Ad-Infinitum*, a three-screen, computer-animated visual environment produced at MIT with the cooperation of programmer Wade Shaw, were made possible by the introduction of an electronic stylus drawing tablet similar to Becker's program, but with a faster response. Currently, in cooperation with Tom Walters and Jim Gunther in the computer department at the University of South Florida, VanDerBeek is using the high-speed plotter to make etchings and silk-screens from computer-driven programs.

Obviously, the requirement for making graphics with computers is not only an artist who can learn to work with such complex machines, but also physical proximity to the machine itself. It is this prerequisite that has earned VanDerBeek the designation (self-applied), "migrant fruitpicker of technology." Different parts of the world get interested in computer-generated experimental films at different times—and often with this interest comes an invitation or a grant for Stan VanDerBeek. As he still does not make and distribute his films commercially, these invitations and grants are VanDerBeek's means of survival. The "survival route" of this one-man film production migrant looks like this: Ford Foundation grant for experimental films, 1963–64; Rockefeller grant for experimental films and studies in non-verbal communication, 1967–68; associate professor in animation and film production at Columbia University, 1963–65; associate professor in film projects at New York State University at Stony Point, 1967–73; MIT fellowship in the Center for Advanced Visual Studies, as artist/fellow with director Gyorgy Kepes, 1969–70; associate professor of filmmaking summer institute, University of Washington, Seattle, 1968. He has also been film artist-in-residence at University of Southern California, 1967; University of Illinois, 1967; Colgate University, 1968; MIT, 1969–70; California Institute of the Arts, 1971–72; and currently at University of South Florida, Tampa. Add to this an impressive listing of mixed-media performances, awards, published articles; and guest lectures and screenings at colleges, and a video workshop at NET, New York City. He jokingly admits that he would like to be "artist-in-residence to the world," only he doesn't know where to apply....

From *Poem Fields* (1967–1969) by Stan VanDerBeek and Ken Knowlton. Eight short films of computer-generated images combine words with fast-moving patterns.

"For the artist, moving into the area of computers is extending his mind with a tool technically as responsive as himself," VanDerBeek says. "To think about his work is, for the artist, doing his work. An abstract notation system for making movies and image storage and retrieval systems open a door to a kind of mental attitude of movie-making—the artist is no longer restricted to the exact execution of the form; so long as he is clear in his mind as to what he wants, eventually he can realize his movie or work on some computer somewhere. Technology becomes the amplifier for the human imagination." With the computer, VanDerBeek is pursuing an early preoccupation with the idea of a river of images that never end: the computer offers the possibility of combining virtually unending combinations of images. VanDerBeek "keeps trying lots and lots of combinations, puttering with my computer (like a jazz musician jamming) until the right combination happens to come along, that 'exquisite moment when things get combined,'—and I have a movie."

VanDerBeek's "river of endless images" has demanded more and more screens until, now, he requires a hemisphere as the appropriate kinetic environment in which to create his mixed-media performances, with maximum use made of the information devices now available. Since these audio-visual systems and techniques really only count where they are finally applied, VanDerBeek used his 1967 Rockefeller grant for studies in non-verbal communication to erect a hemispheric Movie/Drome at Stony Point, N.Y. This dome-shaped prototype theater (a planetarium is also adequate for his purposes) is the medium on which he foresees combining audio-visual devices into an educational tool. By projecting simultaneous images (on such subjects as mathematics, geography, dance) on the entire dome-screen, "the resulting effect of image flow and density," says VanDerBeek, "is to penetrate toward the emotional denominator of all men." The audience lies down at the outer edge of the Movie/Drome, feet toward the center; thus almost the complete field of view is taken up by the dome-screen. Thousands of images are projected on this screen in the form of a collage and the audience derives what it can or wants from the presentation.

In a similar project in February at University of South Florida's planetarium, VanDerBeek (with his associate Ruth Abraham) introduced Cine Naps, a four-hour-long version of Cine Dreams, a multimedia event which he calls "dream theater." The audience, invited to watch and nap, was surrounded with an endless stream of visual and aural images created by computer-generated

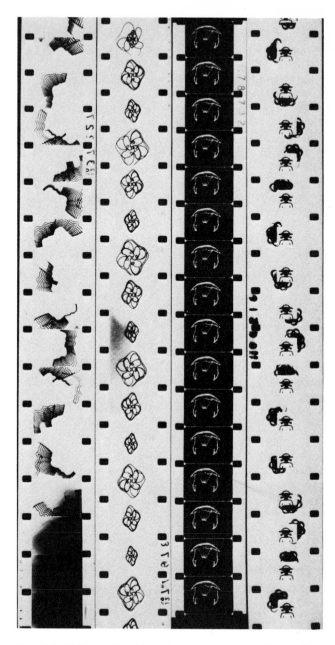

From *Ad-Infinitum* (left) and from *Symmetricks* (right) by Stan VanDerBeek, strips from recent computer films.

film, animated cinematography, quadrasonic tapes, lights, and the planetarium's apparatus for projecting star images. Afterward, audience members called in on a special telephone line to record their dreams, to see if the experience stimulated any common dream content.

In the future, VanDerBeek says, a similar dome could receive its images by satellite from a worldwide library source, store them, and program a feedback presentation to the local community. Dialogues with other centers would be likely, and instant reference material via transmission television and telephone could be called for and received at 186,000 miles-per-second from anywhere in the world. (VanDerBeek and Ruth Abraham transmitted a 6 × 20-foot mural from MIT to six other locations in 1970, using a Xerox telecopier and a telephone conference hookup [see *Print*, January/February 1971]). Cinema could become an instant art-and-image library, with artists-in-residence orchestrating the image material at their disposal, integrating it with live actors and performers. This could lead to a new art-cinema form.

Technological imagination, says VanDerBeek, is still in its infancy, and he optimistically sees the possibility of "an entirely new graphic system with a very big future." But the interaction among people that these new technologies promise presents another imponderable. Humans started out talking one-to-one; technology then made a one-to-400 million talking ratio possible through the invention of TV media. According to VanDerBeek, sophisticated use of technologies that make new sensory discoveries in human cognition may well mean that this intervening third party—media—will disappear and we will be talking one-to-one to each other once again.

(From *Print* Magazine, March/April 1973.)

Students lying on the floor of VanDerBeek's Movie/Drome, watching a multi-media performance of simultaneous projections.

Peter Foldes

Peter Foldes, at his easel.

Hanover Gallery in 1949. His work attracted considerable attention, and with the money that he received from his paintings Foldes bought a motion picture camera and made his first film *Animated Genesis*. Visually, it was a bold film composed entirely of mobile expressionistic paintings. *Animated Genesis* won a grand prix at the Cannes Film Festival and a British Film Academy award. In 1954 he made his second major animated film, *A Short Vision*, an imaginative account of the world's destruction by atomic warfare. Because of its subject matter and interesting graphic treatment, the film was highly successful, winning a grand prix at Venice in 1956.

These two films, however, did not lead to further animation work; Foldes moved to France and concentrated on his painting for the next ten years. In 1965, he returned to animation and has since been creatively active in the field. His recent films, which are basically composed of powerful line-drawings on a white background are markedly different from the painterly style of his earlier work. By using a form of graphic metamorphosis to carry the action, rather than traditional cutting or editing techniques, Foldes creates a dreamlike flow of constantly changing subject matter. His films, unlike conventional cartoon animation, consist of human forms and objects which are graphically transformed by an abstract evolutionary process. Since the early 1970's Foldes, who works with the French Television Research Center, has produced his erotic and often violent surrealistic imagery with the aid of computer technology. In the following article, Peter Foldes relates his experiences while working with computer animation at the National Research Council of Canada.

Peter Foldes, an accomplished painter turned animator, is one of the most outstanding experimental film-artists working in Europe today. Hungarian by birth, he is a naturalized British subject at present working in Paris. Foldes came to England in 1946 at the age of 22 and studied art at the Courtauld Institute of Art and the Slade Art School. He had his first one-man show at the

THE COMPUTER AND I

by Peter Foldes

When I was much younger I was a painter and came to making animated films through paintings. It seemed to me inevitable that in this age of motion, transformations, and continuous change, paintings have to move too. Motion pictures could be motion paintings.

So I believed that motion paintings (animated films) will replace the static canvas. That, of course, was not true; it may yet become true when the cassettes really arrive. Painting survived and animation became something else—as it should.

There are two ways to make animated films: either as a direct personal art form (the movie maker does everything—story, drawings, animation, shooting) or as a communal art form, like the big or small studios.

The lone filmmaker, like myself and most Europeans, suffers from the inevitable slowness of repetitive work. I cannot produce more than two to three minutes a month alone.

This is why I have recently got interested in working directly with computers, which can take a large amount of complicated quantitative work off the creative artist's shoulders.

However, it became soon evident that computer-aided animated films will not replace the handmade ones. The computer is able to do other things—help to create other styles, other movements than the human hand. So I firmly believe that computer-made, or rather computer-aided, animation will simply enlarge the field and produce new creative possibilities, without harming hand animation. I think the expression computer-aided films is correct, because no computer will do anything without human will. Exceptions are the computer-made films utilising random principles, which are quite outside my interest. I think the future lies in domesticating the computer for the artist, and I am trying to use it simply as a tool, asking it to perform complex, precise, and exactly foreseeable, controlled tasks. At present it is probably much more difficult to make a film this way than by hand, but it is a great challenge to the creative mind. The two will complement each other.

I am glad to present at the First USA-IAFF *Narcissus*, my film made by computer, in collaboration with the Research Center. (ORTF) This film was made with a highly sophisticated computer.

My other computer film, *Metadata*, was made with a digital computer at the National Research Council of Canada, utilising the program that N. Burtnyk and M. Wein have developed there. The production is by the National Film Board of Canada.

We are developing this technique and have made tremendous progress in the production and creative possibilities. The new film is called *Hunger* and will be completed by the end of the year. This we believe will be the first fully animated figurative film made using computer techniques. I am now working on a new script for a feature film (my second) utilising a mixture of video and computer animation with hand animation. It deals with the humorous adventure of a young girl in search of love, understanding, and even some kind of a god.

Animation is a means to reach the fantastic—the dreamlike—the far out. It can do everything that cannot be made in live action. It is a field that has hardly been scratched at the surface as yet.

(From the program notes of the International Animation Film Festival in New York, 1972.)

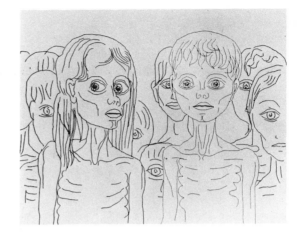

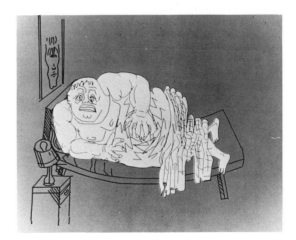

From *Metadata* (1972) by Peter Foldes. A kinetic composition of computer-generated hand-drawn images.

From *Hunger* (1973) by Peter Foldes. In this computer film, full figurative animation is used.

Ed Emshwiller

Ed Emshwiller.

Filmmaker and video artist Ed Emshwiller was born in Lansing, Michigan, in 1925. He graduated in 1949 from the University of Michigan where he was an art major and studied painting at the Ecole des Beaux Arts in Paris before working as an illustrator in the United States. His first film, *Dance Chromatic*, (1959) which combines live action with animated abstract painting, was completed in 1959 and received an Award of Exceptional Merit from the Creative Film Foundation. Shortly after, Emshwiller made two other films using animation

techniques, *Transformations* (1959) and *Life Lines* (1960). Following these early experimental works he concentrated on cinematography and, in addition to creating a dozen or so of his own films, served as cameraman on numerous television documentaries and independent film projects. In 1966, with the help of a Ford Foundation grant, he completed one of his best known films, *Relativity*, an experimental feature which he describes as a "film poem." While continuing his work in film Emshwiller has in recent years also experimented with video tape as a medium of artistic expression. Since the early seventies he has completed several works employing a new form of video animation, including a major production of his called *Scape-mates*, which was funded by the National Endowment For the Arts.

In the interview which follows, Ed Emshwiller discusses *Scape-mates* (1972) and explains the scanimate process, a real-time video animation technique which was used in the production of his tape. By using this scanimate synthesizer, he has been able to explore the emotional effects of simultaneous imagery, the interplay of abstract animated environments and dancing figures, and the dramatization of surrealistic events. In Emshwiller's real-time animation, the use of light itself and the technique of photography are being re-defined by advanced electronic forms of image-making. He is helping to merge the technique of animation with computerized video technology to create yet another kind of kinetic art.

INTERVIEW WITH ED EMSHWILLER

Q: You have over the years produced an impressive and significant body of work as a filmmaker. Why did you turn to video tape when you made Scape-mates?

Emshwiller: I didn't just turn to video tape to make *Scape-mates*. *Scape-mates* was my third video tape. Previously, I had done *Images Of Ed Emshwiller* at Brooklyn College with Charles Levine and Dave Davies. In it I combined live studio taping with films and tape delay. Then, through the television lab, WNET/13, I did *Computer Graphics #1* at Dolphin Computer Image Corporation. A short version of this is called *Thermogenesis.* In it I animated a half dozen drawings using the scanimate system. Based on that experience, I decided to do a more complex work which became *Scape-mates.* My reason for going to video basically was to explore the possibilities of keying, mixing, and transforming images.

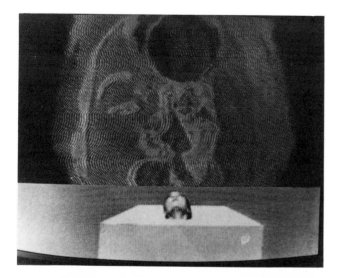

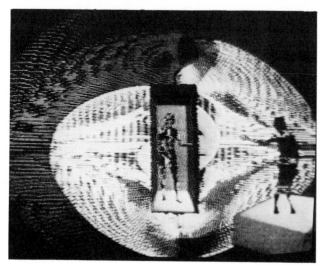

From *Scape-mates* (1972) by Ed Emshwiller, a videotape, electronic dramatization of surrealistic images produced by using the scanimate animation system.

Q: Basically what production process was used to make Scape-mates?

Emshwiller: Scape-mates was made by first designing two dozen black-and-white cels, each having five different grey levels. The cels were standard size acme animation cels and the five grey levels in the art work were made with different shades of zip-a-tone material. These animation cels were then placed before the scanimate computer cameras. There were two computers each having two black-and-white cameras. The computers animated the static art work and colorized it. One computer provided background and the other, foreground. By using a special color encoder, the computers could render each of the grey levels in any hue. The art work was animated in real time while watching monitors which showed what was happening. Selected tapes of the animated art work were then played back in the studio where the dancers were chroma-keyed into the graphic effects. Other tapes of the dancers were processed through the scanimate computers before being chroma-keyed into the final image. Additional texture and transformations were obtained by using the Paik-Abe video synthesizer.

Q: In your tape Scape-mates, *dancing figures moved through an abstract and complicated environment of videographic effects. Was this environment created entirely by using the scanimate animation system?*

Emshwiller: Almost all of the "environment" was created by using computers to manipulate the two dozen animation cels that I made at the start. A few of the background patterns consisted of feedback that was made with the Paik-Abe or scanimate systems. All of the animation, by the way, was real time as opposed to film animation. To give you some idea of the advantage of video animation in this type of work, I should mention that the time spent on the production of this tape was relatively short. In all, I spent two to three days making the cels, two or three days on the computers, two to three days in the studio with the dancers, and two to three days editing. I also spent a week doing the sound score. The actual time spent to create the animated effects for *Scape-mates* was no more than a week. In other words, a fairly complex work took less than three days to animate, once the basic image cels were made. The types of animation that can be done in this way are limited however; when working within those limitations the ability to animate in real time is a tremendous advantage.

Q: Was film used at any point in the process or was it all done on video tape?

Emshwiller: No film was used. It was all video tape used in conjunction with static artwork or live dancers.

Q: Obviously video and the scanimate animation system provided you with many resources that are not available in filmmaking. How would you compare the creative potential of video with film, and what problem, if any, did you have adjusting to this medium?

Emshwiller: Obviously video and film have different physical characteristics which affect the way in which one works and how the completed work appears. A whole book could be written about that. For me, comparing video and film is like comparing engraving and etching or watercolors and oil painting. Each has its own qualities and limitations, and it's a matter of interest and personal taste which you prefer. I like to try different things and so I find the new video possibilities intriguing. In general, I would say video can incorporate film as an element just as film can incorporate music, dance, drama, and graphics. Video also has the capability to smoothly or violently transform any of the images while being monitored in real time. The principal problem that I encountered with video was in trying to make a wide range of spontaneous decisions during the actual taping process. These decisions involved movements and transformations which were not part of the computer program.

Q: Both your video and film work have some relationship to the dance. Could you discuss how this happened and why dance has become a central part of your work?

Emshwiller: I like to work with people, but I don't have a strong desire to use the narrative form in most of my work. Dancers reach us. They express qualities we respond to—kinetic, sensual, abstract—without the need of a plot or story line. I was a painter, not a writer, before entering film and video, and so I am basically concerned with visual rather than verbal concepts. By working with dancers I can deal with esthetic and evocative visual forms that involve people, without using a verbal structure or narrative approach.

Q: Since making Scape-mates, *you have returned to film as a medium of expression. Will you also continue to work with video tape?*

Emshwiller: I generally have a number of projects going at any given time. Since *Scape-mates*, I have continued to work with both film and video tape. My interest in video at this moment may be higher than film, but I find both are interesting and fun to work with.

Q: You and other film artists like Stan VanDerBeek, for example, have produced serious and complicated works using video tape. Do you think there is a trend toward using video tape for artistic experimentation, rather than film?

Emshwiller: Yes, but there is still plenty to do in film and plenty of people who prefer to work with it.

(From a written interview conducted by Robert Russett, August 1974.)

The scanimate animation system is a video synthesizer capable of producing real-time animation. Unlike stop-motion film animation, real-time video animation uses computers to completely calculate, update, and electronically manipulate the artwork during the actual taping process. (Photo courtesy of the Computer Image Corporation, Denver, Colorado.)

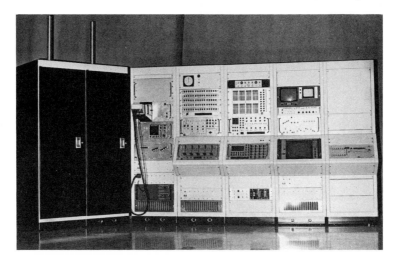

Glossary of Technical Terms

Analog computer A computer using electrical circuits, constructed so as to behave analogously to the real system under study. The analog computer is cheaper and faster than the digital computer, but less accurate.

Animated sound The technique of producing synthetic music from hand-drawn sound waves. These graphic or visual sound waves are made frame by frame and are inscribed on the sound track area either by using a direct drawing technique or a photographic process. The advantage of this technique for the visually-oriented film artist is that both film images and sounds can be animated using a totally graphic approach.

Cel animation The technique of drawing foreground figures on transparent plastic (celluloid) so that the background does not have to be changed for every frame.

Chroma-key The video equivalent of the traveling matte in cinematography. Unlike mechanical cinematic matting, however, chroma-key uses an instant electronic process to insert one image into another. This video process, in addition to creating traditional film-like effects, is also being used to produce entirely new hybrid forms of composite imagery.

Colorizer An electronic video device that converts monochrome pictures into color.

Computer An electronic or electromagnetic device that accepts "input" information, processes it or modifies it according to a logical predetermined sequence, and produces "output" information. See *Analog computer* and *Digital computer.*

Digital computer An electronic machine capable of ingesting and processing quantities that are numerical in nature; furthermore, it is able to perform mathematical operations on these quantities.

Dimensional animation A term used by Carmen D'Avino to describe his three-dimensional or spatial approach to animation. Dimensional animation, unlike most forms of animation, is not produced on a flat two-dimensional surface; rather it consists of drawing and painting, in between exposures of film frames, on surfaces and objects that exist in real space.

Flicker frame technique A cinematic technique essentially consisting of alternating solid black frames with solid white frames in various patterns to create a flashing or stroboscopic effect. Film-artists have varied this technique by incorporating the use of color and imagery.

Hardware Physical equipment that implements programming, such as computers, synthesizers, and video cameras. See *Software.*

Hologram A visually complete three-dimensional image recorded on two-dimensional film. The image is formed on the emulsion of the film by interference between laser light reflected from the scene to be recorded and a laser reference light. The hologram can be reconstructed later by passing laser or strong white light through the emulsion of the film.

Input Information that is fed into a computer for processing.

Laser A device that generates a powerful and totally coherent beam of light. In the photographic technique of holography, lasers are used to form in space a complete three-dimensional image. Although holography is in an early stage of development it is already being experimented with by filmmakers.

Live-action photography The use of the motion picture camera to continuously record events as they actually take place, including real people and settings, as opposed to animation.

Monitor A television set that displays camera video directly, without any intermediate modulation or broadcast transmission.

Moviola A film editing machine.

Multi-media event An environmental audio-visual experience in which film and slide projections, light manipulation, and multiple sound sources are usually used.

Mutoscope An early motion picture peepshow device in which a series of cards with successive drawn or photographed images is flipped rapidly around a revolving core. Variations were used by Fischinger and Crockwell.

Optical printer A device used for copying original footage for the purpose of introducing additional visual effects. Multiple exposures, magnifications, reductions, inversions, and reversals are only a few of the many effects that can be achieved.

Oscilloscope An electronic test instrument which employs a cathode-ray tube to display wave forms, currents, and other visual patterns.

Output Information supplied by the computer as a result of data processing.

Paik-Abe synthesizer A television console or control system that mixes and distorts images. It can create a wide variety of special effects and imaginative pictures, and its name derives from the fact that it was developed by video artist Nam June Paik and engineer Shuya Abe.

Pantograph A mechanical guide attached to the animation stand which is used to precisely plot and execute each drawn movement to be photographed.

Perceptual cinema A form of filmmaking which employs optical or perceptual phenomena as a basis for artistic exploration. The emphasis of perceptual cinema is on the use of purely visual effects such as the orchestration of color and abstract patterns, rather than on the use of figurative or recognizable pictorial subjects.

Periodic phenomena This term, in the artistic sense, relates specifically to the intervals and duration of time in a motion picture or musical composition.

Phenakistiscope A slotted disk, invented in 1832 by the Belgian physicist Joseph Plateau. When turne d before a mirror, the phenakistiscope's phase-by-phase painted images created the illusion of movement.

Pinboard animation An animation system invented by Alexander Alexeieff and Claire Parker in the early 1930s, in which closely placed protruding pins create shadow designs on an upright board which is filmed image by image. Sometimes referred to as pinscreen animation.

Pixillation A term applied by Norman McLaren in the early 1950s to frame-by-frame filming of people and objects in a series of arranged still shots which when projected create new, and often physically impossible, movements.

Praxinoscope A mirrored turning apparatus, patented in 1877 by Émile Reynaud, with removable painted picture strips that prefigure the animated cartoon.

Program A set of coded operator instructions, numerical or verbal, that control the operations of a computer or other mechanical equipment.

Quadraphonic tape A four-track magnetic tape used to record audio signals. Each track of this tape, when played back on a quadraphonic tape deck, is fed into its own individual speaker. Spatial and environmental sound can be achieved by placing the four speakers in various locations. Usually, during a playback performance, one speaker is placed in each corner of a listening area. Also called quadrasonic.

Real-time video animation The process of continuously recording moving computer graphics on tape as though it were live action photography. Unlike stop-motion film animation, real-time video animation uses computers to completely calculate, up-date, and electronically manipulate the artwork during the actual taping process.

Rostrum A term which refers to the animation stand and its individual components. For example, a rostrum camera is an animation camera.

Rotoscope A technique that consists of tracing line drawings one frame at a time from projected live-action footage. Although the technique is traditionally used for producing layouts or traveling mattes, it can also be used experimentally to create a wide variety of special effects.

Scanimate A first-generation video synthesizer that involves various real-time animation techniques in conjunction with synthesizer and colorizer.

Single frame technique The exposure of one frame of motion picture film at a time, as opposed to live-action photography. Animated effects are produced by changing or moving the graphic images or subject matter being photographed, in between the individual exposures of frames which have been stopped or interrupted in their continuous motion through the camera.

Software Computer programs and languages, as opposed to computer equipment, or hardware.

Stop motion photography See single frame technique.

Stroboscopic light Rapidly flashing or flickering light. This effect can be achieved filmically, for example, by alternating short clusters of solid black frames with solid white frames.

Subsonic instrument An electronic device designed, built, and used by John and James Whitney to produce synthetic sound on film.

Synchronization A picture-sound relationship whereby the visual action occurs at precisely the same time as its accompanying sound.

Synthetic sound Sound created visually on the optical track of the film from a non-sound source such as a drawn pattern.

Totalization The term applied by Alexander Alexeieff to his system of filming an illusory solid, which is the total course run by a tracer solid during a sustained period of time. Totalized photographs are animated by slightly modified adjustments to the tracer's movement on the film's successive frames.

Video cassette A video tape which is contained within a cartridge for convenient use and storage. The concept of the video cassette is very similar in principle to the audio tape cassette.

Video feedback Synthetic visual imagery produced basically by focusing a video camera on its monitor. The camera, when pointed at its display monitor, completes an electronic loop or circuit which is capable of producing an infinite variety of complex patterns.

X-Y coordinates Intersecting points on a rectangular grid that are used to plot computer-generated images. By using X-Y coordinates, like X = 15, Y = 32, for example, a picture can be decomposed and represented in terms of numbers. These numbers can then be programmed in a variety of ways to create a wide range of visual displays or graphic effects.

From *The Nose* (1963), by Alexander Alexeieff and Claire Parker.

Notes and Acknowledgments

We are grateful to the many people who helped make this book possible, particularly the filmmakers and their families, and the translators, writers, and publishers whose material is included here.

CHAPTER 1. A RISING GENERATION OF INDEPENDENT ANIMATORS
SOURCES

Source material on Adam Beckett, Laurent Coderre, Caroline Leaf, and Dennis Pies is from written interviews conducted by Robert Russett or statements composed in response to questionnaires sent by Robert Russett. We would also like to acknowledge the assistance of Jules Engel, instructor of animation at the California Institute of the Arts, who contacted us about Dennis Pies and Adam Beckett and helped obtain material on their work. A copy of John Stehura's *Program Notes for the Film* CIBERNETIK 5.3, which were dated May 15, 1975, may be obtained in complete original form by writing directly to the filmmaker at 500 Tuna Canyon, Malibu, California 90265.

CHAPTER 2. PIONEERS OF ABSTRACT ANIMATION IN EUROPE
SOURCES

In addition to sources listed in the Bibliography, valuable unpublished information has been supplied by Lotte Reiniger, Hans Richter, and Mrs. Elfriede Fischinger. Hans Richter's unpublished letter to Alfred Barr, dated November 16, 1942, is in the Film Study Center of the Museum of Modern Art, in New York City. The lengthy Mekas quotation about Richter's old age is from *The Village Voice*, November, 8, 1973. The Brian O'Doherty material is excerpted from a longer essay on Richter, published in the exhibition catalogue for a retrospective exhibition at Finch College Museum, Contemporary Wing. The quotation in the second paragraph of Richard Whitehall's article on Fischinger is from an article by Fischinger called "My Statements are in My Work" which was published in *Art in Cinema*, 1947. Len Lye's "Talking About Film" is taken from an article by that title in *Film Culture*, Spring 1967, and Gretchen Berg's "Interview with Len Lye," *Film Culture*, Summer 1963. The Cavalcanti quotation on Lye is from *Presenting Len Lye*, in *Sight and Sound*, Winter 1947–1948. "The Tusalava Model" is from an autobiographical work-in-progress.

TRANSLATION

The articles by and about Léopold Survage were translated by Cecile Starr, with assistance from Claire Parker, George L. George, and Irene Brun Bowers. Survage's "Color, Movement, Rhythm" and Cendrars's "Birth of the Colors" appear in English here for the first time; both appear in French in *Survage, Rhythmes Colorés, 1912–1913*, published by the Museum of Art and Industry, St. Etienne, and the Museum of the Abbey St.-Croix, Les Sables-D'Olonne, 1973. "The Filmed Symphony," by Leonhard Adelt, on Walter Ruttmann's first film showing, was translated by Paul Falkenberg, who knew Ruttmann in the early 1930s; it is published here in English for the first time. The articles on Viking Eggeling by Kawan and Behne appear in German in Louise O'Konnor's *Viking Eggeling 1880–1925;* they are published here in English for the first time, in translations by Maria Lassnig and Leonard Feinstein.

FILMS

The Eggeling and Richter films are best seen silent, projected at silent speed, as they were originally shown. Surprising changes in visual rhythms can be obtained by varying the screen size for different showings. For a first viewing, the smallest area is recommended, because the eye can follow and enjoy the concentrated moving patterns more easily within a small space. The Ruttmann *Opus* films now circulated in this country are thought to be fragments of the originals; they are in black-and-white, without the musical scores that originally accompanied them. The Fischinger films have been carefully restored and in some cases reconstructed from bits and pieces of long-stored 35mm nitrate film, by Mrs. Elfriede Fischinger and William Moritz. Len Lye's films are owned by the British government, which has not made them available for purchase through an authorized distributor in this country (the Museum of Modern Art offers them for rental only); duped prints are offered for sale by several unauthorized sources, with such poor color and sound that Lye himself deplores their being shown.

Mrs. Fischinger adds that dozens of films and fragments of her husband's work still need to be transferred to safety stock from nitrate originals or from paper/cel drawings.

A number of other European artists planned abstract animation films early in the century. Some of them may have been made and shown, but none seem still to exist. A booklet entitled *Deutsche Filmkunst*, by Simon Koster, includes three frames from a film entitled *Kaleidoskop*, dated 1906 and captioned "Der erste Absolute Film" (the first abstract film). No further information about it has yet turned up. In 1924 Casimir Malevitch, creator of the Suprematist movement, scripted an animation film which was never made. In a recent 13-minute black-and-white film entitled *Malevitch Suprematism* (1971), director Lutz Becker included several abstract sequences based roughly on Malevitch designs (crosses, circles, arcs, and triangles, as well as squares and rectangles), in what the filmmaker calls "a free and personal interpretation of Suprematism." The film is part of a series of art films made by the Arts Council of Great Britain and distributed in the United States by the American Federation of Arts. Perhaps some day an attempt will be made to film Survage's Colored Rhythm designs, according to his plans and wishes as outlined in 1914.

CHAPTER 3. PIONEERS IN PICTORIAL ANIMATION

SOURCES

The Jean Renoir quotation about Lotte Reiniger is from a letter dated September 2, 1975, in response to a query by Cecile Starr. The background material on Berthold Bartosch is based in part upon unpublished information supplied by Alexander Alexeieff, Claire Parker, Lotte Reiniger, and Maria Bartosch. The Reiniger quotation from *Film Art* is from Vol. III, No. 8.

TRANSLATIONS

The André Martin quotation is from "Berthold Bartosch Immobile," *Bulletin de l'ACA* (Paris), March–April, 1959. The interview with Alexander Alexeieff and Claire Parker on Berthold Bartosch was originally compiled by Hubert Arnault; the English translation is by Cecile Starr, with subsequent editing by Alexeieff, Parker, and Maria Bartosch. It appears here in English for the first time. The Alexeieff article on Illusory Solids was translated by Claire Parker and appears in print for the first time.

FILMS

The early Bartosch films, except for those made in collaboration with Lotte Reiniger, are thought by Maria Bartosch no longer to exist. She has also searched without success for a print of the pre-war advertising film Bartosch made for André Shoes. A reel of pre-war advertising films by Alexeieff and Parker, including the puppet film, *Sleeping Beauty*, is deposited in the archives of The Museum of Modern Art Film Library. Some of their post-war advertising films, dating mainly from the 1950s, are circulated in the United States for special showings.

CHAPTER 4. PIONEERS OF ABSTRACT ANIMATION IN AMERICA

SOURCES

The unpublished statement by Douglass Crockwell is in the files of the Film Study Center of the Museum of Modern Art in New York City. Information on Crockwell's specific techniques was sent to Cecile Starr by Douglass Crockwell, Jr., who wrote down the recollections of William Smith, the photographer who assisted Crockwell in filming *The Long Bodies* and *Glen Falls Sequences*, and who had "total recall of what went on in the filming," according to an accompanying note from Crockwell's son. Other important unpublished material on Crockwell—and on Dwinell Grant—is on file at the Anthology Film Archive in New York City, which is now collecting all available information and films of this little-known period of American filmmaking.

At the time of this writing, diligent searches into this period of abstract film work has produced virtually no published information on the animation films of Hy Hirsh and Marie Mencken, and rather little on Francis Lee. Efforts to locate the whereabouts or the films of Robert Bruce Rogers also proved unsuccessful, although numerous queries were made in New York and on the West Coast. Undoubtedly the long-range research of the Anthology Film Archive will turn up important information about these and other filmmakers of the period. The files of Hilla Rebay, who directed the Guggenheim Museum during this same period, are now being catalogued; they also will doubtless reveal some new materials, and new aspects of old materials, on abstract animation during this period.

CHAPTER 5. NORMAN McLAREN AND THE NATIONAL FILM BOARD OF CANADA

SOURCES

The Laurent Coderre quotation is from a statement addressed to Robert Russett in November 1974. Technical notes on most of the Norman McLaren films are available free of charge to filmmakers, teachers, and students, through the National Film Board, P. O. Box 6100, Montreal, P. Q., H3C 3H5, Canada. Other material available from the National Film Board includes a 4-page bibliography on McLaren, with English and French entries to 1971; biographical material; reprints of articles and interviews,

as well as the booklet entitled "How to Make Animated Movies Without a Camera." Some of these materials are available also from the International Film Bureau, in Chicago.

FILMS

Annual catalogues are available from the New York office of the National Film Board, 16th floor, 1251 Avenue of the Americas, New York, N.Y. 10020. These catalogues list all the McLaren films, as well as films by other National Film Board animators and guest animators. Unfortunately dates are not included in the current listings, and some of the wartime animation films have been withdrawn from circulation.

6. CONTEMPORARY IMAGISTS

SOURCES

The "Interview With Robert Breer" by Guy L. Cote was first published in a 1962 Montreal critical review called *Objectif* and also appeared that same year in issue No. 27 of *Film Culture*. The conversation with Coté had been taped at the 1962 Montreal International Film Festival. "The Magic Cinema of Harry Smith" first appeared in Jonas Mekas's *Village Voice* column, "Movie Journal," on March 18, 1965. Jerome Hill's statement, addressed to Cecile Starr shortly before his death in 1972, is published here for the first time. The material on Carmen D'Avino is taken from written and taped material, and from the film, *A Talk With Carmen D'Avino*.

7. EXPERIMENTS IN ANIMATED SOUND

SOURCES AND TRANSLATIONS

John Whitney's article "Moving Pictures and Electronic Music" was translated into German and published in a 1960 edition of *die Reihe*, a publication on contemporary music edited by Herbert Eimert and Karl Heinz Stockhausen. It was later, for some strange reason, translated back into English from the German and published in a 1965 English edition of *die Reihe*. Whitney was unhappy with this double translation because some of the meaning was lost. He therefore sent us a copy of the original manuscript, which appears in print here for the first time. "Notes on the Five Film Exercises" by John and James Whitney was published also in *Art in Cinema*, 1947.

8. ANIMATION AND THE NEW TECHNOLOGY

SOURCES

"A Computer Art For the Video Picture Wall" by John Whitney has previously appeared only in pamphlet form. Although a separate article about James Whitney does not appear, we hope that the information included in Chapters 7 and 8 will indicate his outstanding individual contribution to the art and technique of film animation.

"The Computer and I" by Peter Foldes first appeared in the program notes for the 1972 Animation Festival in New York and we wish to thank Fred Mintz, the festival's director, as well as the filmmaker, for permission to reprint it.

In addition, I would also like to acknowledge the assistance of those who have contributed in other important ways to making this project a reality. I am indebted to the Museum of Modern Art, the Whitney Museum of American Art, and the Anthology Film Archives, and Film Forum, all in New York, the American Film Institute, the Creative Film Society, the Dupre Library at The University of Southwestern Louisiana, the National Film Board of Canada, and The Edward MacDowell Colony in Peterborough, New Hampshire.

Among the many individuals who have been helpful and encouraging are Ron M. Jones, Sam L. Grogg, Jr., Kate Valery Manheim, Jonas Mekas, Mary Jane Coleman, Karen Cooper, Professor William Moreland, Professor Fred Packard, Hugh Wallis, Dan Roth, Lois Bing and particularly Professor Herbert Levine, a good friend and helpful advisor, who suggested that I write a book about animation.

Above all, I want to thank my co-author Cecile Starr and to express my deepest respect and admiration for her spirit of cooperation, professionalism, enthusiasm, and for her vast knowledge of cinema. Warm thanks are also due to our editor Judith Vanderwall Werner for editing the manuscript and guiding us through the final stages of the book. Finally, my task was made much easier by the assistance and encouragement of my wife, Cecile Russett, and by her inexhaustible patience. *R.R.*

In addition to the filmmakers and their families, and those mentioned elsewhere in these notes, I would like to thank the following for their help: Louise Beaudet, La Cinémathèque Québeçoise; Arthur and Corinne Cantrill; Mary Corliss, The Museum of Modern Art Still Collection; Guy Glover, National Film Board of Canada; Jim Hillier, British Film Institute; Françoise Jaubert, National Film Board of Canada; Raymond Maillet,

Association Française pour la Diffusion du Film d'Animation; Gordon E. Martin; Kate Manheim, Anthology Film Archive; Emily Sieger, Film Study Center, The Museum of Modern Art; P. Adams Sitney, Anthology Film Archive; and Anthony Slide, American Film Institute.

Mark Langer has been a diligent research assistant, has supplied basic information on the origins of cartoon animation, and has made many helpful suggestions regarding the manuscript. Nancy Farrell, Susan Mace, Jo Kaufman, and Mary Newhouse have been helpful with special aspects of the research. I am grateful also to Judith Vanderwall Werner and to Alba Lorman of Van Nostrand Reinhold for their interest in film as an art. Most of all, I wish to thank my husband, Aram Boyajian, who for more than eighteen years has encouraged me to do the work I want to do, because I like doing it and because I think it should be done. My special thanks goes also to Robert Russett for thinking up a project well worth doing, and giving me the chance to share it with him. *C.S.*

Bibliography and Filmography

BOOKS

Anderson, Yvonne. *Teaching Film Animation to Children.* New York: Van Nostrand Reinhold, 1970. Special and unconventional techniques used at Yellow Ball Workshop are described and illustrated for parents, teachers, and group leaders.

Curtis, David. *Experimental Cinema, A Fifty-Year Evolution.* New York: Universe Books, 1971; Dell paperback edition, 1971. While mainly concerned with live-action films, this enthusiastic illustrated study has considerable information (with some hand-me-down misstatements) on the early animators (Ruttmann, Eggeling, Richter, Alexeieff and Parker, Bartosch, Len Lye, McLaren, and John and James Whitney) as well as on a number of later animators such as Breer and VanDerBeek.

Film Society Programmes, 1925-1939, New York: Arno Press, 1969. A reprint of unedited notes on films shown at the famous London Film Society, with a new introduction by George Amberg.

Halas, John and Manvell, Roger. *Art in Movement: New Directions in Animation.* New York: Hastings House, 1970. Although the emphasis is on the cartoon approach to animated form, many other graphic techniques are represented. Especially valuable for its fine reproductions, many of which are in color, and its discussion of film animation as a branch of contemporary kinetic sculpture and mobile art.

Halas, John and Manvell, Roger. *The Technique of Film Animation.* New York: Hastings House, 1968, rev. ed. Concerned primarily with cartoon techniques, but includes chapters on puppet and silhouette films, the work of Norman McLaren, and some special techniques (pinscreen, totalized animation, computer animation, and so on.)

Kranz, Stewart. *Science and Technology in the Arts.* New York: Van Nostrand Reinhold, 1974. Includes interview material on Len Lye, Stan VanDerBeek, Carmen D'Avino, and others.

Lawder, Standish. *The Cubist Cinema.* New York; New York University Press, 1975. Primarily about Fernand Léger's *Ballet Mechanique,* the book also includes important information and pictures on Survage, Ruttmann, Eggeling, Richter and their contemporaries, and draws the historical relationship between film and modern art, primarily painting, from 1895 to 1925.

MacPherson, Kenneth and Bryher, Winifred, eds. *Close Up (1927-1933).* New York: Arno Press, 1969. Unedited facsimile reproduction of an innovative European periodical in English, with many references to early animators.

Manvell, Roger, ed. *Experiment in Film.* New York: Arno Press, 1970. Includes interesting material about Eggeling, Fischinger, Len Lye, Bute, Ptushko, and others, with good illustrations. (Originally published in 1949 by the Grey Walls Press, London.)

Mekas, Jonas. *Movie Journal, The Rise of a New American Cinema, 1959-1971.* New York: Collier Books, 1972. Selections from Mekas's originative column in *The Village Voice,* mainly live-action, but including material on Breer, Conrad, D'Avino, Emshwiller, Harry Smith, VanDerBeek, Larry Jordan, and others who use animation as a form of artistic expression.

Moholy-Nagy, L. *Vision in Motion.* Chicago: Hillison and Etten, 1965. A visionary and beautifully illustrated book on the multiple aspects of contemporary design, art, and communication. Of particular interest is a chapter on motion pictures in which the author analyzes the basic elements of cinema and discusses the technique of synthetic sound from the standpoint of his own pioneering experiments with opto-acoustic notation.

Renan, Sheldon. *An Introduction to the American Underground Film.* New York: Dutton, 1967. An especially helpful text for beginners, this concise history of American avant-garde film is enriched by detailed accounts of individual filmmakers and their work, including many prominent contemporary animators.

Singer, Marilyn, ed. *New American Filmmakers*. New York: The American Federation of Arts, 1976. Program notes, essays, quoted texts, and over 200 stills relating to independent films selected from the Whitney Museum of American Art and now distributed by the American Federation of Arts, including films by Breer, VanDerBeek, Conrad, Jordan, James Whitney, Harry Smith, and others.

Sitney, P. Adams, ed. *Film Culture Reader*. New York: Praeger, 1970. An important contribution to film esthetics, this anthology of writings from *Film Culture* traces the evolution of the American noncommercial cinema, and includes articles on Peter Kubelka, Robert Breer, Paul Sharits, Tony Conrad, and others.

Sitney, P. Adams. *Visionary Film*. New York: Oxford University Press, 1974. An in-depth study of the theories and achievements of the avant-garde cinema, including excellent chapters on absolute animation and the graphic cinema, and an analysis of the visionary strains within the experimental film movement.

Starr, Cecile. *Discovering the Movies*. New York: Van Nostrand Reinhold, 1972. Introductions to the work of Richter, Fischinger, Len Lye, D'Avino, Alexeieff and Parker, McLaren, and Jerome Hill, with numerous illustrations in black-and-white and color.

Stauffacher, Frank, ed. *Art in Cinema*, New York: Arno Press, 1969. Reprint of a 1947 San Francisco Museum of Art publication that includes important articles, film notes, and illustrations by and about Hans Richter, John and James Whitney, Fischinger, and others.

Stephenson, Ralph. *Animation in the Cinema*. New York: Barnes and Company, 1967. This study of international animation as a popular art form includes a wide variety of approaches, ranging from the films of Walt Disney and Norman McLaren to the works of Jan Lenica and Yoji Kuri.

Vogel, Amos. *Film as Subversive Art*. New York: Random House, 1974. Dealing with areas of film rarely covered by standard histories, this controversial and well-illustrated book discusses many experimental animators and their work.

Youngblood, Gene. *Expanded Cinema*. New York: Dutton, 1970. An inspiring and well-illustrated study of the new technological extensions of the motion-picture medium. Includes extensive information about computer animation, multiple projection environments, video experiments, and other forms of advanced imagemaking.

SELECTED PERIODICALS
Artforum, 667 Madison Avenue, New York, New York 10021.
Film Culture, G.P.O. Box 1499, New York, New York 10001.
Film Library Quarterly, Box 348, Radio City Station, New York, New York 10019.
Filmmakers Newsletter, P.O. Box 115, Ward Hill, Massachusetts, 01830.
Sight and Sound, 81 Dean Street, London W1V 6AA, England.

FILMOGRAPHY
Annency Impromptu (52 minutes, color), an overview of the work of Alexeieff and Claire Parker, who demonstrate some of their animation devices and comment on their films as exhibited at the 1975 Animation Festival at Annency; includes interviews with several film critics and with younger animators who discuss their own work. Produced by S. F. P. Films (Paris) in 1976, English and French versions. Distributed by Cecile Starr.

Alexeieff at the Pinboard (8 minutes, b&w), demonstrations by Alexeieff and Claire Parker of how they make simple designs on the pinboard—an apple, a branch of a tree—with particular reference to the still illustrations for the book, *Doctor Zhivago*. Produced by Cinema Nouveau (Paris) in 1960; English version produced by Cecile Starr in 1972. Distributed by Cecile Starr.

The Art of Lotte Reiniger (14 minutes, color), demonstration of the moving and filming of the silhouette figures used in *Papageno*, with excerpts also from one of Reiniger's color cutout films. Produced by Primrose Productions (London) in 1971. Distributed by Macmillan/Audio/Brandon Films.

Computer Generation (29 minutes, color and b&w), with Stan Van-DerBeek making computer films at MIT. Produced by CBS-TV's "Camera Three," in 1972. Distributed (for rental only) by Film-Makers' Cooperative.

The Experimental Film (28 minutes, b&w), round-table discussion that includes statements by Robert Breer, Jan Lenica, Norman McLaren, and others, with excerpts of their films and comments by a panel of belligerent critics. Produced by the National Film Board of Canada in 1962. Distributed by Contemporary/McGraw-Hill Films.

Experiments in Motion Graphics (13 minutes, color), an on-camera explanation by John Whitney of the elaborate processes involved in making his film *Permutations*. Produced by John Whitney in 1968. Distributed by Pyramid Films.

The Eye Hears, The Ear Sees (58 minutes, color), a full-length profile of Norman McLaren, interviewed by Gavin Millar about his films, theories, and techniques, with many film excerpts and some delightful demonstrations. Produced by the British Broadcasting Corporation, with the cooperation of the National Film Board of Canada, in 1971. Distributed by the National Film Board of Canada, Learning Corporation of America, and International Film Bureau.

Pen Point Percussion (7 minutes, b&w), a demonstration of McLaren's system of synthetic sound hand-painted directly onto the sound track. Produced by the National Film Board of Canada in 1951. Distributed by International Film Bureau.

Pinscreen (38 minutes, color), a demonstration on the small pinboard (pinscreen) acquired by the National Film Board of Canada, with guests Alexander Alexeieff and Claire Parker, and NFB animators Ryan Larkin, Bernard Longpré, Grant Munro, and others. Produced by the National Film Board of Canada in 1972. Distributed by the National Film Board of Canada.

Richter on Film (14 minutes, b&w), a filmed interview with the artist-fimmaker at the age of 82, which includes recollections of events leading up to the making of *Rhythm 21*, and the relationship of his early films to his abstract paintings and scrolls (film excerpts included). Produced by Cecile Starr, in 1971–72. Distributed by Cecile Starr.

The Shape of Films to Come (26 minutes, color), an overview of unusual film techniques, including those of Stan VanDerBeek, and John Whitney. Produced by CBS-TV's "21st Century," in 1968; directed by Willard Van Dyke. Distributed by Contemporary/McGraw-Hill Films.

A Talk With Carmen D'Avino (8 minutes, color), a filmed television interview that includes samples of D'Avino's colorful "doodle" animation films, as well as his thoughts on animation as an art. Produced by Cecile Starr in 1968; released in 1972. Distributed by Cecile Starr.

VanDerBeekiana (29 minutes, color and b&w), a talk with Stan Van-DerBeek about his early collage films (with film excerpts), his movie-drome, and his theories about animation. Produced by CBS-TV's "Camera Three," in 1968. Distributed (for rental only) by Film-Makers' Cooperative.

ADDITIONAL REFERENCES TO THE FILMMAKERS

CHAPTER 2
SURVAGE:
Putnam, Samuel, *The Glistening Bridge: Leopold Survage and the Spatial Problem in Painting*, Covici-Friede, New York, 1929.
Survage 1879-1968, Greer Gallery, New York, n.d.

EGGELING:
O'Konor, Louise, *Viking Eggeling, 1880-1925, Artist and Filmmaker, Life and Work*, Almqvist and Wiksell, Stockholm, 1971. A major study.
Viking Eggeling 1880-1925, National Museum, Stockholm, 1950.

RICHTER:
O'Doherty, Brian, *Hans Richter*, Byron Gallery/Finch College Museum of Art, New York, 1968.
Hans Richter by Hans Richter, edited by Cleve Gray, Holt, Rinehart and Winston, New York, 1971. A major study.

FISCHINGER:
Moritz, William, "The Films of Oskar Fischinger," *Film Culture*, Nos. 58-59-60, 1974. A major study.
Whitehall, Richard, *Bildmusik, Art of Oskar Fischinger*, Longbeach (California) Museum of Art, 1970.

LEN LYE:
Mancia, Adrienne, and Van Dyke, Willard, "The Artist as Film-maker: Len Lye," *Art in America*, July-August 1966.

CHAPTER 3
REINIGER:
Reiniger, Lotte, *Shadow Theatres and Shadow Films*, Watson-Guptill, New York, 1970.
White, Eric Walter, *Walking Shadows*, Leonard and Virginia Woolf, London, 1931.

BARTOSCH:
White, Eric Walter, *Walking Shadows*, Leonard and Virginia Woolf, London, 1931.

ALEXEIEFF AND PARKER:
Alexeieff, Alexander, "The Synthesis of Artificial Movements in Motion Picture Projection," translated by Guy Glover and Norman McLaren, *Film Culture*, Winter-Spring 1970.
Pasternak, Boris, *Doctor Zhivago*, Pantheon Books, New York, 1958. (Pinboard illustrations by Alexeieff.)

CHAPTER 4
BUTE:
Markopoulos, Gregory, "Beyond Audio Visual Space," *Vision*, New York, Summer 1962. (Contains a Bute filmography.)

ROGERS:
Rogers, Robert Bruce, "Cineplastics: The Fine Art of Motion Painting," *The Quarterly of Film, Radio, and Television*, Berkeley, Summer 1952.

CHAPTER 5
McLAREN:
Cutler, May Ebbitt, "The Unique Genius of Norman McLaren," *Canadian Art*, May/June 1965.
McWilliams, Donald, "Talking to a Great Film Artist," *McGill Reporter* (Montreal), April 28, 1969.

CHAPTER 6
ROBERT BREER:
Mekas, Jonas and P. Adams Sitney, "An Interview with Robert Breer"; Levine, Charles, "An Interview with Robert Breer; "Letter From Robert Breer to Jonas Mekas"; "Robert Breer Filmography"; all appearing in *Film Culture*, Spring, 1973.

CHAPTER 8
JOHN WHITNEY:
Brick, Richard, "John Whitney Interviewed"; Whitney, John, "Excerpts of a Talk Given at California Institute of Technology"; "John Whitney Bibliography"; "John Whitney Filmography"; all appearing in *Film Culture*, Spring, 1972.

From *Circles* (1933), by Oskar Fischinger.

Film Distribution Sources

Note: It is advisable to check with local and regional film libraries (in public library and university collections), which may own many of the films described in this book. The following are primary, or specialized, sources, many of which will send free catalogues or listings upon request:

American Federation of Art
41 East 65th Street
New York, New York 10021
  (Beckett, Belson, Breer, Conrad, Jordan, Mouris, Noyes, Pies, Russett, Schwartz, Sharits, Smith, Spinello, James Whitney, John Whitney, and others)

Adam K. Beckett
28945 Kenington Road
Val Verde, California 91350
  (Beckett)

Blackhawk Films
1235 West 5th Street
Davenport, Iowa 52808
  (Starevitch, Ruttmann's *Berlin, The Symphony of a Great City*, purchase only.)

Carmen Educational Associates, Inc.
Box 205
Youngstown, New York 14174
  (Reiniger)

Contemporary/McGraw-Hill Films
1221 Avenue of the Americas
New York, New York 10020
  (Trnka, Noyes, Starevitch)

Creative Film Society
7237 Canby Avenue
Reseda, California 91335
  (Knowlton, Russett, Stehura, James Whitney, John Whitney, Hy Hirsh, Oskar Fischinger, and others)

Cyclops Films, Inc.
1697 Broadway
New York, New York 10019
  (Noyes)

Ed Emshwiller
43 Red Maple Drive
Wantagh, New York 11793
  (Emshwiller)

Film-Makers' Cooperative
175 Lexington Avenue
New York, New York 10016
  (rental only: Breer, Conrad, Emshwiller, Hill, Mencken, Richter, Sharits, Smith, Spinello, VanDerBeek, and others)

Fischinger Studios
8925 Wonderland Park Avenue
Hollywood, California 90046
  (Fischinger)

Film Images, Inc.
17 West 60th Street
New York, New York 10023
  (early animation films of Reynaud, Cohl, Starevitch)

Film Planning Associates
305 East 46th Street
New York, New York 10017
  (Lee)

German Consulate-General
460 Park Avenue
New York, New York 10022
  and from other German consulates in other key cities
  (*loan only to educational groups:* Ruttmann's *Opus II, III, and IV*)

Dwinell Grant
Solebury, Bucks County,
Pennsylvania 18963
  (Grant)

Grove Press Film Division
53 East 11th Street
New York, New York 10003
  (D'Avino, Breer, Emshwiller, Mencken, VanDerBeek, and others)

International Film Bureau Inc.
332 South Michigan Avenue
Chicago, Illinois 60604
  (McLaren, Coderre, and others)

Larry Jordan
15 Allyn Avenue
San Anselmo, California 94960
  (Jordan)

Learning Corporation of America
711 Fifth Avenue
New York, New York 10022
  (Foldes, McLaren, Noyes, and others)

Macmillan Audio Brandon Films
34 MacQuesten Parkway South
Mount Vernon, New York 10550
  (Reiniger's *Adventures of Prince Achmed*, Trnka, and others)

The Museum of Modern Art Department of Film
11 West 53rd Street
New York, New York 10019
  (*rental only to educational groups:* Eggeling and Richter, Fischinger, Lye, Léger, Crockwell, Breer, John Whitney, Jordan, and others)

National Film Board of Canada
1251 Avenue of the Americas
16th floor
New York, New York 10020
  (various NFB animators and guest animators)

Ted Nemeth Studios
36 West 62 Street
New York, New York 10023
  (Bute)

Phoenix Films
470 Park Avenue South
New York, New York 10016
  (Leaf, Noyes, Trnka, Mouris, and others)

Dennis Pies
15242 Rio Nido Road
Guerneville, California 95446
  (Pies)

Pyramid Films
Box 1048
Santa Monica, California 90406
  (Fischinger, Mouris, John Whitney, VanDerBeek, and others)

Robert Russett
P. O. Box 1097, USL
Lafayette, Louisiana 70501
   (Russett)

Cecile Starr
50 West 96th Street
New York, New York 10025
   (Richter, Eggeling, Alexeieff and Parker,
   Bartosch, D'Avino interview)

Lillian Schwartz
524 Ridge Road
Watchung, New Jersey 07060
   (Schwartz and Knowlton)

Trans-World Films
332 South Michigan Avenue
Chicago, Illinois 60604
   (*rental only:* early compilation reels of
   National Film Board of Canada, including
   films no longer in active distribution:
   Alexeieff's *En Passant,* McLaren's *Dollar
   Dance, V for Victory, C'est L'Aviron,* and
   others)

Vision Resources, Inc.
1 Lincoln Plaza
New York, New York 10023
   (VanDerBeek, Breer, and others)

Vision Quest, Inc.
7715 North Sheridan Road
Chicago, Illinois 60626
   (Richter, Alexeieff and Parker, Bartosch)

List of Illustrations and Picture Credits

Index

ANIMATION FILM TITLES/(and filmmakers)

GENERAL INDEX

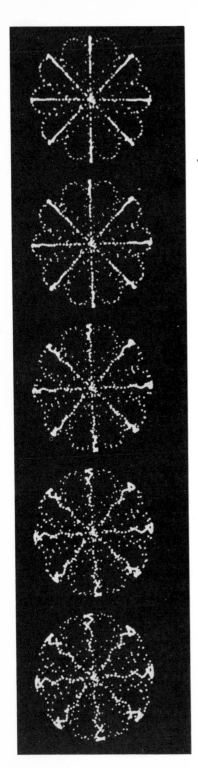

From *Permutations*, by John Whitney.